Budgeting Practice and Structure

Budgeting Practice and Organisational Structure

David Dugdale
Department of Accounting and Finance, University of Bristol

Stephen Lyne
Department of Accounting and Finance, University of Bristol

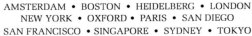

AMSTERDAM • BOSTON • HEIDELBERG • LONDON
NEW YORK • OXFORD • PARIS • SAN DIEGO
SAN FRANCISCO • SINGAPORE • SYDNEY • TOKYO

CIMA Publishing is an imprint of Elsevier

CIMA Publishing
An imprint of Elsevier
The Boulevard, Langford Lane, Kidlington, Oxford, OX5 1GB
30, Corporate Drive, Burlington, MA01807

First Edition 2010

British Library Cataloguing in Publication Data
A catalogue record for this book is available from the British Library

Library of Congress Cataloging-in-Publication Data
A catalog record for this book is available from the Library of Congress

ISBN: 978-0-08-096590-1

For information on all Elsevier publications
visit our website at books.elsevier.com

Transferrred to Digital Printing 2009

Working together to grow
libraries in developing countries

www.elsevier.com | www.bookaid.org | www.sabre.org

ELSEVIER   BOOK AID
              International   Sabre Foundation

To Christine and Jenny

Contents

Part 2 Budgets and Organisational Structure

Executive Summary

Introduction

The investigation reported here was stimulated by the debates generated by the 'Beyond Budgeting' movement and the interest of the Chartered Institute of Management Accountants in this core technique. The executive summary, like the main report, is divided into two parts. The first part reports conclusions from a survey of financial and non-financial managers that investigated attitudes to budgeting and the problems that it can cause. The second part reports a field study of several companies based on interviews with financial and non-financial managers. This stage of the research revealed the importance of understanding budgeting in context, especially the interaction between budgeting, other control systems and organisational structure.

Part 1

The Literature: Origins and Uses of Budgeting

The emergence of 'scientific management', standard costing and public sector budgeting was followed, in the 1920s, by the development of budgeting for business organisations. Quickly this became budgetary *control* with a budget set out in a manner that would allow later comparison with actual results. Linked with a clear hierarchical organisation structure, budgetary control could provide the basis for responsibility accounting and a cohesive control system. Specific individuals were to be responsible and accountable for delivering the budget plan, and responsibility accounting became a major element of management accounting theory.

Our investigation focused, in particular, on the *uses* of budgets in practice and we therefore extracted the standard uses of budgets from the literature. Following Drury (2004, p. 593):

Budgets serve a number of useful purposes. They include:

1. *planning* annual operations
2. *coordinating* the activities of the various parts of the organization…
3. *communicating* plans to the various responsibility centre managers

4. *motivating* managers to strive to achieve the organizational goals
5. *controlling* activities
6. *evaluating* the performance of managers

Budgeting for the key activities of *planning* and *control* seems simple enough though pinning down these concepts is not so easy. Mintzberg argued that many definitions of 'planning' are so broad as to be useless and concluded that strategic planning is characterised by its formalised and structured nature. This definition makes clear why budgeting, with its institutionalised procedures, is associated with organisational planning.

Control is often associated with 'dominance' but, in management accounting, usually means comparison to plan and acting to correct deviations. Again the link to budgeting is clear as an articulated budget acts as a standard against which actual results can be compared so as to stimulate corrective action. We also note that budgeting can be implicated in assisting managers to direct subordinates, in facilitating control of the agenda and in budgeting's underpinning ideology that insists on the importance of profit and cost control.

Budgeting helped senior managers to construct organisations with clearly defined areas of responsibility with managers monitored through the tool of budgetary control. The link between budgetary control and the delegation of responsibility may have facilitated the growth of large businesses because, as businesses grew, it became necessary for central managers to delegate their authority and they therefore needed some means of ensuring that control was still retained.

Although the theory of budgeting was quickly developed and stabilised this does not imply that companies rapidly adopted the new technique. In fact, take-up was relatively slow and companies taking up budgeting often did so only partially without producing full budgeted profit and loss accounts and balance sheets. However, despite the uneven implementation of the technique, after the Second World War, surveys increasingly found that budgeting was widespread and the most recent surveys indicate that virtually all companies use budgeting systems.

The Literature: Problems with Budgets

Budgetary control could be perceived as managerial, impersonal, controlling, task oriented and designed to hold managers and supervisors to account. Argyris (1952) commented that '…making the tool is a far easier task than learning how to use it…' and, based on his research, concluded that budgets could be used to pressure factory supervisors: leading to endemic conflict because staff 'success' was achieved by reporting supervisors 'failure'. Additionally, responsibility centre budgeting emphasised *individual* accountability and militated against teamwork with supervisors blaming others and indulging in budget games.

Hopwood (1972) and Otley (1978) investigated management control in a Chicago-based steel manufacturer and the UK National Coal Board respectively. Hopwood's findings were similar to those of Argyris. He concluded that a budget-constrained style, based upon the cost-centre head's ability to continually meet short-term budgets, was more likely to result in job-related tension and manipulation and was, therefore, likely to lead to inferior performance. Otley, however, failed to confirm Hopwood's findings. He concluded that, in the NCB, that style of performance evaluation had little impact on subordinates feelings and motivations.

Attempts to reconcile the Hopwood and Otley studies concentrated on differing organisation structures and contrasted interdependent cost centres (more uncertainty) in Hopwood's study with relatively autonomous profit centres (less uncertainty) in Otley's study. We suspect the contrast between cost centres and profit centres is more important than the more abstract concept of 'uncertainty' and the interaction between organisational structures and control systems is a key theme in this study.

Commonsense suggests that budgets need to be set at an attainable (though possibly difficult) level and, in the 1960s, Stedry and Hofstede undertook experiments and field studies that suggested that individuals did, indeed, respond best to a challenging target. If the target was either too easy or clearly unachievable performance was not as good as when the target was 'tight but achievable'. Hofstede noted that translating this finding into action was complicated because of the number of intervening variables such as personality, company structure and plant culture. Additionally, a tight budget that encouraged maximum effort might still not be achieved and was not, therefore, realistic for planning. Unexpectedly, despite earlier findings, Merchant and Manzoni (1989) discovered, in a study of profit-centre managers, that budgets were actually *attainable* most of the time. They reported many advantages: bonuses paid, credibility maintained, commitment to 'winning' strengthened, overspending (driven by a too optimistic budget) avoided, earnings predictable, fewer interventions needed and earnings manipulation reduced.

Again, organisation structure comes into play, Otley's and Merchant & Manzoni's findings relate to profit centres whereas Argyris and Hopwood's relate to cost centres. Also, wider context is important. As Merchant and Manzoni point out, there are many ways to motivate managers such as extra bonuses, recognition, credibility and increased career prospects. Senior managers have many levers at their disposal beside the use of tight budgets.

It is well known that managers sometimes play 'budget games'. Research has revealed that the inclusion of budget 'slack' or 'padding' is commonplace with, for example, Onsi (1973) finding that 80% of managers interviewed were prepared to admit that they bargained for slack. Budget gaming may be a consequence of encouraging participation in the budgeting process as managers use the opportunity to bias the budget either optimistically (if they feel insecure) or pessimistically (to improve the chance of achieving the budget).

Early literature tended to view budget slack as unfortunate and dysfunctional. However, attainable budgets have advantages and contemporary literature indicates that some slack can be desirable, providing some flexibility to operating managers. Managers may take actions that are actually beneficial to the company, for example, by continuing a good project that would otherwise be lost.

Budgetary slack and padding are attempts by managers to game the budgeting system *in advance*. Managers may also game the budget *after* it has been implemented, both by making accounting entries that show their operations in a better light and by operational changes that are driven by desire to report better results. For example, managers may incorrectly book expenses to other cost centres or in the wrong accounting period and, more worryingly, managers may defer important but discretionary expenditures so as to improve short-term results.

The Literature: 'Beyond Budgeting'

The 'Beyond Budgeting' movement stemmed from a feeling that traditional, hierarchical budgeting was at odds with the new 'realities' of global competition and rapid change. Originally CAM-I's[1] interest was in the development of 'advanced budgeting' but Bunce et al. (1995) concluded that a better budgeting system was unlikely. Instead, Bunce and Fraser formed the 'Beyond Budgeting Round Table' (BBRT) and, inspired by the example of a Swedish bank, Svenska Handelsbanken, advocated, not better budgeting, but the abandonment of budgeting.

Hope and Fraser argued that budgeting systems are inflexible, fail to support managers in competitive environments, encourage managerial gaming and are bureaucratic and expensive. They are particularly critical of the use of budgets as a rigid 'performance contract'. Hope and Fraser linked the abandonment of budgeting with the adoption of what they called the 'N-form' organisation that should replace the divisional 'M-form'. In this type of networked organisation with emphasis on open non-hierarchical communication, there would be multiple linkages between managers at all levels, group executives would be 'challengers', middle managers, 'integrators' and SBU managers, 'entrepreneurs'. Rewards to managers would be based on relative performance measures versus competition not on performance related to a preset budget. A thoroughgoing culture change was needed based on responsibility, enterprise, trust and loyalty.

---

[1]CAM-I is an international, non-profit making consortium of companies that works with academics in pursuing industry-based research into management systems. Originally CAM-I focused on computer-aided manufacturing but the consortium played a key role in the spread of activity-based techniques in the late 1980s.

The 'Beyond Budgeting' critique echoes earlier gaming themes: setting low targets, procuring more resources than are needed, spending what is in the budget, making the budget 'whatever it takes', meeting the budget but not beating it. Additionally, Hope and Fraser draw attention to the possibly bureaucratic, rigid and expensive nature of budgets and to the use of budgets in performance contracts. However, Hope and Fraser's analysis is rather one-sided and the budgeting literature provides examples of the *beneficial* use of budgetary slack and *appropriate* emphasis on the budget.

Aims of the Survey

The main aim of the survey was to discover whether the 'Beyond Budgeting' critique had affected attitudes to budgeting and whether budgeting practices had changed in recent years as a result. The attitudes of both financial and non-financial managers were investigated and use of the 'BRICMAR'[2] database of companies generated an acceptable response rate of 40.1% to a survey questionnaire. Forty companies from the industrial and service sectors were represented. A financial manager responded from all these companies (response rate 53.3%) and a non-financial manager responded from 21 companies (response rate 28%). Respondents were asked about the importance of budgeting for planning, control, coordination, communication, authorisation, motivation and performance evaluation and the extent to which they agreed with 20 statements that were critical of budgeting. These questions were based on both the traditional and the 'Beyond Budgeting' literatures.

Findings: Financial Versus Non-financial Managers

We were surprised that there were almost no significant differences between the responses of financial and non-financial managers to statements about the importance of budgeting and to statements criticising budgeting. The only significant result related to the time-consuming nature of budgets, their realism and the need for more budgeting resources. Financial managers were more likely to agree that budgets are too time consuming while non-financial managers were more likely to see budgets as unrealistic and to agree that more budgeting resources were needed.

Findings: The Budgeting Process

All 40 respondents confirmed that their companies set budgets. Budgeting processes do tend to be bureaucratic, typically starting 4–6 months before the start of the financial year and involving a number of iterations. Budgets are usually set for each

---

[2]Bristol Centre for Management Accounting Research.

month in the financial year and the vast majority confirmed that variances between budget and actual results are reported monthly. Most companies also provided previous year data for comparison. Few companies claimed to flex the budget before calculating variances and almost 80% of respondents indicated that the budget was not revised during the financial year. Most respondents felt that the budgeting process was driven by senior managers although a significant number (more than half) also felt that junior managers had a major input. Most (85%) of respondents confirmed that financial forecasts are prepared, usually for the remainder of the financial year.

Findings: Attitudes to Budgets

Almost 95% of financial managers thought that budgets are fairly, very or extremely important, performance evaluation, control and planning being the most important uses. Budgets are also important for coordination, communication and authorisation, but respondents tended not to agree that budgets are important for motivation.

Most financial managers *disagreed* with the statements criticising budgeting. A majority of financial managers agreed or strongly agreed with *only two* (from twenty) of the critical statements. Overall, these results do *not* indicate widespread dissatisfaction with budgets and budgeting processes in the survey companies.

While most respondents were not critical of budgeting some were and an open-ended question asked for reasons for dissatisfaction. There were three causes:

1. The 'top-down' nature of the process that could lead to lack of local ownership.
2. Lack of accountability or involvement of operating managers.
3. Need for a better budgeting process.

When asked directly a significant minority of managers expressed some dissatisfaction. However, the issues raised did not relate to over-emphasis on accounting measures, the budget-constrained style of management, target setting or budget gaming. Instead they were concerned with the budgeting process and the roles of both top managers and operating managers.

Changes in the Budgeting Process

More than half (55%) of the respondents reported some form of change in the past 5 years and three general themes emerged:

1. Greater involvement of junior management in budgeting processes.
2. More detailed analysis.
3. Intensification in the use of budgets.

Traditional budgeting methods are not decreasing in importance and another question indicated that their use in setting bonuses was *increasing* in importance. Change in the past 5 years had not been driven by the 'Beyond Budgeting' movement, instead, respondents reported more sophisticated (traditional) budgeting, and, in some companies, tighter financial controls.

There was also evidence that non-financial performance indicators and the balanced scorecard had become more important in recent years together with increasing emphasis on standard costing and variance analysis.

Exploration of the Data

Generally, this study shows that there is more satisfaction with budgeting when conditions are relatively stable. When there is more certainty budgets become more important for implementation and control and managers are unlikely to agree that budgets cause problems. This is consistent with traditional literature that Otley (2001) summarised '...budgetary control appeared to work reasonably satisfactorily in a relatively stable environment with well-codified business plans.'

If conditions are relatively uncertain then budgeting is generally not so well regarded although we report that it becomes more important for *planning*. Consistent with this, there is more participation in budgeting with more involvement of junior managers and more iterations in the development of the budget. We also note that, in uncertain conditions, managers feel that budgets can be both challenging *and* realistic and, consequent on the involvement of more managers, budget gaming tends to increase.

In 'top-down' companies where *senior management drive the budget* there is a very significant likelihood that the budgeting process will be perceived as more bureaucratic, time consuming and inhibiting.

Analysis of survey data showed that attitudes to budgeting are likely to be most favourable in stable conditions where top management adopts a relatively light touch to the budgeting process.

Conclusion

We conclude that neither the traditional literature nor the 'Beyond Budgeting' diagnosis captures the reality of budgeting practice in contemporary organisations:

- Traditional literature has concentrated on the behavioural consequences of budgeting but, in this survey, there was only limited evidence of budgets leading to a blame culture, excessive gaming or over-stringent targets.

■ The 'Beyond Budgeting' critique identifies the bureaucratic and time-consuming nature of budgets; performance contracts and gaming as problems and similar dimensions emerged from our factor analysis. *However*, there is little to suggest that budgeting is perceived as a major problem by most financial or non-financial managers.

Our observations are consistent with those of Ross (1995) and Frow et al. (2005). Ross failed to replicate the Hopwood and Otley studies and concluded that one possible explanation was that '...a more flexible use of variances for performance evaluation had developed' (p. 8). Frow et al. investigated whether traditional budgeting based on responsibility centres inhibited innovation in a high-tech company and concluded that it did not. These positive findings are consistent with our survey. Budgets are often used flexibly and there is very limited evidence of the various misfortunes that might follow in the wake of budgeting. Budgets can be time consuming, bureaucratic and rigid, managerial ownership might be lost and some managers complained of sometimes unfortunate interventions by senior managers. However, most managers are satisfied with their budgeting systems. Where companies do go 'Beyond Budgeting' they do so by adding additional techniques or analytical detail rather than reducing traditional budgeting.

Part 2

Introduction

A number of interviews were undertaken in order to confirm the findings of the survey and to provide more insight into the changing uses of budgeting. This revealed the importance of understanding the uses of budgeting in organisational context and helped provide a provisional reconciliation of our findings with those that advocate 'Beyond Budgeting'.

The Literature: Business Structures and Control

As small businesses grow, they develop specialised, *differentiated* functions and budgetary control provides a means of *integrating* these, allowing functional directors to set out objectives and plans and delegate authority to responsible managers.

Business structure depends on circumstances and Burns and Stalker (1961) showed that administrative, hierarchical control may lead to loss of flexibility and innovation. In uncertain conditions, they recommended *organic* structures based on individual initiative, lateral communication and shared values. Chenhall (2003) summarised subsequent research noting that organic structures were associated with broad scope and timely information, more subjective evaluation style, participative budgeting and more interpersonal interaction.

Woodward (1965) found that technology (individual, batch, mass) had an important influence on structure and Thompson (1967) provided a categorisation of technologies: pooled, sequential or reciprocally interdependent. Pooled interdependence (e.g. bank branches) refers to relatively self-contained operating units carrying out similar activities. Sequential interdependence (as in many manufacturing operations) arises when the output from one department is passed to the next in serial fashion. Reciprocal interdependence (e.g. in the interaction between marketing, design and development departments) is characterised by work passing back and forth between departments and complex dependencies. Macintosh and Daft (1987) confirmed that pooled organisations tend to use standardised rules and procedures, sequential organisations use more sophisticated accounting and reciprocal organisations need more face-to-face interaction and mutual adjustment.

Decentralisation in Very Large Organisations

Following study of the growth of American businesses, Chandler (1962) showed that very large companies needed to adopt something other than functional (whether mechanistic or organic) structures. Large firms tended to diversify both products and markets but this placed an 'intolerable strain' on existing administrative structures and Chandler concluded that, as companies grew and diversified, they moved towards decentralised, divisional, product–market-related structures.

Divisional organisation structures are now ubiquitous, often with many decentralised divisions, each with its own functional organisation, reporting to a corporate centre that might include a variety of staff functions that support the divisions. There can be many layers with divisions, themselves, internally decentralised into product/market business units while corporate 'centres' themselves report to yet higher corporate levels.

Contemporary and Future Organisations

The application of the principles of decentralisation and mechanistic/organic structures has been adapted to developments such as flexible manufacturing, just-in-time production, total quality management, lean methods and workforce empowerment and an increasingly globalised, deregulated and competitive environment. Researchers expected more team structures and more diversified skills in empowered employees and this is what they found. Generally, recent developments in manufacturing and a more uncertain, competitive environment have tended to promote more organic than mechanistic structures.

Beinhocker (2007) and Hamel (2007) supported the move towards organic structures with a radical attack on traditional economic theory and examples of companies that emphasised encouragement, peer pressure and results-based incentives. Hamel's examples have similarities with the key 'Beyond Budgeting' example, Svenska Handelsbanken and the future of organisations might be ever more organic structures with flat hierarchies and democratically managed and remunerated teams. However, we also note that the companies chosen as examples emphasise innovation and can be organised into relatively small, sometimes pooled units. Flat organisational structures are easier to arrange in these companies than in those companies that focus on efficient execution of complex processes.

Hierarchies and Markets

Arrow (1969) and Williamson (1981a,b) drew attention to transaction costs with markets being efficient when transaction costs are low but, if complex contracts are needed, transaction costs increase and hierarchical organisation becomes more efficient. Paradoxically, as companies grew, the hierarchies became unworkable and, as Chandler explained, this has been met by the introduction of internal market-based structures.

Hierarchies, Markets and Clans

Organisations may be structured as mechanistic hierarchies or they may prefer organic structures where the glue is not the invisible reporting lines that define duties and responsibilities but common beliefs and values. Ouchi (1980) later referred to this sort of organisational control as *clan* control with employees socialised to regard their personal interests as congruent with those of the organisation.

This analysis based on markets (output controls), hierarchies (process controls) and clans (input controls of beliefs and values) provides insights into the transition of growing organisations from markets to hierarchies and then back to the use of markets as very large companies decentralised. Clan controls, appropriate to organic organisations, provide a counterpoint to mechanistic, hierarchical controls with beliefs and values replacing reliance on rules and instructions.

Our summary:

1   A taxonomy of control systems

		Focus of control		
		Input control	Process control	Output control
Method of control	**Formal systems**	**Budgetary control** for authorisation of financial resources. Qualifications, training, induction schemes for control over personnel	**Mechanistic** structures with administrative systems for control over action. Standards, procedures, **budgets**, bureaucracies, hierarchies and role definitions.	Specification of required outputs: product and service quality and volume; financial metrics for performance evaluation. **Markets** for product; incentive schemes for results.
	Informal systems	Company values and culture leading to peer pressure and **clan** control over personnel	**Organic** structures with lateral communications and reliance on interpersonal relationships	If outputs are ambiguous or difficult to evaluate subjective social controls may be needed.

Budgetary control is most likely to be associated with *formal* organisational control especially when that control is over *inputs and processes* and is especially useful when outputs are unambiguously specified and the relationship between outputs and inputs is well understood.

Strategy and Control

Chandler's analysis showed how large, diversified companies opted for decentralised organisation structures and Goold and Campbell's (1987) research found that strategy might be set at the corporate centre (core businesses), at divisional level (diverse businesses) or at business unit level (manageable businesses).

From the late 1970s a number of models were suggested that could help in analysing strategy and in guiding its formulation: the defender–prospector–analyser typology of Miles and Snow (1978); Porter's (1980, 1985) identification of cost leadership and differentiation as generic strategies and the build–hold–harvest–divest strategic missions of Gupta and Govindarajan (1984). Common sense matching between chosen strategy and control systems suggested that defenders and cost leaders would use hierarchical, centralised, mechanistic structures. On the other hand, prospectors following differentiation strategies would use more organic structures with control through interpersonal coordination rather than formal systems. Surprisingly, research did not confirm these expectations.

This caused a re-evaluation of budgeting and Simons (1995) set out his 'levers of control' based on belief systems, boundary systems, interactive systems and diagnostic systems. This echoes several of the themes developed in our literature review: belief systems relate to clan control and organic structures; boundary systems link to input controls; interactive systems imply participation; diagnostic systems link to traditional feedback (or feed-forward) standard costing and budgeting systems.

Simons' analysis leads to the conclusion that the manner in which control systems are *used* is important. While output targets and standards are intrinsic to diagnostic control systems, according to Simons they should not be used in interactive control systems where participants are expected to share problems and opportunities and propose solutions, thus fostering organisational learning. 'For these reasons, control systems *cannot* be used interactively if incentives are linked by formula to fixed, *ex ante* goals' (p. 118).

The Field Study

Visits were made to eight of the companies that had participated in the survey and interviews undertaken either with a finance manager or with both finance and non-finance managers. A semi-structured interview style was adopted.

The companies represented a range of manufacturing industries[3] and varied from a very large cost centre, Aircraft, part of an aerospace multinational, to two small, privately owned companies, Systems and WRL. We visited five companies that could be characterised as 'profit centres': Systems, WRL, Foundations, Frozen Food and Jam. Of the remaining three companies, Aircraft and Laboratory Instruments were cost centres and, at the last company, Food Ingredients, our interviewee

---

[3] Three from the food industry, Frozen Food, Jam and Food Ingredients; one in construction, Foundations; one wholesaling/retailing, WRL; one manufacturer of laboratory instruments, Laboratory Instruments; one engineering consultant, Systems; and one in the aircraft industry, Aircraft.

represented the corporate centre of a major European division. Two companies, Systems and the Jam Group, had plans to float on the stock exchange.

Field Study Findings: Budget Preparation

The field study confirmed the findings of the survey. Typically budget preparation begins 3–6 months before the financial year and follows a carefully structured process. We were impressed by the attention to detail and, where appropriate, the use of probabilities to estimate the likelihood of winning contracts. There were references to the longwinded nature of budgeting (at Aircraft and Systems) and at two companies, Laboratory Instruments and Frozen Food, this had been addressed by reducing the timescale for preparation of the budget by 1 month.

'Ownership' of the budget by responsible managers was an important issue in most of the companies. If profit-accountable managers accept their budget, one would expect them to be motivated towards its achievement and this did seem to be the case. In one company we heard about a failure of budget ownership: agreement to an over-ambitious budget, subsequent failure, demoralisation and the general manager responsible left the company.

The pressure for an aggressive budget varied from company to company. At the two companies that desired stock exchange listing senior managers generated pressure and inserted budget 'tasks'. In other companies realistic (though not easily achieved) budgets were set and, at Foundations, there was a clear mandate from the corporate centre to ensure that the budget was *achievable*. There could be some conflict, for example, at Systems, the Finance Director wanted realism while the general manager wanted more ambition.

The field study supports the results of the survey. In these companies preparation of the budget begins some months in advance of the financial year and preparation can be longwinded with several iterations. Two companies had taken steps to reduce the time taken to prepare the budget and, in some companies, there was recognition that it was a time-consuming and expensive process. This did not lead automatically to dissatisfaction but, in two companies, the interventions of senior managers were criticised.

Field Study Findings: Budgets for Influencing and Controlling Behaviour

Budgets are used for control in all the companies and, at Systems and Laboratory Instruments, the Managing Director set what might be considered a budget-constrained culture. At Systems this led to some job-related tension while, at the cost centre, Laboratory Instruments, managers seemed to accept the need for tight targets and cost control (aggressive targets in Laboratory Instruments' more stable, cost-centre environment may be more acceptable). Whereas Systems and Laboratory Instruments faced personal constraint, enforced by individuals, the large cost centre, Aircraft, seemed to face bureaucratic constraint with complex systems and senior managers involved in detailed reporting.

The profit-centre managers tended to emphasise managerial responsibility rather than control with the need to educate managers to take action even if this involved unbudgeted spend at Foundations and WRL. Managers at Jam seemed to be sand-wiched[4] between corporate managers insisting on aggressive targets and their local culture that emphasised teamwork and supportive budgeting. The budget sets the financial profit but '…not the method of getting there'.

Field Study Findings: Resetting the Budget

All these companies set a budget for the financial year and did not amend it. Aircraft and Systems had previously reset the budget but, at Aircraft, it was felt that this involved a disproportionate finance workload for the benefit obtained and, at Systems, the board felt that, if the budget could be changed, managers did not take it sufficiently seriously.

Field Study Findings: Attitudes to Budgeting

In the survey most respondents continue to see budgets as important and the field study confirmed these perceptions. Budgeting is 'essential', 'pretty important' and the 'primary financial tool'. It 'provided a framework', 'crystallised targets' and allowed 'management by exception'. Although there were some adverse comments, as in the survey, these were outweighed by generally positive comments.

In the survey respondents generally *did not* agree with a list of statements criti-cising budgeting and, similarly, our interviews were generally positive. Where dis-satisfaction was expressed in the survey it was usually because of the process and/or failure to encourage local ownership of budgets and senior management pressure. Again, the interviews reflected these findings. At Aircraft and Systems, budgets were considered longwinded and local budget ownership was an issue. At both these com-panies and Jam the intervention of senior managers was not always seen as helpful.

Implications for 'Beyond Budgeting' and Traditional Literatures

We confirm that *budget processes tend to be longwinded and bureaucratic* although this did not automatically lead to dissatisfaction. Two companies had reduced the length of time given to budget preparation.

---

[4]No pun intended.

We had little evidence that budgeting *fails to meet the needs of managers in competitive environments*. In general, budgeting was seen as helpful for planning and control and, as in Frow et al. (2005), managers seemed to find budgets useful in setting a realistic financial framework rather than inhibiting necessary action.

There was little evidence that *performance contracts are pernicious* although incentive schemes had real and sometimes undesirable effects. At Food Ingredients and Frozen Food budgets might be 'managed' with an eye on potential bonuses and the combination of budget targets and an incentive scheme was criticised at Systems.

There were limited examples of *budgets leading to gaming:* budget contingencies to manage the expectations of Group managers and a danger that, once authorised, operational managers might regard budgets as 'theirs to spend'. Overall, managers were aware of the dangers of budget gaming and did not see this as a major issue.

We saw only one example, at Systems, of *a budget-constrained style having adverse consequences*. In most of the companies we would have characterised the style as more 'profit conscious' than 'budget constrained'.

There was little evidence of *conflicting objectives in setting budget targets*: survey managers did not agree that this was a problem. There was some evidence of budget optimism, especially at Systems and, recently, at Jam. However, even at these companies, there were voices arguing for realism and, generally, companies seemed to set realistic but nevertheless challenging budgets.

The use of budgeting does seem to have moved on since the 1970s with managers generally positive about the benefits of budgeting, aware of the possible risks and prepared to use the budget constructively so long as the culture set by senior managers permits this.

Lessons from the Field Study: Culture, Context and Structure

Local management culture was influenced by the structures adopted. Managers in decentralised, autonomous profit centres adopted flexible approaches to meeting targets while management attitudes at Laboratory Instruments and Aircraft were influenced by their cost-centre status.

Context was important at all the companies. Possible stock exchange listing affected senior management attitudes at Jam and Systems. Serious difficulties at WRL meant budgeting was necessary to reassure creditors. At Laboratory Instruments recent cost pressures had led to a freeze on capital expenditure. At Aircraft the joint venture, trans-European nature of the operation, set the context for budgeting and other systems. At Frozen Food the outperformance of the company allowed the use of contingencies in budgets submitted to Group and increased local flexibility. At Foundations corporate insistence on realism in budgets impacted directly on local practices.

Budgets and Structures

Profit centres were relatively autonomous and, where possible, pushed the profit-centre approach down their organisations: to geographical areas at Foundations; to products at Frozen Foods; to customer segments at Systems and to functions (wholesaling, retailing, leisure) at WRL. Jam could not so easily adopt this approach because its different product lines (and those of the wider group) are often sold to the same powerful customers. The Jam Group therefore has a marketing division that takes a large proportion of Jam's product and there is more centralisation than at other companies.

Where appropriate, standard costing and operating systems were used. Factories at Foundations and Frozen Foods were treated as cost centres, controlled, like Laboratory Instruments, through standard costing and budgeting systems. WRL also has important operational controls with an incentive scheme that rewards warehouse personnel for speedy and accurate stock-picking.

We conclude that control in the organisations we visited was exercised through a number of related systems emphasising control of *outputs* (sales, gross margin, contribution margin) in the sales areas, *processes* in the factories (standards and budgets) and *inputs* (budgeted resources) in the support areas.

Particularly important for our later conclusion was the observation that, even *within* a unit of a much larger group there were complex issues of coordination and control. Budgets at Foundations and Frozen Food help to coordinate activities across the factories, marketing areas and service centres. Budgets are also important in setting the fully absorbed cost used in transferring output from factories to marketing areas and in providing a resource envelope for service areas such as IT and Finance.

Transfer pricing policy was important in several companies. Managers at Jam and Foundations wanted 'arms-length' inter-divisional transfer pricing. There was a similar view at WRL where transfers from the wholesale division to the retail division were at the same price as that used to supply other customers. However, within Frozen Food, a Support Services centre provides its services to the other profit centres and our interviewee emphasised the importance of a relatively high transfer price so as to prevent the delivery profit centres from 'giving the service away'. At Frozen Food a specialised Support Services centre, supplying its services at managed transfer prices, is an integral part of company strategy.

Coordination, Planning and Control

Budgets were useful for different reasons. Foundations, Frozen Food and Jam need systems to *plan* and *coordinate* their production, service and delivery operations and budgets help in *setting transfer prices*. Frozen Food also uses the budget as a *control* mechanism, whereas Foundations and Jam emphasised *interaction*, trusting the managers and encouraging them to think outside the budget when needed.

At Systems and WRL there are fewer coordination issues with relatively autonomous sub-units. In these companies budgets are used for both planning and control. At Systems senior managers reverted to an unchanged budget in order to enforce agreed targets and at WRL a budgeting system was necessary to persuade creditors that the company merited continued support.

Are Budgets Needed?

A key element in the 'Beyond Budgeting' thesis is that, if companies implement radical decentralisation, they will have much less need for budgeting systems. However, *despite extensive decentralisation*, the companies we visited continue to use budgets. We argue that, even after reaching the limits of decentralisation, there was enough complexity and interdependence *within* companies we visited for budgets or other coordinating systems to be necessary.

We conclude that interdependence between business units and the corporate centre and within business units is the key to understanding whether budgets (or other coordination/planning/control systems) are *necessary*. Interdependence can be analysed into vertical, lateral and external dimensions. Vertically the business unit may share corporate services, may be constrained by corporate strategy and may suffer a degree of control both in formulating and in executing plans. Horizontally the business unit may buy from or sell to other business units. Externally, the business unit may share finished good or factor markets with other business units. Within business units the analysis in relation to sub-units proceeds in similar fashion. Sub-units may share services, follow common strategies and be closely controlled. They may take/supply products and services from/to other sub-units and, externally, they may share factor and/or finished goods markets.

This analysis indicates that interdependence varies depending on organisational level. Foundations and Frozen Food are relatively autonomous business units with few vertical, horizontal or external interactions. However, both exhibit considerable *internal* complexity. This leads us to the conclusion that, structurally, these business units could be managed by setting *output* targets but they need budgets or other planning/control systems to manage their *internal* operations.

Implications for the 'Beyond Budgeting' Debate

Partly driven by the Svenska Handelsbanken example a key element of the 'Beyond Budgeting' thesis is that modern organisations need to go beyond hierarchical, divisionalised structures and adopt flat decentralised structures. Our analysis suggests a more complex relationship between organisational structure and budgets in non-pooled organisations. At Foundations, Frozen Food, Jam, Laboratory Instruments and Aircraft we observed complex, differentiated organisations that contrasted with the pooled organisation of Svenska Handelsbanken. Although Frozen Food and Foundations, being relatively autonomous business units, might not need budgets to control them, internal complexity means that, even if budgeting for the business unit itself were abandoned, local managers would probably wish to use budgets to manage their internal operations.

Our conclusion is that there are organisational limits to decentralisation which mean that a coordinating system is often needed and budgeting provides such a system. The need for budgets can vary throughout the organisation and budgets (or another coordinating mechanism) may be needed at one organisational level but not at another.

Those who advocate moving 'Beyond Budgeting' also draw attention to the multiple and conflicting uses of budgets. They argue that budgets with multiple uses lead to logical problems. However, in the cases we have reported, there are few obvious practical problems. While budgets could be used to generate pressure (as at Jam and Systems) they need not be used in this way and several companies provided evidence that budgets could be used to plan and control operations. Additionally, the long-established institutional role of budgeting was valuable in reassuring creditors at WRL.

Budgets can be valuable for a number of purposes and can be important for coordinating activities at various levels in an organisation. However, where appropriate, and, if they are sufficiently independent, the 'Beyond Budgeting' suggestion that such units need not be controlled by complex budgets makes sense. Profit or investment centres are designed to be controlled by their outputs: profit, return on investment, economic value added, cash flow return on assets, etc., and, if the target is agreed, then the method of its achievement need not, in theory, trouble senior managers. In fact, if both targets and method of achievement are set out in detail then the control system might be over-specified. A manager could achieve target but not follow process while another followed process but failed to achieve target. Which manager has done what is required?

Designing Structure and Control Systems

The report concludes with a discussion of structure and control system design. The discussion is informed by the conclusions from the survey and the field study and by a further case, Finrock. This case led us to appreciate the importance of identifying the key value-adding part of the business when designing organisational structure and control systems.

Finrock specialises in drilling and blasting equipment and in loading and handling equipment and has four product divisions with (worldwide) selling organised by region. Transfers of product from the product divisions to the sales companies used to take place at transfer price. However, this made the profits of both sales companies and product divisions sensitive to the negotiated transfer price. Now, emphasis is placed on the profitability of product divisions calculated after an *allocation* of sales costs. At this company, value is added in the complex and engineering-intensive production processes that manufacture, often huge, heavy drilling and rock-moving machines and trucks. Although it is *easy* to attribute revenue to the sales companies, it is much more *useful* to attribute revenue to the product divisions.

Transfer prices still exist because the sales companies are legal entities, operating in several countries. However, within Finrock there are now references to 'consolidated profit' and 'local profit'. Consolidated profit refers to the profit of the product divisions and this is now very important for strategic planning and control. Local profit refers to sales company profits. These are not critical for company planning but are important in evaluating the performance of individual sales companies.

Lessons from the Study: Structure

Although decentralisation might be desirable, there are limits to decentralisation that might impact different tiers of the organisation in different ways. Organisations combine profit centres, cost centres and product/service transfers between these centres in a variety of ways depending on their varying products and markets.

In four field study profit centres we saw that profitability was driven down to sub-units and value is added by these market-facing units. Finrock is different. Its primary value-adding activities are in the design and manufacturing product divisions, not in the sales companies. This has now been recognised by attributing revenue directly to the product divisions.

We conclude that business units tend to use structures that recognise the key value-adding parts of the business. Revenue is usually attributed to value-adding units either directly or at arms-length transfer prices.[5] Centres that are deemed not to be key value-adding units tend to be designated cost centres and their outputs are transferred on some cost-related basis to the value-adding units.

These examples provide insights into the way that structures and systems might be designed and we offer Figure 1 as an overview of the insights this research has generated. It suggests logical links between strategy, structure, control systems, organisational culture and reward systems and these are likely to vary across differentiated organisational functions:

- Identify general strategic aims (cost leader, prospector, etc.) and key product/service/markets.
- Identify key value-adding parts of the business.

---

[5] The exception to this 'rule', in our cases, was the use of managed transfer price in Frozen Food's Service profit centre.

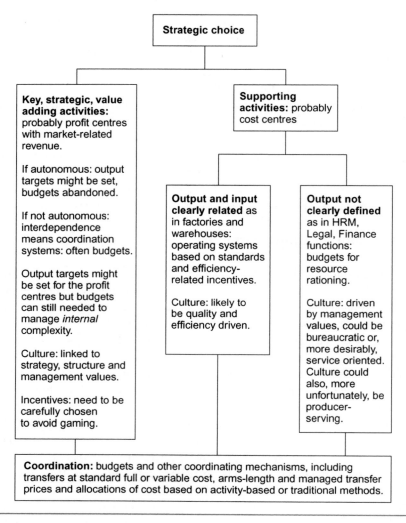

Figure 1 Strategy, structure, control and culture.

■ Design a decentralised structure that emphasises the value-adding operations by attributing revenue to them while recognising limits to decentralisation:
  ○ interactions between units, sub-units, service centres;
  ○ extent of local capability;
  ○ need for central control over strategy and, possibly, operations.
■ Identify supporting operations, probably designating them cost centres.

■ Design appropriate coordination and control systems for different parts of the organisation.

■ Pay attention to culture and recognise that culture might differ between different elements of the organisation with, for example, efficiency in operations but entrepreneurship in marketing.

Lessons from the Study: Coordination

The advocates of 'Beyond Budgeting' see radical decentralisation as a vital part of the cultural change that abandoning budgeting entails. However, the field study companies need coordinating mechanisms either between business units or within the business unit we visited. Our conclusion is that complexity sets limits to sensible decentralisation and the degree of autonomy varies depending on organisational level. Autonomous divisions that have their own IT, HR, Finance, Quality, Engineering and Production functions may not need systems to coordinate operations across the group. However, the divisions themselves, with significant *internal* complexity need coordinating systems.[6]

Lessons from the Study: Control

If budgets are used in order to pressure managers then a number of unfortunate consequences are possible. However, we observed more examples of the constructive use of budgets with little evidence of problems within Jam, Foundations, Frozen Food, WRL or Finrock. Laboratory Instruments probably had a 'traditional' approach to budgeting and the budget was an instrument of tight control in this company. Nevertheless, as a cost centre producing standard product, it was difficult to say that the use of standard costing and tight budgets was inappropriate.

Our conclusion is that budgets can be an important management tool for maintaining control and, generally, managers understand their advantages and disadvantages well enough to ensure that the former outweigh the latter.

The 'Beyond Budgeting' Debate

Our questionnaire survey revealed limited dissatisfaction with traditional budgeting practices and we were puzzled that, contrary to expectations stoked by 'Beyond

---

[6] We note that strategic planning organisations are likely to need coordinating systems across the whole company; strategic control organisations are likely to need such systems within their relatively autonomous divisions and financial control organisations may only need such systems within their relatively autonomous business units.

Budgeting', financial and non-financial managers were united in regarding budgeting as important and not particularly problematic.

A partial reconciliation of our findings with those of the 'Beyond Budgeting' movement resides, we believe, in the interaction between organisational structures and coordination systems. We have suggested that:

- The performance of *independent, autonomous* units can be assessed using market-based, output-related measures.
- Interaction between business units and sub-units makes coordination devices such as budgets necessary.

In our study the focus was on control *within* operating organisations and we saw sufficient complexity to suggest that a coordinating system, such as budgeting, was needed. The 'Beyond Budgeting' movement, on the other hand, emerged from study of the relations *between* corporate managers and operating units. Corporate executives aiming to control relatively autonomous divisions may see target setting and performance measurement rather than budgeting as the key issues. Our conclusion is that control and coordination systems need to be matched to the level of the organisation. It is possible for tiered organisations to adopt output-related measures in managing relationships between corporate and divisional levels and to adopt budgetary systems *within* divisions or other business units.

Context

Finally, budgeting operates within a context that includes organisational strategy, structure, culture and reward and omitting some of these variables means that research models are likely to be under-specified. While many studies now control for organisational size and nature, we argue that researchers need to be aware of multiple interacting variables in complex business environments. Among other things the behaviour of managers in profit and cost centres will be different; organic and mechanistic structures require different behaviours/cultures and budgets may have a range of purposes that may be appropriate (or inappropriate) for particular combinations of strategies, structures and functions.

Part 1

The Uses of and Attitudes to Budgeting

This book reports a study of budgeting practice that started in 2003 with a survey of companies in the South-West of England and continued with visits to several of the survey companies through 2004–2006.

The research was stimulated by the challenge to budgeting posed by the 'Beyond Budgeting' movement that emerged during the 1990s. Business budgeting had developed in the 1920s and, in the space of 70 years or so had come in for its share of criticism. However, until the 'Beyond Budgeting' challenge, it was generally thought that its benefits outweighed its costs or, at least, that it was a necessary evil. However, those advocating 'Beyond Budgeting' suggested that companies could improve their performance by actually abandoning budgets. The first aim of the research was to test whether these views are shared by managers in practice and a questionnaire was designed in order to investigate this.

In the first part of the book we review the development of budgeting practices, the uses of budgets and the problems that budgeting can create. Then we report the findings of our survey on management attitudes to budgeting. Chapter 1 provides a review of the development of budgeting in the early twentieth century and the uses for budgeting that emerged then and subsequently. Chapter 2 reviews the problems that budgeting could generate and the criticisms that were levelled at budgeting in the second half of the twentieth century. This chapter places the contemporary criticisms of the 'Beyond Budgeting' school in context. Chapter 3 reports the findings of the budgeting survey. Companies in the South-West of England were asked to participate in a questionnaire investigation into changes in budgeting practice and the attitudes to budgeting of both financial and non-financial managers. Somewhat to our surprise both financial and non-financial managers saw budgeting as fairly unproblematic and generally they thought it important for a range of reasons.

Chapter 1

The Uses of Budgeting

1. Introduction

The official terminology of the Chartered Institute of Management Accountants (2005 p. 5) provides the following definition of a budget: 'Quantitative expression of a plan for defined period of time. It may include planned sales volumes and revenues; resource quantities, costs and expenses; assets, liabilities and cash flows.' Textbooks provide similar definitions. For example, Seal et al. (2006, p. 494) state that: 'A budget is a detailed plan for the acquisition and use of financial and other resources over a specified time period. It represents a plan for the future expressed in formal, quantitative terms.' For Anthony and Govindarajan (2004, p. 409): '*An operating budget usually covers one year and states the revenue and expenses planned for that year.*' (emphasis as in original)

There is general agreement amongst management accounting writers that budgeting is important, pervasive and forms a key element in most organisational control systems. Merchant and Van der Stede (2003, p. 306) see budgeting as a 'near-universal organizational practice' and, quoting Umapathy (1987, p. 140) as the most recent survey available, note that the vast majority of responding firms had a formal budgeting system; of these, 91% reported that their budgets were for a 1-year period. This is consistent with recent work in the UK by Dugdale et al. (2006). Interviews with financial controllers/directors in 41 companies revealed only one that did not have budgeting processes. The other 40 companies prepared budgets for a period of 1 year and most (37) did not amend the budget during the financial year.

The prevalence of budgeting and the general agreement among textbook writers that it is important certainly suggests that it is useful and, in this chapter we identify the key uses of budgeting. We provide a short historical review of the development of budgeting and argue that, by the 1920s, three key uses of budgeting had emerged: authorisation, planning and control. Later, authors noted that the use of budgets for planning and control led almost automatically to their role as a tool of communication and coordination and it was suggested that the setting of budget targets could also help to motivate managers.

We begin by describing the introduction of budgeting in nineteenth century UK government and then its emergence in private sector companies in the 1920s.

2. Public Sector Budgeting

Budgets, in the sense of making forecasts of and plans for future events, have been around for a long time. Solomons (1952. p. 45) even goes back to biblical times to find the example of Joseph, in Egypt, making a budget of corn supplies.

However, in modern times, the use of budgeting can be traced to its institutionalisation in nineteenth century government. Roseveare (1973) saw the UK Treasury gaining authority as early as the seventeenth century but modern government budgeting had to wait till the nineteenth century. Even the 'modest objectives' of accurately assessing and collecting revenue and honestly disbursing and accounting for expenditure were not easy in the face of 'tenure for life' in English civil administration; connivance in the misappropriation of public funds and the politicisation of Parliamentary Accounts Commissions.

Only after the Exchequer and Audit Departments Act of 1866 could Roseveare speak of the completion of the 'circle of control' and the emergence of positive principles of financial management. Now there was:

(a) a technique of estimate, by which the annual requirements of forthcoming public expenditure could be accurately assessed, and (b)... parliamentary appropriation, by which funds could be strictly allocated to these needs. It also required (c) an independent agency (the reformed Exchequer) empowered to issue these appropriated funds to (d) responsible, non-political paymasters, disbursing funds on behalf of government departments. Finally it required (e) effective machinery for the independent audit of this expenditure and (f) the submission of the balanced, annual account to the scrutinizing committee of the House of Commons. (p. 47)

Thus, budgeting became a key tool in planning public expenditure and authorising the expenditure of public funds by non-political paymasters acting on behalf of government departments.

In the US, public budgeting lagged than in Europe but, in the late nineteenth century, municipal budgets were developed in New York, Philadelphia, Boston, Chicago and other large cities. Then, between 1911 and 1919, 44 states developed budgets and the budget and accounting act of 1921 mandated a national budget.[1]

3. Emergence of Budgetary Control in the Private Sector

The late nineteenth century and early twentieth centuries saw the development of budgeting in the public sector and this was also a very fertile period in the history of organisational and management theory. The late nineteenth century saw the birth of scientific management and what Solomons (1952, p. 17) called *'The Costing Renaissance'*. These developments and the emergence of budgeting in the public sector provided the background against which private sector budgetary control emerged. Interest in costing developed apace in the last years of the nineteenth and early years of the twentieth century and interest in budgetary control in the private sector followed in the wake of this with the 1920s being a particularly fruitful period in the development of budgeting theory.

Quail (1997, p. 619) referred to: 'J.O. McKinsey's pioneering work *Budgetary Control* [that] appeared in 1922.' And he quoted Elbourne (1926, p. 11): 'By 1926 an English observer could say "of all the many forces at work in American business today there is nothing so new, so arresting and so much in men's minds as Budgetary Control" '. Hayes (1929, p. 106) noted that budgeting in the US had been confined 'almost entirely' to government bodies but: 'A decade ago budgeting for business enterprises began to attract and to hold the attention of business executives.' And Harrison (1930) was enthusiastic: 'The vivid interest which accountants are taking today in budget and the predetermination of profits and costs is one of the most significant and encouraging signs of the times,...' (p. 24).

Already, in the 1920s, one of the authorities on the subject, McKinsey (1927) was able to spell out the outline of a budgetary control system:

> *[Budgets] ...are a statement of future accounts expressed in terms of unit responsibility...It is essential that that the budgets be made in such form that they will present a statement of future accounts, for otherwise it is difficult, if not impossible, to make such comparisons between the estimated and actual*

---

[1] *Source*: Budgetary Control in Manufacturing, p. 5, National Industrial Conference Board, 1931.

results... The budget should be expressed in units of responsibility because responsibility must be placed upon specific individuals... (p. 363)

Comparison of this definition with those in Section 1 reveals that budgets and budgeting have had similar forms and purposes for almost a century. Budgeting in the private sector quickly became a means of assigning financial responsibility and accountability to managers and a means of checking whether actual results were in line with those budgeted for each part of the organisation. Very soon 'budgeting' became 'budgetary control' and when linked with clearly specified organisation structures budgetary control was a means of enforcing accountability. The early literature saw budgeting as not only providing a plan of action but also a check on progress against that plan. And specific individuals were to be held responsible and accountable for delivering the plan. The themes of feedback control and hierarchical, delegated responsibility rapidly became pervasive in the budgeting literature.

Budgetary control developed alongside the other child of scientific management, standard costing. Although the National Association of (Cost) Accountants in the US noted that their initial development was largely separate, it was later realised that:

...both were merely applications of the same management philosophy and they were complementary parts of a complete program of cost control. (N.A.(C.)A. Research Series 11 (1 February 1948 quoted by Horngren, 1962, p. 180))

Harrison (1930) spelled out this common philosophy:

It may be asked what objective can we set up in our books for the executive. The answer is obvious: whereas the objective of the superintendent is decreased costs of production, that of the executive is profits. ...

No man can realize his fullest possibilities, whether he be a five-dollar-a-day trucker in the factory or a fifty-thousand-dollar-a-year executive, unless he has before him at all times (1) a carefully determined objective, (2) record showing the relation between accomplishment and this objective, and (3) if he has failed to realize his objective, information as to the causes of such failure. Standard costs furnish the factory superintendent and the factory foreman with this information as regards factory costs, and standard profit or budget systems give the executive this information as regards profits. (p. 28)

Thus standard costing and budgetary control provided a management philosophy that revolved around setting out a plan and holding individuals responsible, through clear delegation, for delivering the plan.

In the mid-twentieth century, budgeting was seen as an extension of control outside the factory. The Institute of Cost and Works Accountants (ICWA) (1950) noted that both budgetary control and standard costing require: predetermined standards/targets; measurement of actual performance; calculation of variances between standard/target and actual and follow-up action. The techniques were then differentiated by their focus of application:

By common usage the application of these principles to the operation of the business as a whole, or of its departments, is termed Budgetary Control, whereas the application of these principles to the detailed production operations and products is termed Standard Costing. (ICWA, 1950, p. 7)[2]

There are plenty of examples of the emphasis on *control* in budgetary control. For example, Willsmore (1932) in what was claimed to be the first British book on budgeting argued that: '...budget control entails more than a mere forecast of the future. It involves a concerted plan of action based on a careful consideration of all relevant tendencies and factors, and it is, in itself, a complete system for controlling costs and preventing waste." (Preface to first edition, 1932, reproduced in Willsmore, 1949, p. viii, quoted by Boyns, 1998)

Similarly, Peirce (1954, p. 60) suggested that budgeting and control are inseparable:

I am referring to control, which is the eternal complement of planning. Neither one is useful without the other, and to budget even the smallest unit of a business, implies the presence of control also.

The ubiquitous use of the term budgetary *control* in twentieth century texts clearly meant what it said. When budgeting systems were introduced they reflected a particular approach to management. This was an approach born of the scientific management movement where managers were expected to know how to get things done the right way and to ensure that they were done that way. The key aspects of budgetary control are, first, the comparison of actual results with plan and, second, the delegation of responsibility and authority. We consider these in turn.

4. Feedback Control and Flexible Budgets

Boyns (1998) notes that Solomons (1952, p. 48) traces the idea of flexible budgeting to an article by Henry Hess in 1903. However, the idea does not appear to have

---

[2] The ICWA report sees budgetary control and standard costing as inter-related but not absolutely inter-dependent. Budgetary control might be appropriate in industries where standard costing would not make sense. And standard costing could be applied without a formal system of budgetary control. The National Industrial Conference Board survey (1930) had indeed noted that: 'Numerous companies classified in the survey as having no budget did have standard costs in their operating departments... [But standard costs only] afford a basis for currently measuring certain operations. They do not forecast trends or constitute a program.'

been pursued in earnest until the late 1920s. Ralph E. Case (who had been trained by Harrison) then worked with a group of engineers who developed a system of budget allowances to a standard cost system at the Westinghouse Company in 1928. (Sizer, 1968, quoted by Boyns, 1998)

The emphasis on 'control' pervades the development of 'flexible budgets' for the budget is flexed *after the event* when the actual level of output and sales is known. The point is to facilitate a meaningful comparison of resources *used* with what *might have been expected* for the given level of output/sales.

Standard cost systems allow this to be easily achieved for direct costs such as materials and labour by multiplying the unit standard cost by actual volume achieved. However, for overhead costs, incurred both inside and outside the factory, matters can be much more complex. As Horngren (1962) notes: '... (1) the size of individual overhead costs usually does not justify elaborate individual control systems; (2) the behaviour of individual overhead items is either impossible or inconvenient to trace to specific lots or operations; (3) various overhead items are the responsibility of different people; and (4) the behaviour of individual overhead items differs drastically'. (p. 193)

The last point is the focus of most textbook treatments. It is presumed that overheads behave as semi-fixed costs that can be split into their fixed and variable components and then it is possible to calculate the cost for a given level of activity by adding the variable cost allowance (volume × variable cost per unit) to the budgeted fixed cost.[3]

5.   Responsibility Accounting

We have already seen that budgeting facilitates the delegation of authority and responsibility and more references could be found. For example, delegation of responsibility was implicit in Harrison's (1930) example of a company that supplied radio spares. He wrote: 'A number of factors contributed to the satisfactory showing of the business referred to, but, without question, the primary reason for the success of the company was the fact that a definite realizable objective was set for every responsible member of the organization.' (pp. 29–30)

---

[3] Of course, it must be remembered that the categorisation of costs as either fixed or variable is an over simplification. In practice both may be 'step' costs – but fixed costs remain fixed within a 'relevant range' of activity levels and variable costs, though often stepped, can be approximated by assuming that they are proportional to level of activity. Other costs can have a more complex relationship to level of activity but, in principle, such costs can be accommodated within flexible budgeting so long as the behaviour is well understood.

Evans-Hemming (1952) linked standard costing, (flexible) budgetary control and responsibility accounting:

> *One essential feature of Flexible Budgetary Control and Standard Costs is the decentralisation of cost responsibility to departments, and therefore to departmental managers...As a plan is prepared for each department the departmental executive is consulted, and by this means his interest is aroused in operating his department according to the plan laid down, this interest being sustained by the continuous measurement of his actual performance. (pp. 2–3)*

Budgetary control provides not only a standard by which the whole business can be judged it also provides a standard for each separate department and thus a means of evaluating the performance of each departmental manager.

Similar sentiments were expressed in the ICWA's (1950) publication 'An Introduction to Budgetary Control Standard Costing Material Control and Production Control'. This report, planned in 1946/47, was based on contributions from members of the Institute and a draft submitted to the 19th National Cost Conference in 1948. The principles of authority, responsibility and controllability come through strongly. For example, the section dealing with the *Production Cost Budget* advises that: '...it be analysed departmentally according to responsibility. Every item of cost then becomes the responsibility of a person whose duty is to ensure that expenditure is controlled and does not exceed the allowance prescribed'. The section goes on to advise that items should only be included in a person's budget if: '...that expense is actually incurred by departments or functions under his control...' Budgetary control could be: '...an instrument of management policy whereby the extension of the scheme to lower levels of management enables top management to decentralise responsibility and centralise control'. (p. 8)

In the second half of the twentieth century, budgetary control and responsibility accounting was *de rigueur* in management accounting texts. In an echo of McKinsey's earlier comment, Horngren (1962) states that: '*Budgets are basically forecasted financial statements.*' (p. 168, emphasis as in original). This facilitates the comparison of actual results with budget. And responsibility accounting can be achieved through the nesting of organisational responsibilities. Horngren's example shows how controllable overhead items in the Assembly Foreman's report appear as a single line in the superintendent's report. The controllability principle is central: only items subject to the manager's control should be included in their reports.

Control, feedback and hierarchical responsibility accounting remain key themes in late twentieth century texts. Miller (1982) goes so far as to suggest that, if necessary, the organisation should be restructured to accommodate the efficient operation of budgetary control. 'Where significant interdependencies are present, the organizational structure should be examined and restructured with the purpose of either centralizing interdependent segments or redefining their controllable inputs and outputs.' (pp. 35–36)

6.   A Note on Definitions

Our review of the historical origins of budgeting refers to planning and control, and we assume that the reader has a feel for what is meant by these terms. However, careful consideration of terms like planning reveals that its definition can be rather elusive. Mintzberg (1994) discussed five different views of strategic planning. First, there is a school of thought that sees planning as a very broad term that refers to future thinking. Unfortunately, this definition would include most human activity and would therefore be unhelpful. Second, planning could refer to controlling the future: designing the future or controlling change in the environment. Unfortunately, again, this would encapsulate most human activity since virtually everything that we do is oriented to shaping the future, including, for example, deciding what to have for lunch. Third, planning is sometimes seen as decision making. For some authors planning is about choosing (deciding) between alternatives and this involves identification of options, their analysis, choice and identification of the actions/ resources needed to achieve the desired goal. For Mintzberg, this definition reduces to the first. for it is difficult to envisage human activity that does not involve making decisions and 'planning again becomes synonymous with everything managers do' (p. 10). Fourth, planning is integrated decision making. Although apparently similar to the third definition this is more distinctive with its emphasis on organising, grouping or batching decisions. Finally, Mintzberg introduces the key idea of formalisation and defines (strategic) planning as 'a formalized procedure to produce an articulated result, in the form of an integrated system of decisions'. (p. 12)

For Mintzberg this definition of planning, with its emphasis on formalised procedure and explicitly articulated results, is the one that most closely corresponds with what organisational planners actually do. Although it might be too restrictive for some authors and some purposes, it serves as an operational definition of organisational planning. Mintzberg's conclusion allows us to see more precisely why budgeting is almost invariably associated with planning. If organisational planning in practice means formal procedure and explicit statement, then budgeting processes fulfil both criteria to perfection and the taken-for-granted view that budgets are useful aids to planning is easily rationalised.

'Control' also poses problems of definition and Giglioni and Bedelan (1974) noted that several authors had pointed out that 'control' can mean different things depending on context. In organisational theory, control tends either to mean control over subordinates or '...the evaluation of the desired outcome of an activity and the making of corrections when necessary' (p. 293). Giglioni and Bedelan ignored control where it refers to the directing of subordinates and concentrated on control as a cycle of plan, do, compare and correct. Their review of writings in the period 1900–1972 revealed a general view among management writers such as Emerson, Diemer, Fayol, Robinson and Urwick: control involved a comparison of present performance with previously set standards/expectations/direction and knowledge of the means to correct divergences.

Giglioni and Bedelan's distinction between control as directing and control as evaluation/correction was also important to Otley and Berry (1980). They noted that, in the many possible uses of 'control', the 'most common idea it suggests is dominance' (p. 231) but their focus would be on the '...second strand of meaning that emphasises the idea of regulation and the monitoring of activities... In this paper the term "control" will be used in its full cybernetic sense of both monitoring activities and then taking action'. (pp. 231–232). Otley and Berry employ Tocher's analysis of cybernetic control based on an objective, a means of measuring results, a predictive model and choice of alternatives. They draw out issues such as whether an organisation can have objectives since they must be set by individual(s); that predictive models will under-specify operations and a trade-off is needed between efficiency and adaptability in such models; that measures are needed in relation to both the dimensions of the objective and also the variables in the predictive model(s) and the range of actions available: changing system inputs, changing the objective, amending predictive model(s) and changing the system itself.

These considerations show why budgeting systems are associated with the idea of control, particularly the correction of deviations from plan. No matter how *objectives* may be set or negotiated, they usually emerge through explicit budget statements. Links between budgeting and the accounting system implicate budgets with the *measurement* of revenues and expenses. Budgets embody the outcomes of *predictive models* for expense and investment. And the budgeting system provides the instrument that allows *actions* such as resetting objectives and redesign of the system to be articulated. Thus, while most managers would simply observe that budgets can be used for control, analysis of the literature, especially that which sees control as monitoring and correcting, confirms that there are good reasons to associate budgetary systems with organisational control.

Separately we can reflect that budgets can also be implicated in control as dominance or direction. Lukes (1974) identified three dimensions of power: as imposing one person's will over another's; as controlling the agenda; and through shaping beliefs and values. Budgeting can be implicated in all these dimensions. In the next chapter we will see that budgets can be used to pressure subordinates and to depersonalise management processes. Second, supervisors or more senior managers may follow secretive budgeting processes, using these processes to control the agenda.

Third, the budgeting system can help to shape organisational values with its explicit focus on the importance of profit and implicit prioritising of shareholder interests.

7.   The Uses of Budgets

Our review of the development of budgeting systems has emphasised two key uses of budgets, in planning and control. The systematic nature of budgeting and its formal statement through the accounting system in terms of revenue, expense and responsibility codes ensure the association of budgeting with planning. And the design of budgeting systems to facilitate the feedback loops beloved of cybernetics with comparisons of actual results with budget benchmarks by responsibility centre means that budget processes are readily associated with organisational control.

To these primary uses a number of secondary uses of budgets have been added and these seem to follow naturally from the main purposes and structure of budget systems. If what distinguishes budget-based planning from more widely drawn definitions of planning is the emphasis on process that ensures organisational direction then it is easy to see why budgeting is an aid to communication within organisations and an aid to coordination of organisational activities. And, if feedback control through budgets facilitates the comparison of agreed targets with actual results, neatly aligned with the responsibilities of cost or profit centre managers, then the use of budgets in evaluating managerial performance is also easily understood.

These considerations have led late twentieth and early twenty-first century management accounting texts to general agreement on the uses of budgets and we can gain a flavour of the consensus by reference to texts that have dominated in the US since the 1960s and in the UK since the 1980s. Anthony and Horngren were the first writers to codify managerial accounting and their US-based texts, now in their tenth and eleventh editions respectively, and written in partnership with co-authors, spell out the uses of budgets. For Horngren et al. (2000, p. 179):

Budgets are a major feature of most management control systems. When administered wisely, budgets (a) compel planning including the implementation of plans, (b) provide performance criteria, and (c) promote coordination and communication within the organization.

While for Anthony and Govindarajan (2004, p. 411):

Preparation of an operating budget has four principal purposes: (1) to fine-tune the strategic plan; (2) to help coordinate the several parts of the organization; (3) to assign responsibility to managers, to authorize the amounts they are permitted to spend, and to inform them of the performance that is expected of them; and (4) to obtain a commitment that is a basis for evaluating a manager's actual performance

Drury's (2004, p. 593) dominant UK text includes the following summary of budget uses:

> *Budgets serve a number of useful purposes. They include:*
>
> planning *annual operations*
>
> coordinating *the activities of the various parts of the organization...*
>
> communicating *plans to the various responsibility centre managers*
>
> motivating *managers to strive to achieve the organizational goals*
>
> controlling *activities*
>
> evaluating *the performance of managers*

Thus we have a view of what budgeting is and the uses that it performs. Budgets are usually set for a period of 1 year, identify projected revenues and expenses by both account code and responsibility centre and aid in planning, coordinating, communicating and controlling activities and in motivating and evaluating responsible managers.

8.   The Take-up of Budgetary Control

As with many innovative management practices there is a danger that the reader is persuaded by the articulate views of theorists, that the technique, providing a solution to managerial problems, was eagerly and rapidly adopted across industry and commerce. This was not the case. In practice new techniques tend to be adopted cautiously and sporadically and companies that implement them sometimes backtrack, giving up the new methods and reverting to earlier practices.

As noted, forms of budgeting can be found in antiquity and examples can be found before the developments of the early twentieth century. Solomons quoted De Cazaux who, in 1825, devoted a chapter in his work on agricultural accounting to budgeting: 'Future conduct is to be traced from an account of successes and failures of the past. Thus one can determine one's needs in the coming year and can compare them with the resources one will have.' (De Cazaux, quoted by Solomons, 1952, p. 45) And Quail (1997) referenced Chandler (1977) in noting that 'Budgets had been in use on some U.S. railroads from 1881. Nevertheless, the use of budgeting in business does not seem to have become prevalent until at least the inter-war years.'

In America, the National Industrial Conference Board (1931) reported the extent of 'Budgetary Control in Manufacturing Industry' (title) based on a survey of 294 large US companies. Of the 294 companies replying to the survey, 162, or 55% had budgets of some kind. However, while most responding companies had budgets for sales, production, manufacturing expense, marketing expense and administrative expense, only 78 (48%) produced budgeted P&L statements and only 37 (23%) produced budgeted balance sheets (p. 18). Additionally the report acknowledges some bias in its concentration on large companies and, in addition, it was likely that companies employing budgets would be more likely to respond. Bearing in mind that the use of budgets by many of the surveyed companies was only partial, one can conclude that, although budgeting existed in a significant minority of US companies in 1930 it was neither prevalent nor, yet, sophisticated.

It is generally presumed that the take-up of budgeting techniques was slower in the UK than in the US. Boyns (1998) notes that US companies being larger than in the UK might be expected to adopt budgeting practices more extensively and, possibly, British practitioners might have been less inclined to report their practices than their US counterparts. Nevertheless, even in large British companies, Quail's (1997) study of pre-war budgeting does little to suggest that budgeting had been widely embraced before the Second World War. While Austin Motors and Lever Brothers developed budgetary control systems, the London Midland and Scottish Railway (LMS) and ICI did not. And the budgetary control system at Austin Motors 'disappeared without trace' (p. 625) when Austin died in 1941. Quail's analysis suggests idiosyncratic reasons for the use or non-use of budgeting in UK businesses. The technique allowed Herbert Austin to maintain control of the company even after creditors had forced it into receivership in 1921. On the other hand the traditional structure at LMS whereby committees of the board exercised tight control over departments might not have been conducive to the introduction of budgetary control. 'Delegations to managers to spend within budget figures would have appeared to be an invasion of directors' prerogatives.'

If the take-up of budgeting practices was patchy before the Second World War there is plenty of evidence that budgeting became much more commonplace thereafter. Sord and Welsch (1958) undertook interviews in 35 companies and received 389 usable responses to a mailed questionnaire to companies in the US and Canada. They found that 385 (91%) of their 424 companies prepared a detailed plan of operations and over 90% prepared reports for general and administrative expenses, sales reports and profit reports, comparing actual with budget in each case. More than 80% of their respondents prepared budget versus actual reports for distribution expense and factory overhead expense. (p. 207)

By the 1980s budgeting was a near universal practice in US firms. Umapathy (1987) received 400 replies to a question concerning the use of formal budget programs and 389 (97%) answered that they did use such programs. The nature of budgeting was also very uniform: 'Budgets are prepared annually and are broken down by quarters (79%) or by months (11%) in most firms.' (p. 82) Umapathy compared his results with those of Sord and Welsch and noted that budget manuals were used by 64% of responding firms compared with 49% in the earlier survey. Interestingly, however, Umapathy reported that the number of firms fully matching performance reports to organisational authority and responsibility had fallen from 56% to 18%. This was a matter of 'grave concern' although Umapathy noted that it could be a consequence of increasing organisational complexity.

Almost certainly the adoption of budgetary control systems in the UK lagged that in the US but, eventually take-up of the technique approached 100% in the UK. Drury et al. (1993) took it for granted that their respondents would be using a budgeting system concentrating not on *whether* a system existed but on *how* it was used. And Dugdale et al. (2006), in a field study of 41 manufacturing companies, reported that all but one had adopted budgeting systems.

9.   Conclusion

We have seen how the theory of budgeting developed rapidly in the twentieth century. Emerging from the public sector and early twentieth century debates concerning costing and, especially, standard costing, budgeting became a key technique in the developing edifice of management accounting theory.

However, it was not budgeting itself that focused the minds of theorists and managers; it was budgetary control. Budgetary control together with its soulmate, standard costing, promised a scientific approach to management. Methods, times and costs could be specified; plans made and responsibilities delegated. Reporting designed to allow easy comparison of budget with actual results then permitted management by exception and closure of the feedback loop. Flexible budgeting would help to generate meaningful budget/actual comparisons and not only would reports be designed to facilitate actual/budget comparisons, the organisation itself might be designed to facilitate responsibility accounting.

Thus was budgetary control constructed as a cohesive approach to management. Not only did it offer a solution to the problems of operational management, it also facilitated decentralisation. Senior managers could construct an organisation with clearly defined areas of responsibility and the efforts of responsible managers could be monitored through the tool of budgetary control. The key link between budgetary control and the delegation of responsibility may have facilitated the growth of large businesses because, as businesses grew, it became necessary for central managers to delegate their authority and they therefore needed some means of ensuring that control was still retained. Quail (1997, p. 619) references Sloan (1986, Chapter 8) in noting that: 'Without the central control which budgetary control based business planning gave, decentralization into divisions might well have been too risky.'

Budgeting promised a solution to some of the key problems of management and some of the uses of the technique became clear very quickly. Within a decade of the introduction of the technique in American business, budgeting had provided an institutionalised approach to planning, delegation via clear responsibility centres and accountability through systems that efficiently compared actual results with those budgeted by responsibility centre. In summary, budgeting was quickly seen as a key technique for *planning*, for *authorisation* and for *control*.

Despite the very persuasive arguments set out by those that promulgated the theory of budgetary control, take-up of the technique was not rapid and, where it was implemented, the technique was often criticised. Perhaps because of the emphasis on *control* in budgetary control, budgeting came to be associated with pressure and a managerial style that was at odds with the human-relations approach to management that emerged in the 1930s. And, in their 'Beyond Budgeting' critique, Hope and Fraser argue that the 'command and control' style of hierarchical organisation often associated with budgetary control was becoming inappropriate in late twentieth century competitive conditions.

We consider these issues in the next chapter.

Chapter 2

Problems with Budgets

1. Introduction

Perhaps because of the emphasis on budgetary *control*, the new technique was not without its problems. A technique that could be perceived as managerial, impersonal, controlling, task oriented and designed to hold managers and supervisors to account was bound to meet some resistance. In this chapter, we identify some of the problems that budgeting and budgetary control created.

Our review is organised under four main headings. First, we consider the use of budgets as pressure devices that can lead to tension, stress and under-performance. This was the key theme in Argyris's seminal study and was further investigated by Hopwood and Otley in the 1970s. Second, we consider the manner in which budget targets might be set and, in particular, the consequences of setting slack or tight targets. Third, we consider the propensity of managers to bias budgets by creating budget slack. Fourth, we pull together the findings on budget gaming, a theme that runs through the budgeting literature.

It is easy to overstate the potential problems associated with budgets, but it is also clear that budgeting, used inappropriately, can lead to a number of unfortunate consequences. In the late twentieth century, these possibilities have been emphasised by those advocating that companies move 'Beyond Budgeting' and we review the origins of the 'Beyond Budgeting' movement, its main themes and prescriptions. It is claimed that the adverse consequences of budgeting are now so severe that companies need to abandon the technique if they are to compete effectively in the twenty-first century.

Our study includes an exploration of the attitudes of contemporary managers to budgeting and budgetary control systems, and this chapter summarises the literature on which our exploration of 'attitudes to budgeting' was based. Our review allows some consideration of whether the 'Beyond Budgeting' critique adds to or simply restates the problems revealed in the traditional literature.

2.   Recognition of Behavioural Problems in Budgeting

As long ago as 1930, Harrison wrote:

...a budget is not a cure-all and when improperly applied a budget may do more harm than good. For a budget to be effective, it is of vital importance that those who are called upon to live up to it be entirely sold upon the possibility of so doing (p. 30).

He noted that 'depending on their temperaments' an over-optimistic budget might disgust, amuse or discourage individuals. And 'A budget is of little use unless it can be shown that the goal which has been set up, though possibly a hard one, is nevertheless not an impossible one...' (Harrison, 1930, p. 30).

Already Harrison had identified the stringency of the budget target as a key factor in budgetary control and the importance of the budgetee's personality in shaping his or her reaction to the budget.

As firms adopted budgetary control systems, practitioners became increasingly aware of their possibly unfortunate consequences and Peirce's (1954) personal reflections suggested that he had seen most of the things that could go wrong:

It is in the control area that the colossal mistakes of budgeting are made. It is here that the amateurs have censured their subordinates for exceeding budgets, without realizing that they themselves were to blame for inadequate training. It is here that men have become so frustrated under maladministered budgets that they have resorted to all sorts of tricks to conceal the actual results and have padded their budgets to give themselves breathing room. It is here that staff men have usurped authority, merited pay increases have been denied because of budget limitations, and tales have been carried around supervision and up to the top under the guise of budget reporting (p. 61).

A growing concern with the possible human consequences of budgeting led, in 1951, to an exploratory study sponsored by the Controllership Foundation. Dr. Chris Argyris undertook this seminal study assisted by Frank Miller under the direction of Dr. Schuyler Dean Hoslett. Argyris's (1952, 1953) work is commonly seen as the starting point for behavioural budgeting research and we report his findings in the next section.

3. Argyris's Study: Budget Pressure and Human Consequences

Argyris (1952) noted (Foreword) that, in the case of budgeting, '...making the tool is a far easier task than learning how to use it...[and]...many controllers suspect that the difficulties in using it have been underestimated.' His study was based on interviews with budget people and supervisors in four plants.

The plants that Argyris visited seem to have been extreme examples of the mis-application of budgetary control, and it seems that the budget administrators were uniformly unfeeling in their application of budgetary control principles. One saw himself as 'the watchdog of this company' (p. 6) and budget people strived for improvement, putting pressure on supervisors even though: '...he may be batting his brains out already on the problem, but our phone call adds a little more pressure...'. They instantly reported problems to top management and were clear that budgets '...serve as a constant reminder that a goal *has* to be met' (p. 7). According to budget people, this helped to motivate factory personnel.

Not surprisingly, given these attitudes, the factory supervisors had some earthy comments to make about budgets and budget people:

1. It would be folly to show budget figures to the workers: 'No, no, I couldn't even use a budget in front of my people. I just wouldn't dare. And, mind you, I *don't think* my top management would want us to. We wouldn't get any production out if we did' (p. 10).

2. Budgets contain only results but: 'Budgets never show the reasons *why* they have not been met. They never take into account all variables that affect production' (p. 11).

3. Budgets emphasise history, using projections from the past to predict the future, but one supervisor felt that this was wrong: 'It's today, today, that is important' (p. 12).

4. Budgets are rigid: 'Somehow the budget people freeze the figures in their minds and they just don't want to change' (p. 12).

5. Budgets incorporate moving targets: 'If I meet this budget, those guys up there will only raise it. Or, You can't let them know that you made the budget without too much trouble. If you do they'll up it sure as hell' (p. 12).[1]

6. Budgets are not seen as motivators, instead supervisors emphasised intrinsic motivation: '…[we] do our job, and *we do the best job we can*. That's it. No matter what comes out, we know we've done our best' (p. 13).

7. Budgets are set unrealistically high: 'What good is it? If a man doesn't meet it, he's going to say, "to hell with it"…If you ever want to discourage a guy, just give him a budget you know he can't meet' (p. 13).

Several of the themes are important to our investigation of managerial attitudes. In particular note the narrow financial emphasis of budgets (2), their (possible) rigidity and historical emphasis (3 and 4) and the problems related to target setting and (lack of) motivation (1, 5, 6 and 7).

Argyris's analysis raised several issues.

First, some managers believe workers are inherently lazy and budgets help to pressure them. This unites the workforce against management and the tension thus generated falls largely on supervisors. Frustration, stress and under-performance may result.

Second, there may be endemic conflict because the budget supervisor's 'success' is in demonstrating 'failure' on the part of factory supervisors. Such failures are reported directly to top management so as to demonstrate that the budget administrator is doing a good job. Not surprisingly, given this behaviour, budget administrators are defensive and their obfuscation of the budgeting process helps to shield them; meanwhile, factory supervisors complain about their lack of understanding of budget processes.

Third, budgetary control leads to 'department-centred supervisors'. The responsibility accounting system continually emphasises '…*his* department's mistakes, *his* department's errors, *his* department's production… In other words, the budgets emphasise that the supervisor should constantly examine his department as *against* the other departments.' Argyris provides vivid examples to illustrate how much time and energy can be wasted in a game of blame and counter-blame.

Argyris's analysis points to the structural consequences of a budgetary control system. The apparently infallible logic of delegating authority to clearly responsible managers and holding them accountable for their results can lead to a narrow, departmental outlook and a blame culture. This consequence is more likely if tensions build between line supervisors and budgeting staff – possibly consequential on the use of the budgeting system as a pressure device.

---

[1] This point might appear to contradict the previous one. However, the fourth point almost certainly relates to (unacknowledged) problems arising during the budget period while the fifth point relates to the consequences for the next budget period if the current budget is exceeded.

4. The 'Budget-Constrained' Style: Hopwood's and Otley's Studies

4.1. Hopwood's Study

In the 1970s, Hopwood (1972) and Otley (1978) published their influential studies. Hopwood noted that accounting measures could only supply a partial measure of performance and, additionally, they might be contaminated by uncontrollable elements and biased by attempting to serve several purposes. The unenlightened use of financial measures might, therefore, be expected to have unfortunate consequences, and Hopwood set out to test this in his study of budget cost centre managers in a large, Chicago-based, steel manufacturer.

Hopwood identified three styles of evaluating managers. The budget-constrained style was '...primarily based upon the cost center head's ability to continually meet the budget on a short-term basis.' The profit conscious style was based on '...ability to increase the general effectiveness of his unit's operations in relation to the long-term purposes of the organization.' And, in the non-accounting style, 'Accounting data play a relatively unimportant part in the supervisor's evaluation of the cost center head's performance' (p. 160).[2]

Hopwood did not attempt to directly analyse the impact of different managerial styles on performance because of the interaction between 'true' performance and 'reported' (possibly manipulated) performance. However, he found that a budget-constrained approach was more likely to be associated with high job-related tension and manipulation. He also noted that the budget-constrained style could mean distrust and rivalry between cost centre managers and difficult supervisor–supervisee relations. He concluded that:

The evidence is certainly suggestive that a Profit Conscious style is likely to result in a higher general level of efficiency than in the Budget Constrained style (p. 176).

Thus Hopwood's study supported the findings of Argyris when budget measures were (over)-emphasised. In the literature, this came to be known as 'reliance on accounting performance measures'. However, budgets could also be used in a more enlightened, 'profit conscious' manner and then:

Cost center heads are satisfied with an increased absolute importance being attached to both their concern with costs and the extent to which they meet the

---

[2] Hopwood also identified a fourth style, the budget-profit style where managers were concerned with both meeting the budget and with costs. However, there were fewer managers in this group than the other three and Hopwood concentrated his analysis on the budget constrained, profit conscious and non-accounting styles.

budget, the latter possibly helping to clarify the job environment and goals. They are satisfied with the Profit Conscious style of evaluation even though it certainly does not result in easier job requirements (pp. 174–175).

Hopwood's study, though limited by its concentration on one company, was based on the statistical analysis of managers' responses and was thus better grounded than Argyris's work. It corroborated Argyris's findings when budgets were over-emphasised but also indicated that problems were mitigated if budgets were used as part of a package of controls in a 'profit conscious' manner.

4.2.   Otley's Study

Otley (1978) attempted to replicate Hopwood's study at the National Coal Board in the UK. The Coal Board was divided into relatively autonomous profit centres and the investigation centred on the attitudes of the managers of these centres which, typically, had revenue of several million pounds per year.

Otley used a similar scale to Hopwood's but amended for use by profit centre rather than cost centre managers. Managers were asked to rank the three items they considered most important when group managers evaluated their performance. Two items frequently appeared in the top three: 'how well I meet budget' and 'how efficiently I run my unit'. Otley took these to be broadly equivalent to Hopwood's items: 'meeting the budget, but not concerned with costs' and 'concern with costs, but not meeting the budget'. If meeting the budget but not efficiency was in the top three this was considered 'budget constrained' while ranking efficiency but not meeting the budget in the top three was considered 'profit conscious'.

Otley failed to confirm Hopwood's findings noting that '...the style of performance evaluation perceived to be used by the superior manager had little effect on a subordinate manager's feelings about his job.' He went on: 'Equally, the state of these feelings was only loosely associated with performance, and possibly with the pattern of causation running from performance to feelings rather than vice versa' (p. 135).

Otley found that '...when the profit budget was relatively high, the output budget was more nearly attained; when it was relatively low, the output budget was significantly underachieved. This result strongly suggests that the budgetary standard is manipulated in an optimistic direction when expected profits are low' (p. 138). The subtleties in the situation are captured in Otley's conclusion:

...it was found that there were considerable interactions between style of budget use, budget accuracy, and unit profitability. A situation had evolved where profitable units produced accurate budgets which were subsequently used as a basis for evaluation, whereas unprofitable units produced optimistic

budgets which gave the impression of profitability, but which were not then used in evaluating unit and managerial performance (p. 146).

We conclude that budgets can be used in a rigid or punitive manner and Argyris and Hopwood discovered that, in the organisations they studied, such use of budgets led to increased job-related tension and, possibly, poorer performance. However, Otley's study showed that the contingent nature of these results for, in his study, the same consequences were not observed.

The conflicting results of the Hopwood and Otley studies led to strenuous efforts to reconcile them. The obvious intervening contingent variable was taken to be organisational structure with interdependent cost centres in Hopwood's study contrasted with relatively autonomous profit centres in Otley's study.[3] The relation of budgeting systems with organisational structure is central to our study and this subject is reviewed in Chapter 5.

5. Budget Targets: Can They Be Set 'Correctly'?

We have already noted Harrison's commonsense view that a budget needed to be set at an attainable (though possibly difficult) level, and Stedry (1960) undertook an experimental investigation of the impact of budget difficulty on performance. As might be expected, he demonstrated that participants tended to respond to stiffer targets by working harder, but only up to a point. After that, participant performance fell as the target became harder.

Stedry's doctoral thesis, though award winning, was somewhat unsatisfactory in that its conclusions were reached in very artificial conditions. Specifically, students were asked to solve 'water jar' problems[4] with different performance targets. The students might be asked for an aspiration level before or after the target ('budget') had been set. In order to test the results in a field setting, Stedry and Kay (1964) undertook further experiments but with supervisors in industry. Although limited by a small sample size, the results were consistent with the earlier experimental findings.

Hofstede (1968) studied six plants in five (large) Dutch companies employing 260–750 (average 530) people. One hundred forty interviews were undertaken with staff (48 interviews), first level line managers (51 interviews) and higher level

---

[3] One might add that comparing a US-based steel manufacturer with a nationalised, UK-based, coal manufacturer that employ not only differing structures but also had different managerial histories might easily lead to differing results. As Otley says, the particular way of using budget targets had evolved over time, in the jargon, the use of management control systems is likely to be 'path-dependent'.

[4] For example, given three jars that can hold 9, 5 and 3 pints of water; devise a sequence of steps to obtain 7 pints of water. (Pour 5 pints into the 3 pint jar leaving 2 pints in the 5 pint jar. Put these 2 pints in the 9 pint jar and add 5 pints to them.)

line managers (41 interviews). He explored the relationships between inputs to the budget (policies concerning standards and participation, contribution of staff departments and different leadership styles) and the consequent outputs (profitability of the enterprise and the well-being of people working in it).

Hofstede (1968) confirmed the finding of Stedry and Kay that loose budgets are poor motivators and budgets motivate more as they become tighter. However, over a certain limit, motivation becomes poor again. Hofstede argued that aspirations become higher as the budget is tightened but, when the budget becomes too tight, aspiration levels fall dramatically (because there is no point trying to achieve what is perceived to be an unrealistic budget).

These findings have complicated implications because, in order to obtain the best actual outcome, a tight budget should be set. Aspiration levels would therefore be increased and, so long as the budget is not too tight, a good outcome would be achieved. Unfortunately, this 'good' outcome would, typically, meet neither managers' aspiration levels nor the (challenging) budget. Such instrumental top management behaviour would have obvious consequences for budgetees' confidence and might affect their long-term performance. Additionally, if a challenging budget is unlikely to be achieved, perhaps a second, more realistic, budget is needed for planning.

In addition to these general observations, there are a number of practical difficulties in seeking the 'best' budget targets. Hofstede identified psychological, organisational, personal and sociological variables that affect the appropriate budget level:

■ First: 'Personality and cultural differences, like differences in job involvement, are important determinants of people's reactions to a certain level of standards' (p. 160).

■ Second: 'Situational data like hierarchical levels, the time people have in their jobs, and people's age, influence the way in which people react to standard levels' (p. 161).

■ Third: '...plants have different "informal budget levels" and different degrees of internalization of standards into personal aspiration levels'(p. 160).

Although tight budgets might motivate the best results, setting them in practice is not easy and Merchant and Manzoni (1989) found that, in their field study, practice differed from the nostrums of theory. Otley's study of profit centre managers had failed to replicate Hopwood's study of cost centre managers and, similarly, Merchant and Manzoni's field study of profit centre managers failed to discover the tight budgets that might be predicted. Instead, they found that budgets were *attainable* most of the time. In fact, in 54 profit centres from 12 corporations, more than half of the managers reported that the budget was achieved more than 90% of the time and 87%

of the managers reported that the budget was achieved more than 75% of the time. Despite the experimental evidence that demonstrates the value of tight budgets, it seems that profit centre managers have achievable budgets. However, this does not imply that the budgets were 'easy':

> *...almost all the PC [profit centre] managers interviewed objected to this term. As one manager put it: We have to work very hard to make it happen... Each day is a struggle for us... It's not like we're coasting (pp. 506–507).*

Merchant and Manzoni reported a host of advantages in setting achievable budgets. First, from the managers' point of view, bonuses are paid, credibility is maintained, emotional commitment to 'winning' is strengthened, there is some flexibility and an optimistic budget with concomitant (over) spending commitment is avoided. Second, from top management's point of view, earnings are predictable, over-commitment to spending is avoided, managers are committed, fewer interventions are needed, 'slack' in the budgets gives trusted managers flexibility, the incentive to indulge in earnings manipulation is reduced and the payment of bonuses can ensure that pay is competitive.

It is not surprising that these advantages are judged to outweigh some possible loss of motivation. In fact, it seems that even this theoretical drawback is not serious because, *in practice*, budgets are part of a wider control system:

> *...virtually all the managers interviewed stated their belief that their corporation's management systems have been structured to give PC managers reasons to strive for (and produce) earnings in excess of their budget targets (p. 512).*

The systems included extra bonuses, recognition, credibility and increased career prospects. In addition, senior managers not infrequently asked for extra profit in order to compensate for unforeseen problems elsewhere in the organisation.

It seems that the well-validated psychological finding that a tight target motivates the best performance might not translate simplistically into a recommendation that budgets should be set 'just out of reach'. Despite this being implicit or explicit in most textbooks, Merchant and Manzoni cast doubt on the efficacy of the recommendation in practice, particularly for profit centre managers.

6.   Budget Bias and Slack

Peirce (1954) had noted the issue of slack in budgets when he commented that managers might be driven to this device to provide 'breathing room', and there is little doubt that the creation of budgetary slack is a common occurrence. Schiff and

Lewin (1968) concluded that there was as much as 25% slack in the budgeted operating expenses of the three large firms they investigated. Onsi (1973) found that 80% of managers interviewed were prepared to admit that they bargained for slack. And, in Merchant and Manzoni's (1989) study, budget slack is implicit in the finding that profit centre managers generally achieve their budget targets.

There are complex inter-relationships between the various aspects of the budgeting process. As we have just noted, degree of slack in the budget is intertwined with the notion of degree of budget difficulty; tight, challenging budgets have less slack than achievable, 'easy' budgets. And Lowe and Shaw (1968) found a link between participation and the creation of budget slack. In their investigation of a retail chain they found that, although involving sales managers meant that the budget was based on sounder operational information, managers had the opportunity to bias their budgets. The reward system (based on league tables of achievement versus budget) encouraged downward bias so that the budget could be more easily achieved. However, poorly performing, insecure managers might introduce upward bias so that, in the short run, superiors would be pleased. This echoes Otley's finding that poorly performing profit centres tended to be set ambitious targets while the better performers were set realistic targets.

The early literature tended to view budget slack as unfortunate and dysfunctional. Schiff and Lewin (1970) saw a conflict between individuals' personal goals and their duty to further the organisational goals as a cause of slack because, as Williamson (1964) noted: '...managers can best achieve both their personal goals and the firm goals in a slack environment...'. However, we have seen in Merchant and Manzoni's (1989) study that top management can have good reasons for permitting and even encouraging some slack in budgets. We also note that, although the early literature assumed a conflict between personal and organisational goals as a cause of slack, managers may employ the slack they have created in the organisation's interests. They may maintain valuable projects that would otherwise be lost and they may be more creative than otherwise.

Contemporary literature has reinforced the idea that slack can be desirable as well as dysfunctional. For example, Nohria and Gulati (1996) noted that slack could act as a buffer that was necessary for organisational adaptation. Van der Stede (2000) found that slack could facilitate strategy in business units pursuing differentiation. And Davila and Wouters (2005) reported that budget slack could be helpful when the demand on business processes increased and other targets such as service quality became more difficult to achieve.

A key theme in our conclusions will be the interaction between budgetary control and organisational structure and, already, in 1970, Schiff and Lewin had interesting points to make on this theme. Decentralised organisations were becoming increasingly prevalent and financial controllers, while still responsible to the corporate controller, were also key members of divisional top management. According to Schiff and Lewin in this role, '...the divisional controller appears to have undertaken the task of creating and managing divisional slack and is most influential in the internal allocation of this slack' (p. 263).

7. Budget Gaming

The propensity of managers to 'game' the budgeting process is a recurring theme in the literature, and the whole topic of budgetary slack and padding can be seen as an attempt by managers to game the budgeting system *in advance*.

Managers also tend to game the budget *after* it has been implemented both by making accounting entries that show their operations in a better light and by operational changes that are driven by desire to report better results. In his study, Hopwood showed that such behaviour is more likely if managers are evaluated in a budget-constrained manner and analysed manipulative behaviour in his study organisation into three main forms:

> *First, cost center heads attempted to charge items of cost to other cost centers... [Second] ...cost center heads...tended to time the expenditures in the light of their effects on the short-term variances... A third form of manipulation was available to relatively few persons. Some cost center heads did, however, attempt to influence the volume and type of production... (pp. 170–171).*

Merchant (1985) also found that managers were more likely to create budget slack if they frequently had to deal tactically with budget overruns and, in another study of financial controls on profit managers in a large US corporation, he provided further evidence of the interaction between financial pressure and budgetary manipulation:

> *'We're under considerable pressure to meet our short-term goals, and sometimes to meet them I've had to do some things I'd rather not have done, such as deferring preventative maintenance'.*

> *'Sure, I've seen a lot of managers play games to meet their budget targets. Last year a manager I know sold some of his raw material inventory ... at year-end for the profit even though he knew he would have to buy it back later at higher prices'.*

> *'When times are tight, as they have been, we're squeezed on expense dollars, particularly discretionary program expenditures. I know a couple of managers who have hidden programs in variable costs in order to keep them going'.*

> *'Capital is not a problem – expense is. So I've gotten some expense money charged into capital accounts...' (Merchant, 1990b, p. 299).*

The first two instances impinge on operations while the second two examples 'merely' relate to accounting manipulations. While the first two are obviously detrimental, it is not clear that the second two actually hurt the company. In fact, managers are trying to do what they think is best in spite of the system. There is a certain similarity to the use of slack in budgets – if the slack is used in the company's best interests then it may actually help to meet future targets.[5]

Statistical analysis showed significant correlations between pressure to generate financial results and the manipulation of performance measures. There was a particularly significant correlation between pressure to meet net income targets and the manipulation of expenditures in order to accelerate the recognition of profit. Merchant also found significant correlation between pressure to meet financial targets and the discouragement of new ideas:

> *'Our planning processes usually deteriorate into a discussion of the forecasts of profitability over the next five years, with the focus on the next two years. The effect has been to discourage new product ideas because it is clear that the focus is on cost improvements, not better products'* (p. 299).

Hopwood's and Merchant's examples of budgetary manipulation are related to budget-induced financial pressure. However, even in an organisation that did not seem to be subject to excessive budget-related tension, Otley still noted that managers knew all about budget games:

> *As one very experienced manager observed: 'There are always games associated with the budget. You learn the short-cuts for getting a bit more output today at the expense of tomorrow. There's always some cost that can be held over. It's a bit farcical really. I mean, I wasn't here last year so I pushed as much (expenditure) as I could into last year'* (p. 136).

There is little doubt that budget manipulation and gaming is widespread, and it is probably more prevalent in organisations that place significant reliance on accounting performance measures and emphasise budget targets.

---

[5] We prefer not to discuss the feelings of the accountants who are persuaded/coerced into charging discretionary expenses to variable costs and, conversely, expenses to capital. The latter practice is, of course, especially dangerous as it leads to short-term over-statement of profit. In an interview with the controller after the data were available, Merchant reports the following comment: 'If we catch [the profit center managers] pulling in future profits constantly, we tell them to stop it. We'll never know what the true operating results are' (p. 310).

8.   The 'Beyond Budgeting' Critique and Prognosis

8.1.   Origins

The 'Beyond Budgeting' movement can be traced to work initiated by CAM-I[6] into 'advanced budgeting'. Bunce et al. (1995) reported the group's interest in developing advanced management systems that would overcome the deficiencies of traditional budgeting. Budgeting was seen as '...concerned with top-down planning for financial performance, built on organizational hierarchies, and intended as a control over operational expenditures' (p. 255). This was at odds with the 'new realities' of 'global competition, rapid commercialization of technology, and the use of new management techniques... The market has become volatile, highly competitive and customer-driven' (p. 254). The study group identified five objectives for advanced management systems: linking activity plans with strategy; linking resource consumption with outputs; supporting continuous improvement; building congruent behaviour and adding value through planning and budgeting. Investigation in four large case-study companies revealed the importance of a process-oriented (rather than functional) approach to planning; linkages between operational plans and vision, mission and strategy; target costs and benchmarks; the development of team-working, good communications and an appropriate culture; and continuous improvement based on rolling forecasts and simple, process-based organisation structures. The group concluded that traditional budgeting was dysfunctional but, to their disappointment, '...the key goals will not be met simply by finding a better budgeting system to replace the old one' (p. 263). Peter Bunce and Robin Fraser collaborated in this research and, joined by Jeremy Hope, in 1998, they formed the 'Beyond Budgeting Round Table' (BBRT).

8.2.   Overview

The CAM-I investigation had, at least initially, continued the pursuit of the holy grail of 'advanced budgeting' and, while criticising 'traditional' budgeting systems, had assumed that a budgeting system of some kind was necessary. Researchers were concerned to establish the conditions in which different forms of budgeting were appropriate, not to challenge the usefulness of budgeting itself. However, this changed in the 1990s as Hope and Fraser (1997, 1998, 1999, 2003ab) mounted a wide-ranging

---

[6]CAM-I is an international, non-profit making consortium of companies that works with academics in pursuing industry-based research into management systems. Originally, CAM-I focused on computer-aided manufacturing, but the consortium played a key role in the spread of activity-based techniques in the late 1980s.

critique of the manner in which budgeting systems are typically implemented. They observed and described budgeting systems highlighting: the often bureaucratic and expensive nature of the budgeting process, the failure of budgeting to meet the needs of managers in uncertain and competitive environments and the likelihood that budget systems would lead to managerial 'gaming' of the numbers.

Hope and Fraser reached these conclusions following study of a number of, mainly Scandinavian, companies that had abandoned or radically modified their budgeting systems. Not only had budgeting changed but, in some of these companies, new systems had been introduced, organisation structure modified and the whole management culture revised. In the next sections, we review Hope and Fraser's views on the problems caused by budgets, the key case of Svenska Handelsbanken, recommendations for organisational structure change and the prescriptions of the 'Beyond Budgeting' school.

8.3.   Problems with Budgets

Advocates of 'Beyond Budgeting' emphasise the adverse consequences of budgeting and Hope and Fraser (2003b, p. 3) claim that '...the balance of opinion has swung decidedly in favour of the "very dissatisfied" '. Hope and Fraser's (2003b) contemporary analysis of the problems inherent in budget practice identifies three 'primary factors' that account for '...such high levels of dissatisfaction with budgeting: ...(1) budgeting is cumbersome and too expensive, (2) budgeting is out of kilter with the competitive environment and no longer meets the needs of either executives or operating managers, and (3) the extent of "gaming the numbers" has risen to unacceptable levels' (p. 4). In support of their claim that budgeting is cumbersome and expensive, they note that budgeting often takes 4 months, involves many managers and multiple iterations and can put considerable pressure on the finance team. In support of the claim that budgets are now out of kilter with the competitive environment, they cite IBM's 1970s' extensive and expensive budgeting bureaucracy that was unable to cope with a changing competitive environment where customers became more demanding and competitors more nimble and adaptable. Finally, they claim that the use of budgets as integral in 'fixed performance contracts' might provide a clear understanding between organisational levels but '... in the wrong hands, such a contract leads to undesirable and dysfunctional outcomes at every level of the organization' (p. 11).

For Hope and Fraser, the use of budgets in creating a 'performance contract' is one of the most pernicious aspects of contemporary budgeting systems. This leads to a number of problems including the creation of 'the lowest targets' and 'more resources than you need' etc. (see Figure 1).

Budgeting leads to:

- The lowest targets;
- More resources than you need;
- Making the bonus 'whatever it takes';
- Competing with other divisions, business units and departments;
- Spending what is in the budget;
- Providing inaccurate forecasts;
- Meeting the target but not beating it;
- Not taking risks.

Figure 1   Hope and Fraser's critique of budgeting.
(*Source*: Adapted from Hope and Fraser, 2003b, pp. 13–14.)

8.4.   The Svenska Handelsbanken Case

Hope and Fraser have been greatly impressed by their study of Svenska Handelsbanken:

> '... our greatest source of inspiration has been the philosophy of radical decentralisation as exemplified by Svenska Handelsbanken ...' (Hope and Fraser, 2003b, frontispiece).

This case is central to the exposition of 'Beyond Budgeting' and has been important to Hope and Fraser's thesis since the mid-1990s:

Svenska Handelsbanken abandoned traditional budgeting as long ago as 1979 and has since achieved dramatic success. It is now the largest bank in Scandinavia and the most efficient of the big banks in Europe...

By operating each branch like an independent business, adopting a unique profit-sharing scheme based on performance relative to competitors, and developing a fast and open information system so that one branch can compare its performance against another, its cost/income ratio has been reduced to 45% (and falling)...

Hope and Fraser (1997, p. 22)

The Svenska Handelsbanken organisation structure is based on independent, profit-oriented branches and radical decentralisation has been a key theme in the 'Beyond Budgeting' literature. An important element of this is the use of relative performance measures so that the bank as a whole aims for better return on equity (ROE) than its rivals; regions compete with each other on ROE and cost/income ratio and branches compete with each other on cost/income ratio, profit per employee and total profit. Branches do not compete with each other for customers (Hope and Fraser, 2003b).

The Svenska Handelsbanken management model includes a profit sharing scheme based on the performance of the whole bank; individuals can access their share of profit at the age of 60 so: 'It is not intended to be an incentive for individuals to pursue financial targets rather, it is intended as a reward for their collective effort and success' (Hope and Fraser, 2003b, p. 62). At Svenska Handelsbanken, the decentralised structure is reinforced by an internal market whereby central staff functions have to 'sell' their services to regions and branches. 'Regional and branch managers have every right to challenge these costs and even reject them' (Hope and Fraser, 2003b, p. 64). Finally, there are no central targets but control is achieved by focusing on a few metrics such as ROE and cost/income ratios together with a sophisticated and an efficient information system that gives decentralised managers rapid access to all the information they need.

8.5.　Beyond Budgeting and Organisation Structure

In their earliest writings on the Beyond Budgeting theme, Hope and Fraser (1997) linked the abandonment of budgeting with new organisational forms. In a world where the most important asset had become intellectual capital, command and control, hierarchical systems were no longer appropriate and what they called the N-form (network) organisational model was needed. In this type of organisation, with multiple linkages between managers at all levels, group executives would be 'challengers', middle managers, 'integrators' and SBU managers, 'entrepreneurs'. A thoroughgoing culture change was needed based on responsibility, enterprise, trust and loyalty, and care was needed to prevent management behaviour 'snapping back' to its old command and control style.

8.6.　Beyond Budgeting Prescriptions

The two most important recommendations of those advocating 'Beyond Budgeting' are that budgeting should be abandoned and that organisations should adopt radically decentralised, entrepreneurial structures. We note that banks appear regularly as examples of organisations moving 'Beyond Budgeting'[7] and observe that the

---

[7] Referring to six examples of performance improvement, Hope and Fraser (2003b) include two banks: Fokus Bank and Svenska Handelsbanken and go on to mention the Swiss bank, UBS, as a further example.

change might be more difficult in more complex organisations where there are limits to decentralisation. Nevertheless, Hope and Fraser found complex organisations such as Volvo Cars that were prepared to make radical changes to their budgeting systems and management culture:

> As Johannesson notes, 'we recognised the extent of the cultural change needed. We wanted less and less of order giving, victims of circumstance, administration, checking, reactive positions, functional ties and hierarchical thinking, and more of creating opportunities, communication, development, confidence-building, proactive positions, network ties and process thinking'...
>
> Strategy and forecasts are [now] reviewed and updated several times a year with four distinct cycles apparent. Each month a 'flash' forecast is prepared covering the next three months; each quarter a two-year rolling forecast is updated; and each year sees a revised four-year and ten-year strategic plan...

> Hope and Fraser (1999, p. 19)

Other examples include Borealis, a large petrochemical company, and Rhodia, a manufacturer of speciality chemicals. At Borealis, uncertainty made the budget out of date as soon as it was completed and it was replaced by benchmarking, the balanced scorecard, activity accounting and rolling forecasts. 'Forecasts are used in conjunction with actual results to show trends for high-level key performance indicators such as return on capital, profitability, volumes and so forth. These typically show the last eight quarters' results and the next five quarters' forecasts' (Hope and Fraser, 2003b, p. 59). At Rhodia, the budgeting process that took 6 months to complete was replaced by 5-year goals for return on capital and free cash flow together with the development of action plans based on a strategy cycle and a short-term operating cycle. Managerial bonuses are 40% based on personal results and 60% based on wider business results.

Hope and Fraser listed 10 'principles and practices' for managing without budgets (Figure 2).

9.   Concluding Comments

9.1.   Budget Padding and Gaming

Hope and Fraser's contemporary analysis of problems in budgeting echoes several earlier themes in the literature. Their references to setting low targets, procuring more resources than are needed and spending what is in the budget reflect attempts to pad the budget by ensuring that more resources are obtained than are strictly necessary

> **Target setting** to maximise long-term value and beat the competition, not the budget
> **Strategy** devolved to the front line, continuous and open, not an annual event
> **Growth and improvement** by challenging people to think radically not incrementally
> **Resource management** over the lifetime of an investment, not on short-term budget allocation
> **Coordination** by managing cause and effect relationships, not through departmental budgets
> **Cost management** by challenging whether costs add value, not by increase or decrease compared with last year
> **Forecasting** using rolling forecasts for managing strategy and making decisions, not keeping on track
> **Measurement and control** using a few leading and lagging indicators, not a mass of detailed, historical reports
> **Rewards** based on company and unit-level competitive performance, not personal financial targets
> **Delegation** by giving managers freedom to act

Figure 2 Ten 'principles and practices' for managing without budgets. (*Source*: Adapted from Hope and Fraser, 1999, p. 18.)

for the planned level of activity. The references to making the budget 'whatever it takes' and meeting the budget but not beating it refer to subsequent gaming in order to align actual results with those budgeted.

These issues have been explored in the accounting literature, and there is a general consensus that managers may indeed pad budgets in advance and manipulate reported figures after the budget has been set. Schiff and Lewin (1968) and Onsi (1973) indicated that budget padding was widespread. Hopwood (1972) and Otley (1978) quoted the comments of managers who charged expenses to incorrect codes and manipulated expense and revenue timings. And Merchant (1989, 1990b) reported that data manipulation was common with results controls with 'widespread shifting of funds between different budget items in order to avoid adverse budget variances' (reported by Drury, 2004, p. 651).

Having said this, it is important to recognise that this 'gaming' of budgets is not necessarily all bad. The key issue here is the often implicit assumption that managers game the budget either for personal gain (better bonuses) or for an easier life. This assumption may be unfounded and the work of Nohria and Gulati (1996), Van der Stede (2000) and Davila and Wouters (2005) indicates that budgetary slack may actually be used to further organisational adaptation and strategy. Similarly, some of

Merchant's (1985) examples suggest that managers can adopt gaming behaviour in an attempt to do what they perceive to be in the best interests of the company.

9.2. Departmentalisation and Unhealthy Competition

A key element of the Hope and Fraser 'Beyond Budgeting' thesis is that the 'old', hierarchical, command and control structure needs to give way to an N-form, networked organisation. Traditional organisation can easily lead to competition between different parts of the organisation as business units compete in the same markets for customers and possibly for resources.[8] This point goes to the heart of budgetary *control* and Argyris's seminal study pointed to the dangers of over-emphasis on *departmental* results, encouraging parochialism and the manipulation of reporting through incorrect coding of expenses.

In Chapter 5, we shall see that the coordination of departments and business units has long been a central issue for organisational theorists, and it is certainly possible to develop inappropriate structures and systems that encourage divisive and unfortunate behaviour. Nevertheless, there are circumstances where the hierarchical organisation, based on clear designation of authority and responsibility, can be efficient. Conversely, *organic* structures have been developed that depend on interpersonal and lateral rather than hierarchical communication and, in essence, these structures correspond to Hope and Fraser's N-form organisation.

9.3. Targets

Hope and Fraser emphasise the possibility that managers might negotiate 'soft' targets, which is another possible budgeting problem. This possibility is recognised in the traditional literature as an aspect of budget padding. However, the traditional literature also points to the possibility that budgets might be 'tight' and suggests that tight budgets actually motivate the best performance. The problems associated with a tight budget relate to the likelihood that it will not be achieved and its lack of realism for planning purposes. Thus the traditional literature suggests that budgets cannot easily perform the functions of both motivating managers and providing a realistic basis for planning and coordinating.

Although experiments do suggest that individuals can (usually) be best motivated by relatively stringent targets, we noted that Merchant's study indicated that, in practice, profit centre managers usually had *achievable* budgets. This was convenient for a number of reasons and the embedding of budgets within a package of controls package meant that, in practice, managers had plenty of motivating factors.

---

[8]Note that the Svenska Handelsbanken branches compete in relation to output metrics such as profit, not for customers.

9.4. Budget-Constrained Style and Reliance on Accounting Performance Measures

Argyris pointed out that budgets could be used as pressure devices and Hopwood saw the budget-constrained style of management as less than optimal. For Hope and Fraser, this translates into the use of budgets as a 'performance contract' and this leads to a range of unfortunate consequences.

However, Otley's attempt to replicate Hopwood's research but based on profit (rather than cost) centre managers failed to confirm Hopwood's results and, since the late 1970s, there has been a burgeoning stream of research that has attempted to reconcile the conflicting findings of the Hopwood and Otley studies. This research indicates that emphasis on the budget is not necessarily problematic so long as circumstances are appropriate and/or a participative style of budgeting is adopted.

9.5. Hope and Fraser's Critique in Historical Context

Hope and Fraser's critique of traditional budgeting resonates with a number of themes from previous research. They emphasise problems in budgeting and, like other authors, note that budgets can lead to managerial games in setting targets that include slack; in manipulation/smoothing of accounting numbers; in actions that are sometimes at odds with business needs; and in unhealthy departmental rivalries.

Although Hope and Fraser note that budget targets might be too loose, they do not mention the possibility that targets might be too demanding. And their critique differs from traditional analysis in two other ways. First, they do not refer to (over) reliance on accounting-related measures and a budget-constrained management style. Instead, they draw attention to what they call the possibly pernicious effects of budget-related performance contracts. Second, they observe that budgeting processes can be long, time consuming, bureaucratic and expensive. Although many managers would agree that this can, indeed, be the case, this particular aspect of budgeting has received little attention in the academic literature.

▌ 10. Conclusion

We conclude that Hope and Fraser's analysis of contemporary budgeting practices reinforces some of the traditional themes. Additionally, Hope and Fraser draw attention to the possibly bureaucratic, rigid and expensive nature of budgets and to the use of budgets in performance contracts that might lead to a range of gaming behaviours. We note that Hope and Fraser's analysis is rather one-sided and the budgeting literature provides examples of the *beneficial* use of budgetary slack, *appropriate* emphasis on the budget and, especially in profit centres, the absence of evidence that targets are too tight or that budget emphasis leads to stress and under-performance.

Both the traditional and the 'Beyond Budgeting' literatures provided the basis for a questionnaire instrument that included 20 critical statements about budgets and budgeting. The results are reported in the next chapter.

Chapter 3

The Survey

1. Introduction

The main aim of the survey was to discover whether the 'Beyond Budgeting' critique had affected attitudes to budgeting and whether budgeting practices had changed in recent years as a result. The attitudes of both financial and non-financial managers were investigated, and the use of the 'BRICMAR'[1] database of companies generated an acceptable response rate to a survey questionnaire. Descriptive statistics for the questions asked can be found in Appendix 1 (p. 169).

2. The Survey Questionnaire

The survey questionnaire was developed in a number of sections.

The first section focused on budgeting context. The uncertainty of the environment was investigated using a nine-point question and a separate question investigated the degree of competition faced. A further question investigated the sophistication of the internal (IT) environment.

The second, third and fourth sections investigated budgeting processes. There were questions that asked for the relative influence of top and junior managers; what information was reported; whether the budget was flexed; how variances were

---

[1] Bristol Centre for Management Accounting Research.

dealt with and whether the budget was revised during the financial year. There were also questions about forecasting practices: how often they were prepared and the period to which they related; and about incentive schemes and the use of budgets in performance appraisal.

The fifth section, investigating attitudes to budgeting, was particularly important. One set of questions asked about the importance of budgeting in relation to planning, control, coordination, communication, authorisation, motivation and performance evaluation. Two questions investigated satisfaction with budgeting processes. And a 20-point question investigated whether respondents agreed with a variety of statements that criticised budgeting. These questions were based on both the traditional and 'Beyond Budgeting' literatures. They aimed to discover whether respondents thought budgets were too bureaucratic and whether they led to gaming, a blame culture, lack of cooperation, failure to innovate and de-motivation through unrealistic targets. This section also included a 13-point question to investigate the importance of a range of non-financial indicators.

The sixth and final section investigated the extent of change in the previous 5 years. Questions asked for the most important change in budgeting during the past 5 years and whether budgeting and other practices had become more or less important over the time period. Finally, a 10-point question was included to check whether new initiatives such as activity-based costing and the balanced scorecard had led to successful outcomes.

The survey was mailed to companies, and by using companies that were members of the BRICMAR panel, an overall response of 40.1% was obtained. We requested a completed questionnaire from both a financial and a non-financial manager in each company and 40 companies from the industrial and service sectors were represented in the survey. A financial manager responded from all these companies (response rate 53.3%) and a non-financial manager responded from 21 companies (response rate 28%).

3.   Comparison of Responses from Financial and Non-financial Managers

One of the distinctive features of the survey was the comparison of the views of financial and non-financial managers. The Mann–Whitney test was used to test for significant differences between their responses.

We compared the responses of financial and non-financial managers concerning the importance they attached to budgeting. Our expectation was that financial managers would see budgeting as more important than did non-financial managers. In fact, the reverse was true; non-financial managers tended to regard budgets as more important than did financial managers. *However, the difference in the responses of the two groups was not significant.* There was no significant difference between the two groups when we compared their answers concerning the importance of budgets for particular purposes: planning, control, coordination, communication, authorisation, motivation and performance evaluation.

We were also very interested in the attitudes of financial and non-financial managers towards budgets and budgeting. Twenty questions asked respondents to what extent they agreed with critical statements such as budgets are too bureaucratic, are too time consuming, are unrealistic, promote game playing, etc. The Mann–Whitney test revealed *no significant difference between the answers of finance and non-finance managers to 19 of these 20 questions.*

Virtually all the tests revealed no significant differences[2] in the responses of financial versus non-financial managers in their attitudes to budgeting. The only significant result was related to the time-consuming nature of budgets. Financial managers agreed more strongly with the statement that 'budgets are too time consuming for the results achieved' than did non-financial managers. This is not surprising because financial managers actually do most of the work in preparing, disseminating and updating budgets. It provides an indication that non-financial managers *do not* necessarily see budgets as overly time consuming and counterproductive.

A second test was undertaken using the Wilcoxon signed ranks test on matched pairs of financial and non-financial managers and this confirmed virtually all the results of the Mann–Whitney tests. There were, however, two further significant results. Non-financial managers were more likely to agree that 'budgets are unrealistic' and also that 'budgets are too inaccurate, more resources and technology needs to be devoted to them'. These results are consistent with each other for, if non-financial managers believe that budgets are too unrealistic, it is logical for them also to want more resources devoted to their preparation.

Overall, these groups of financial and non-financial managers have similar views about budgeting, its uses and consequences. Non-financial managers are likely to see the budget as more important in managing the company and less time wasting than their financial colleagues although they are more likely to consider the budget unrealistic. In view of these perceptions, it is not surprising that non-financial managers would like to see more resources and technology devoted to the preparation of the budget than their financial counterparts.

▌ 4. The Budgeting Process

A series of questions dealt with the budgeting process itself and the following description of typical budgeting processes is based on the responses of the 40 financial managers. It has already been demonstrated that the views of financial and non-financial managers are very similar but, in any case, financial managers would be best placed to answer these descriptive questions.

---

[2] At the 5% level (two-tailed test).

Take-up of budgeting: All 40 respondents confirmed that their companies set budgets thus reaffirming the findings of Umapathy (1987) in the US and of Dugdale et al. (2006) in the UK. Budgeting is a near universal practice across all sizes and types of company.

Preparation of the budget: The budgeting process typically starts 4–6 months before the start of the financial year and 80% agreed that there were frequent revisions to the budget during its preparation. The time needed for preparation and concerns about the bureaucratic nature of the process in some companies are consistent with the observations of Hope and Fraser (2003b).

Level of detail: 95% confirmed that the budget was broken down by month throughout the budget year, and this would appear to be a significant change since Umapathy (1987) reported that 'Budgets…are broken down by quarters (79%) or by months (11%)' (p. 82). There is no doubt that the availability of computers in the past 20 years has markedly increased the number of companies that produce detailed budgets.[3]

Budget variances: More than 90% reported both month and year-to-date figures showing budgets, actual results and variances. Most (80%) also showed some past year data for comparison (either actual figures, variances or both).

Flexing the budget: Few companies flex the budget before establishing variances; just 7 (17.5%) respondents claimed to do this.

Budget revisions: Revisions of the budget during the year are infrequent with 79.5% of respondents reporting that no changes were made, 12.8% respondents reported a change at the half-year and 7.7% reported quarterly changes.

Top-down or bottom-up budgeting: 34 respondents (85%) agreed or strongly agreed that top managers drove the process. However, 23 respondents (57.5%) also thought that junior managers had a major input to the process.

Forecasting: About 85% of respondents reported that they prepared a forecast separately from the budget. Of those preparing forecasts, about 50% do so every month, 36% every quarter and 12% half-yearly. Most (78%) forecasts are for the remainder of the financial year. The extent of forecasting reported in this survey is consistent with the findings of Dugdale et al. (2006) where 90% of companies generated a rolling forecast or a forecast to the end of the financial year.

5. Attitudes to Budgets

Table 1 reveals that our financial managers hold a near universal view that budgets are important. Almost 95% of financial managers thought that budgets are

---

[3] One of the authors was surprised by Umapathy's finding. The company he worked for in the 1980s broke the budget down by month, initially manually and then, about 1983, using microcomputers and the spreadsheet, Lotus 1-2-3. He had assumed that this practice was widespread.

Table 1   Perceptions of the Importance of Budget Uses by 40 Financial Managers

	Almost irrelevant (%)	Not very important (%)	Fairly important (%)	Very important (%)	Extremely important (%)
Overall		5.1	23.1	53.8	17.9
Planning	2.5		25.0	55.0	17.5
Control		5.0	20.0	52.5	22.5
Coordination	5.0	12.5	37.5	35.0	10.0
Communication	5.0	12.5	35.0	40.0	7.5
Authorisation	2.5	7.5	40.0	42.5	7.5
Motivation	10.0	27.5	30.0	25.0	7.5
Performance evaluation	7.5	5.0	22.5	35.0	30.0

fairly, very or extremely important. Although Table 1 relates to financial managers, as discussed in Section 3, the same sentiments apply to all the responding managers.

Performance evaluation, control and planning are the most important uses of budgets in the survey companies. These might be regarded as the 'core' uses of budgets. Budgets are not seen as quite so important for what might be considered the 'secondary' purposes of budgeting: coordination, communication and authorisation. Slightly less than 50% of respondents saw budgets as very or extremely important for these purposes. Notably, budgets are seen as less important as a means of motivating managers. Only 32.5% saw budgets as very or extremely important for this purpose while a greater percentage (37.5%) considered them almost irrelevant or not very important.

Of course budgets can be important but still have unfortunate consequences and the 'Beyond Budgeting' critique suggests that, while appreciating their importance, managers would be unhappy with their budgeting systems on a number of counts. We investigated this by asking managers if they agreed with 20 statements that criticised budgeting. The results are presented in Table 2.

Table 2 reveals only limited evidence of dissatisfaction with budgeting. Highlighted figures relate to responses from more than 50% of the sample of financial managers and most of the highlighted figures show *disagreement* with the critical

Table 2   Attitudes to the Consequences of Budgeting from 40 Financial Managers (Responses Exceeding 50% Highlighted in Bold)

Question	% agreeing or strongly agreeing	% neither agreeing nor disagreeing	% disagreeing or strongly disagreeing
Process too bureaucratic	35.3	32.4	32.3
Too time consuming for results achieved*	**56.4**	17.9	25.6
Budget process demotivates managers	23.1	17.9	**59.0**
Budgets set are unrealistic*	25.6	17.9	**56.4**
Too many budget games and padding of budgets	40.0	25.0	35.0
A culture of blame, recrimination, buck passing	12.5	22.5	**65.0**
Budgets 'challenging' but therefore unrealistic	22.5	12.5	**65.0**
Budgets too rigid and difficult to change	40.0	22.5	37.5
Planning in financial years not logical	35.9	20.5	43.6
'Streetwise' managers build empires	27.5	32.5	40.0
Managers stay in budget instead of taking necessary actions	**52.5**	20.0	27.5
Links to bonus system make this an over-riding concern when budgets are set	30.0	32.5	32.5
Budgets must be realistic so cannot be challenging	17.5	22.5	**60.0**
Too much emphasis on budget targets, not enough on actions to benefit the business	20.0	35.0	45.0
Battle with HQ too time consuming and unproductive	41.0	30.8	28.2
Budgets focus too much on the past	25.0	20.0	**55.0**
Budget process inhibits innovations and change	17.5	30.0	**52.5**
Budgets focus too much on financial performance	35.9	25.6	38.5
Budgets inhibit cross-functional thinking	30.0	35.0	35.0
Too inaccurate, more resources needed*	28.3	28.2	43.5

For these questions there were significant or almost significant differences between the attitudes of financial and non-financial managers.

statements made. Generally, financial managers do *not* think there are particular conflicts between the need for realism in budgeting and the setting of challenging targets and they do not accept that budgets are unrealistic. Neither do most accept that budgets inhibit innovation and change, de-motivate managers or lead to a culture of blame and recrimination.

A majority of financial managers agreed or strongly agreed with only two of the critical statements: that managers might not take necessary actions because of the need to meet budget targets and that the budget process was too time consuming for the results achieved. (However, on the time-consuming nature of the budget process, non-financial managers had a different view; only 33.3% of them agreed or strongly agreed with the statement.)

Overall, these results do *not* indicate widespread dissatisfaction with budgets and budgeting processes in the survey companies although some respondents agreed that budgets can be time consuming and inhibiting. Some responses also indicated that budgets may lead to 'gaming', can be rigid and difficult to change and may focus too much on the past. However, these possible consequences must be kept in perspective. There is general agreement that budgets are important in managing businesses, and views on the potential drawbacks are very equivocal.

There was, perhaps, slightly more evidence of dissatisfaction in the responses to two questions that asked directly for the degree of satisfaction with budgets. A significant minority of respondents (30% of financial managers and 33.4% of non-financial managers) were not satisfied.

A separate, open-ended question asked for reasons for dissatisfaction. The main reasons were:

■ the 'top-down' nature of the process that could lead to lack of local ownership (5 companies);

■ lack of accountability or involvement of operating managers (5 companies);

■ need for a better budgeting process (6 companies);

■ concern that the budget became out of date and '…I would like to see rolling budgets' (1 company).

When asked directly, a significant minority of managers expressed some dissatisfaction. However, the issues raised did not relate to over-emphasis on accounting measures, the budget-constrained style of management, target setting or budget gaming. Instead, they were concerned with the budgeting process and the roles of both top managers and operating managers. The majority of respondents were satisfied with their budgeting processes and, overall, this survey reveals only limited dissatisfaction with budgeting.

6.   Changes in the Budgeting Process

This section is based on the written comments in response to a general question asking for changes in the budgeting process during the last 5 years. More than half (55%) of the respondents reported some form of change in the past 5 years and three general themes emerged:

- greater involvement of junior management in budgeting processes (7 companies);
- more detailed analysis (10 companies);
- intensification in the use of budgets (8 companies).

In three more companies, change was driven by changes in ownership. Two companies were now part of a major aerospace manufacturer and had adopted a common, centralised format. However, change in ownership does not automatically lead to budgeting changes; in a third company, relatively little change had been occasioned by the merger of two major manufacturers.

In only one company did there seem to be a *less* intensive approach to budgeting with monthly sales targets abandoned in favour of a 6 monthly target. This was intended to encourage managers to concentrate on maximising monthly sales (presumably instead of just meeting the monthly target).

6.1.   Changes in the Importance Attached to Specific Practices and Techniques

Table 3 suggests that a number of techniques and practices have become more important.

Most obviously, the use of traditional budgeting methods is not decreasing in importance. The responses concerning traditional budgeting and the use of budgets in setting bonuses indicate their *increasing* importance.

The increased emphasis on traditional budgeting has taken place in parallel with increased emphasis on non-financial performance indicators with a massive majority of respondents indicating their increased importance. Increasing emphasis on the balanced scorecard is also consistent with more intense use of non-financial performance indicators. These results are consistent with a recent survey of the use of non-financial performance measures in UK manufacturing by Abdel-Maksoud et al. (2005).

Similarly, this survey indicates that standard costing and variance analysis are increasing in importance. Some 50% of respondents indicated an increase and less

Table 3   Changes in the Importance Attached to Specific Techniques
(39 Financial Managers)

	Less important (%)	No change (%)	More important (%)
Traditional budgeting	7.9	50.0	42.1
Budgets as basis for bonuses	5.6	50.0	44.4
Use of non-financial performance indicators	0	21.1	78.9
Balanced scorecard	0	47.0	53.0
Activity-based costing	11.1	55.6	33.4
Economic value added	2.9	60.0	37.2
Standard costing and variance analysis	10.5	39.5	50.0

than 11% reported that these methods had declined in importance. This is at odds with a recent field study of 41 UK manufacturers by Dugdale et al. (2006), which found that standard costing and variance analysis were used selectively in manufacturing companies.

The results in relation to activity-based costing and economic value added are more equivocal with only about one-third of respondents reporting that these techniques are now more important, and, in the case of activity-based techniques, about 11% reported that they had become less important.

6.2.   Summary

All the companies surveyed used budgeting systems, and this study reveals very little difference in the attitudes to budgeting of financial and non-financial managers.

Budgeting processes are similar across the companies surveyed. Budgets relate to financial years and preparation of the budget begins some months in advance. There are usually several iterations in preparing the budget with the process driven by senior managers but also usually involving more junior managers. Subsequently, actual results are compared with the budget and, often, with previous year results. Forecasts are undertaken in most companies, usually every month or quarter, and the most common forecast period is to the end of the financial year. The budget is usually unchanged throughout the year and very few companies flex the budget before calculating variances between actual results and budget.

Over half the respondents felt there had been changes in the past 5 years but, generally, these were not driven by the 'Beyond Budgeting' movement. Changes usually related to greater involvement of junior managers, more sophisticated techniques or a revised organisation structure. Generally, the change was towards more sophisticated (traditional) budgeting, and, in some companies, financial controls had been tightened.[4]

Most respondents felt that traditional budgeting methods had become more rather than less important. There was also evidence that non-financial performance indicators and the balanced scorecard had become more important in recent years together with increasing emphasis on standard costing and variance analysis. Evidence for the increasing importance of activity-based costing and economic value added was weaker.

It seems that traditional budgeting is now more likely to be combined with increased use of non-financial indicators. However, this does not seem to be signalling the demise of traditional methods or the rise of 'Beyond Budgeting'. The vast majority of respondents continue to see budgets as fairly, very or extremely important, and for all the usual reasons: but especially performance evaluation, control and planning. The respondents generally *did not* agree with a list of statements criticising budgeting. Where dissatisfaction was expressed it was usually because the process failed to encourage local ownership of budgets. In some cases, this was blamed on senior management pressure.

7. Exploration of the Data Using Factor Analysis

7.1. Introduction

Factor analysis allows responses to be analysed for underlying themes and, in this survey, the technique was useful in analysing responses to the question concerning the importance of budgets for different uses and the question that investigated attitudes to budgeting. These analyses were based on 61 responses from both financial and non-financial managers.[5]

---

[4] One company had actually gone 'Beyond Budgeting' but, following several profit warnings, had returned to more traditional methods.

[5] The SPSS package was used to undertake principal component analysis; the varimax rotation method was adopted and factors with eigenvalues greater than 1 (the Kaiser criterion) are presented.

Table 4   Rotated Component Matrix for Question 19, 'How Important is the Budget for Each of the Following Uses?'

Budget uses	Factor 1: Implementation, control and evaluation	Factor 2: Planning
Performance evaluation	0.840	
Motivation	0.822	
Communication	0.778	
Coordination	0.755	
Control	0.583	
Authorisation	0.556	
Planning		0.943

Two factors account for 66.1% of the total variance in the variables. Factor 1: 50.5%, Factor 2: 15.6%.

7.2.   Uses of Budgets

The factor results for Question 19, asking how important were a range of uses of budgets, are presented in Table 4.[6]

This reveals that budget uses can be analysed on two dimensions. The first factor groups together several variables related to 'implementation, control and evaluation'. It seems that managers associate all these uses of budgets and this was confirmed by a Cronbach Alpha statistic of 0.848. The use of budgets for planning is separated into a second factor. This would suggest that there are two dimensions of use in budgeting:

- Planning: relating to the preparation of budgets *prior to* the period under consideration.
- Coordination, communication, control and performance evaluation: relating to the use of budgets *after* they have been approved.

---

[6]Factor analysis is a statistical technique for reducing the number of variables. In this example, a single underlying factor, labelled 'planning', can explain 50% of the variance in the variables: six variables can be grouped together and replaced by a single variable. The variable 'planning' *cannot* be grouped with the other six variables.

7.3.   Attitudes to Budgeting

Table 5 reports the factor analysis relating to the key question concerning respondents' agreement or disagreement with critical statements concerning the consequences of budgeting. It can be seen that six underlying factors were identified in relation to the possibly unfortunate consequences of budgeting and these were named:

	Cronbach Alpha Statistic
Factor 1: Bureaucratic, unrealistic and inhibiting	0.880
Factor 2: De-motivation and blame culture	0.737
Factor 3: Games and empires	0.438
Factor 4: Rigid and hierarchical	0.625
Factor 5: Realism versus challenging	
Factor 6: Constrained	0.676

We compared this factor analysis with the literature reviewed in Chapter 2. It will be recalled that the traditional literature identified a number of possible adverse consequences of budgeting. First, an aggressive, *budget-constrained*, style might inhibit managers and lead to gaming; second, *stringent targets* might de-motivate and third, budgets might encourage the creation of *organisational slack*.

Our analysis broadly supports these themes. However, there are some subtle differences between traditional analysis and the current survey.

Budget constraint has features that match survey factors (1) and (6). Both these factors link budgets with inhibition and constraint. However, neither Factor (1) nor Factor (6) is quite the same as the 'budget-constrained' theme derived from the literature where aggressive *use* of the budget as a tool of control and evaluation leads to tension, stress and under-performance. Examination of the specific variables that comprise Factors (1) and (6) suggests instead that rather impersonal features of budgets, in particular their often bureaucratic and rigid nature, inhibit managers in relating to other managers and in pursuing innovation.

Over-stringent targets leading to de-motivation and poor performance seem to match Factor (2). This factor certainly suggests that an overly challenging budget might have undesirable consequences. However, it also links an overly challenging budget with a number of other issues. As the budget is set, managers may be overly concerned with prospective bonuses and, after the budget is set, there may be further consequences as managers indulge in buck passing, etc.

Creation of slack is easy to map against Factor (3), labelled games, padding and empires. This factor is easier to interpret than some of the other factors as it brings together just two variables that relate to padding and empire building.

Table 5 Rotated Component Matrix for Question 22, 'Do You Agree or Disagree with the Following Statements'?

Critical statements	Factor 1	Factor 2	Factor 3	Factor 4	Factor 5	Factor 6
Budgets inhibit cross-functional thinking	0.800					
Budgets focus too much on financial performance	0.780					
Too time consuming for results achieved	0.744					
Budget process inhibits innovations and change	0.738					
Budgets set are unrealistic	0.660					
Process too bureaucratic	0.564					
Budgets 'challenging' but therefore unrealistic		0.689				
Links to bonus system make this an over-riding concern when budgets are set		0.674				
Budget process demotivates managers		0.576				
A culture of blame, recrimination, buck passing		0.541				
Too inaccurate, more resources needed		0.513				
Too many budget games and padding of budgets			0.804			
'Streetwise' managers build empires			0.702			
Planning in financial years not logical				0.813		
Battle with HQ too time consuming and unproductive				0.677		
Budgets too rigid and difficult to change				0.574		
Budgets must be realistic so cannot be challenging					0.816	
Budgets focus too much on the past						0.745
Too much emphasis on budget targets, not enough on actions to benefit the business						0.563
Managers stay in budget instead of taking necessary actions						0.554

Six factors account for 72.5% of the total variance in the variables. Factor 1: 20.8%, Factor 2: 12.5%, Factor 3: 11.2%, Factor 4: 10.6%, Factor 5: 8.9%, Factor 6: 8.5%.

While it is possible to map this factor analysis against traditional themes, we found it easier to compare our factors with Hope and Fraser's analysis of issues in contemporary budgeting. It will be recalled that Hope and Fraser considered (1) budgeting to be cumbersome and too expensive, (2) budgeting to be out of kilter with the competitive environment and no longer meeting the needs of either executives or operating managers, (3) the extent of 'gaming the numbers' has risen to unacceptable levels' and (4) the use of budgets as integral in 'fixed performance contracts' can lead to undesirable and dysfunctional outcomes at every level of the organisation.

Budgets can be bureaucratic and expensive can be mapped against Factor (1). This factor includes reference to the bureaucratic and time-consuming nature of budgeting, and these variables are linked with the possibly inhibiting nature and narrow financial focus of budgets.

Budgets fail to meet competitive needs can be mapped against Factors (4) and (6). These factors link together variables relating to the rigid and hierarchical nature of budgets and the impact they can have on managers who focus on the budget rather than actions needed to benefit the business.

Gaming the numbers can be readily mapped against Factor (3) relating to padding and empire building.

Fixed performance contracts map against Factor (2). This factor suggests that there are links between incentive schemes, target levels and gaming behaviours.

Factor analysis of attitudes to budgeting is consistent with Hope and Fraser's contemporary analysis of the possible unfortunate consequences of budgeting. We therefore feel that Hope and Fraser's analysis of possible problems with budgeting systems may be more relevant than the older budgeting literature. However, factor analysis only indicates possible dimensions of analysis. It does not indicate that budgets actually lead to particular consequences. As we have seen, managers in this survey tended to *disagree* with statements criticising budgets.

7.4.   Environmental Uncertainty

Factor analysis was also undertaken on one of the background questions that aimed to identify the respondent's perceptions of certainty and uncertainty in tasks undertaken and in the organisational environment. Nine questions were asked concerning the degree to which managers' perceived uncertainty in the environment and in the tasks that had to be addressed. Analysis revealed four factors that were labelled: task, judgement, environment and information certainty/uncertainty. We had not expected so many factors from only nine variables although this is certainly consistent with prior research that revealed environmental uncertainty to be a multi-dimensional concept. In particular, the first factor relates to certainty about the best method and how it should be carried out. The separation of this factor is consistent with earlier literature that has explored the impact of task uncertainty on MCS (Abernethy and Brownell, 1997; Brownell and Dunk, 1991; Daft and Macintosh, 1981).

8. Correlation Between the Uses and Consequences of Budgets and Contingent Variables

8.1. Influences on the Nature of the Budgeting Process

Three questions were designed to elicit information concerning the nature of the business: the sophistication of the company's IT system, perception of the competitive environment and the degree of uncertainty in the environment, analysed into the four factors described earlier (task, judgement, environment, information certainty/uncertainty). We explored the correlation between these six independent variables and three variables that elicited information about the nature of the budgeting process. Table 6 summarises Kendall's tau test results based on a one-tail test (because the direction of association can be readily hypothesised).

These results are not surprising, and can be summarised as follows:

■ Junior managers are more involved in budgeting in conditions of increased competition, greater judgement uncertainty and difficulty in obtaining information.

■ As task and judgement uncertainty increases, the number of iterations before the budget is finalised increases.

Table 6 Kendall's Tau Test Statistics for Contingent Variables and the Budgeting Process

'Dependent' variable: contingent variable	Senior managers drive the budget	Junior managers affect final budget	Many iterations of the budget before finalised
Sophistication of IT	0.208^1	0.167	0.183
Competitive situation	−0.004	0.201^1	0.091
Task certainty/uncertainty	0.020	0.018	$−0.314^2$
Judgement certainty/ uncertainty	0.064	$−0.170^1$	$−0.170^1$
Environmental uncertainty/ certainty	−0.017	−0.149	0.007
Information uncertainty/ certainty	−0.076	0.175^1	0.126

[1] Indicates significance at the 5% level (one-tail test).
[2] Indicates significance at the 1% level (one-tail test).

A sophisticated IT system correlates with senior managers driving the budget. However, it also correlates strongly with junior managers having an impact on the budget (significant at the 10% level).

8.2. Influences on the Uses and Consequences of the Budgeting System

Next we considered the degree of association between the contingent variables (now expanded to include characteristics of the budgeting system) and the uses and consequences of budgeting. There are nine dependent variables in Table 7. The first three are: (1) the importance of budgeting in managing the company; (2) the importance of budgets in implementation/control and (3) the importance of budgeting for planning. The remaining six variables relate to the six factors that were established concerning the possible consequences of budgeting: (4) bureaucracy; (5) poor culture; (6) gaming; (7) rigidity; (8) realism versus challenge and (9) constraining.

Table 7 reveals a number of significant associations between the contingent variables and the budgeting process and two contingent variables, task certainty/uncertainty and the number of iterations before the budget is finalised, have significant correlations with four dependent variables. We consider each in turn.

Where there is relative *task certainty*, budgets become more important for implementation and control but *not* for planning (where there is a significant negative relationship).[7] In these circumstances, managers are unlikely to agree that budgets cause problems.

This result is intuitively sensible and consistent with previous research that revealed greater emphasis on accounting controls in conditions of greater task certainty (Abernethy and Brownell, 1997; Daft and Macintosh, 1981; Hirst, 1983). These results are also consistent with Chapman's (1998) finding that, in a study of four cases, accounting had a *planning* role to play in conditions of *uncertainty*.

This finding is also broadly consistent with Otley's (2001, p. 253) overview where, referring to assumptions made in the 1960s and 1970s, he noted that 'Although a unidimensional representation of a more complex reality, budgetary control appeared to work reasonably satisfactorily in a relatively stable environment with well-codified business plans.' However, this study suggests that, in a stable environment, budgets are important for control, *not* planning. When business is predictable the budget may not be needed as a planning device, but given 'well-codified business plans' it becomes valuable as a control device.

If there are *many iterations in the budgeting process*, budgets are likely to be seen as important. This is not surprising because, if several iterations are considered necessary, this indicates that managers consider them worth undertaking. If there

---

[7] This finding is also consistent with the *negative* correlation between environmental uncertainty and the importance of budgets for implementation and control.

Table 7 Kendall's Tau Test Statistics for Contingent Variables Versus Uses and Consequences of Budgeting

Dependent variable: Contingent variable	Importance of the budget in managing company	Budget important for implementation and control	Budget important for planning	Budget bureaucratic, time consuming, inhibiting	De-motivating, leads to culture of blame and recrimination	Budget leads to gaming and empire building	Budgets rigid and hierarchical	Budgets must be realistic and so cannot be challenging	Budgets historically oriented and constrain managers
Sophistication of IT	0.007	0.110	0.082	0.044	0.044	0.096	0.063	−0.003	−0.016
Competitive situation	−0.015	0.082	−0.136	−0.077	−0.039	0.121	−0.115	−0.354[2]	0.126
Task certainty/uncertainty	0.138	0.147[1]	−0.161[1]	−0.300[2]	−0.076	−0.161	−0.094	0.052	−0.216[1]
Judgement certainty/uncertainty	0.099	0.007	0.007	−0.081	0.041	0.072	0.094	0.045	−0.023
Environmental uncertainty/certainty	−0.132	−0.152[1]	−0.040	0.112	0.118	0.136	0.034	−0.13	−0.145
Information uncertainty/certainty	0.196[1]	0.056	0.049	0.127	−0.025	−0.043	−0.030	−0.092	0.105
Senior managers drive the budget	0.015	0.028	−0.023	0.316[2]	−0.053	−0.162	0.170	0.107	−0.010
Junior managers affect final budget	0.104	0.047	0.084	−0.061	−0.130	−0.146	−0.111	−0.157	0.018
Many iterations of the budget before finalized	0.251[1]	0.076	0.231[1]	0.107	−0.099	0.252[1]	0.163	−0.321[2]	0.000

[1] indicates significance at the 5% level (one-tail test).
[2] indicates significance at the 1% level (one-tail test).

are many iterations the budget is likely to be important for planning and, remembering that *iterations* is correlated with uncertainty (Table 6), we can therefore infer that an uncertain environment tends to lead to budgets being important for planning. Again, this is consistent with Chapman's (1998) case-study-based finding that accounting had a *planning* role to play in conditions of *uncertainty*.

We make two further observations concerning uncertain environments and importance of budgets for planning. First, in uncertain, competitive environments, there are very significant correlations indicating that managers tend to disagree with the statement that realistic budgets cannot be challenging.[8] Second, there appears to be a downside in the extensive use of the budget as a planning tool because it seems that, with more budget iterations, there is likely to be more scope for game playing and empire building.

Where there is more *environmental uncertainty*, managers are more likely to see budgets as counterproductive (more positive associations with propositions concerning the unfortunate consequences of budgets) and there is a significant *negative* association with the importance of budgets for control and evaluation. This is consistent with Ross (1995) and Chenhall and Morris (1986) who found increased uncertainty related to less budget emphasis, broader information and/or a more subjective style but not with Ezzamel (1990) and Merchant (1990b) who found environmental uncertainty linked with emphasis on budget measures and targets.

Finally, we note one other very significant correlation. In 'top-down' companies where *senior management drive the budget*, there is a very significant likelihood that the budgeting process will be perceived as more bureaucratic, time consuming and inhibiting than in companies where a less 'hands-on' approach by top management is adopted.

Overall, these results make a good deal of sense. Budgeting for implementation and control (not planning) is most obviously satisfactory when there is relative task certainty. In these circumstances, managers tend to disagree with critical statements about the consequences of budgeting and, in particular, they do not perceive the process as bureaucratic and constraining. As uncertainty increases, budgets tend to be perceived as less satisfactory, but, nevertheless, they become increasingly important for planning. These observations are confirmed by the correlations reported in Table 8.

8.3.   Influences on Satisfaction with Budgeting Processes

Finally, we consider all the variables so far considered to be contingent, analysing their relationship with satisfaction with the budget process. There are two variables.

---

[8] There is a significant correlation between *iterations* and disagreement with the statement that a realistic budget cannot be challenging. Similarly, a competitive situation is correlated with disagreement with the statement that a realistic budget cannot be challenging.

Table 8   Significant Associations Between Contingent Variables and
Satisfaction With the Budgeting Process

Contingent variable	Managers' satisfaction with budgeting system	Personal satisfaction with budgeting system
Task certainty/uncertainty	0.263^2	0.268^2
Judgement certainty/uncertainty	0.226^1	
Environmental uncertainty/certainty	-0.280^2	-0.301^2
Importance of budgeting in managing the company	0.259^1	0.290^2
Importance of budgeting for control and evaluation	0.355^2	0.375^2
Bureaucracy, time wasting and inhibition caused by budgeting	-0.459^2	-0.514^2
De-motivation and culture of blame caused by budgeting	-0.514^2	

[1] *Indicates significance at 5% level (one-tail test).*
[2] *Indicates significance at 1% level (one-tail test).*

The first is the respondent's assessment of managers' views; the second is the respondent's personal satisfaction with the budgeting system. Because of the number of contingent variables, only those variables that have significant associations with the satisfaction variables are listed in Table 8.

Not surprisingly, there is greater satisfaction when budgets are judged to be important and not considered bureaucratic or de-motivating. These conditions are most likely when there is task and judgement certainty and low environmental uncertainty.

9.   Further Analysis of Correlation Between Variables

Given the significant associations between a number of variables, some further multivariate analysis was undertaken in order to check the interpretation of the data based on bivariate analysis. This analysis confirmed the findings described earlier. There was, however, one further finding of note. When the intermediate variables, 'senior managers drive the budgeting process' and 'junior managers affect the final budget', were introduced, one *very* significant regression equation was discovered.

Table 9 Drivers of Attitudes to the Budget Process

Independent variables	Standardized coefficients	T	t sig
Task certainty	0.446	3.573	0.001
Top managers drive the budget process to ensure outcome is acceptable	−0.425	−3.399	0.002

Dependent variable: *budget bureaucratic, time consuming and inhibiting; a higher score indicates increasing disagreement with this statement.*

Table 9 shows that managers were more likely to disagree with the proposition that budgets can be bureaucratic and inhibiting in conditions of task certainty but more likely to agree with the proposition if top managers drive the process.

An adjusted R^2 value of 0.345 and an F statistic significant at the 0.001 level indicate a *very* strong statistical result, and task certainty and top management involvement account for almost 45% and over 40%, respectively, of deviation in the dependent variable. The implication is that budgets are seen as less bureaucratic when tasks are perceived to be well defined and top managers are not seen as driving the process.

▌ 10. Contingency Relationships

This survey may indicate a changing emphasis in the way that budgets are used but, insofar as relationships between budgeting and contingent variables are concerned, it tends to confirm longstanding results. In particular, budgets are judged to be most satisfactory when tasks are well understood and predictable. In such circumstances, managers are more likely to register their satisfaction with budgeting processes and to disagree with criticisms of budgeting. However, in relatively certain conditions, this survey emphasises the importance of budgeting for control, not planning.

There was a negative correlation between task certainty and the importance of budgets for planning: as task uncertainty increases budgets become less important for control but *more* important for planning. This is likely to mean more iterations in preparation of the budget, more junior management input and more managerial gaming.

There is confirmation that organisational culture can impact on perceptions of budgeting and, in particular, the over-involvement of top managers in driving budgets can lead to perceptions of a bureaucratic process and inhibition of junior managers. Mintzberg (1979, pp. 291–292) hypothesised that 'All members of the organization typically seek power... [and] managers of the strategic apex promote centralization…' The evidence supporting this hypothesis is 'anecdotal, but plentiful' and the '…structure can easily become excessively centralized.' Similarly, Lyne (1992) found that senior managers sought increased use of the budget for control purposes while managers and accountants desired more decentralisation. This study shows that a competitive, uncertain environment tends to counter centralising tendencies through the involvement of junior managers. And the possibility that structures can become 'excessively centralised' is supported by the finding (Table 7) that top management driving the budget process can lead to perceived bureaucracy and the inhibition of junior managers.

11.   Budgeting in the Twenty-First Century

This survey provides little evidence of widespread dissatisfaction with traditional budgeting, and both financial and non-financial managers tended to disagree with propositions that budgets cause a variety of organisational problems. Although selective quotations could easily make a case against budgeting, the more comprehensive analysis based on the systematic use of questionnaire findings cautions against this.

This survey suggests that there has been change in budgeting practice in recent years but that little of it has been driven by 'Beyond Budgeting' ideas. Instead, there appears to have been an intensification of *traditional* budgeting processes. This has been coupled with increasing importance of standard costing and variance analysis, the use of non-financial performance indicators and the balanced scorecard. Interest in activity-based costing and economic value added has increased but much less markedly.

The changes in the use of budgets indicated by this survey suggest that neither the traditional literature nor the 'Beyond Budgeting' diagnosis captures the reality of budgeting practice in contemporary organisations:

- Traditional literature has concentrated on the behavioural consequences of budgeting but, in this survey, there was only limited evidence of budgets leading to a blame culture, excessive gaming or over-stringent targets.

- The 'Beyond Budgeting' critique identifies the bureaucratic and time-consuming nature of budgets; performance contracts and gaming as problems. It was relatively easy to map our factor analysis against the 'Beyond Budgeting' critique of budgeting, and there is some evidence that managers can find budgets time consuming, bureaucratic, rigid and constraining. *However*, there is little to suggest that budgeting is perceived as a major problem by most financial or non-financial managers.

Our observations are consistent with two other studies. We consider each in turn.

11.1. Ross (1995): Attempted Reconciliation of the Hopwood and Otley Studies

Ross (1995) set out to replicate the work of Hirst (1981). Hirst had failed to reconcile the conflicting results of the Hopwood and Otley studies, and Ross argued that this might be because of his definition of performance evaluation styles and/or his student-based sample. Ross aimed to avoid these pitfalls by using the original Hopwood/Otley instruments for performance evaluation style and, like Hopwood and Otley, surveying responsibility centre heads. Like Hirst, he attempted to reconcile the findings of Hopwood and Otley by showing that environmental uncertainty was an important intervening variable in the relationship between style of performance measurement and job-related tension.

Ross's first hypothesis was that:

■ *in conditions of low uncertainty* a budget-constrained style would lower job-related tension.

The results did not support this hypothesis. 'At low levels of perceived environmental uncertainty the results indicate that the style of performance evaluation does not affect job-related tension' (p. 8).

Ross's second hypothesis was that:

■ *in conditions of high uncertainty* a budget-constrained style would lead to higher levels of job-related tension.

The results did not support this hypothesis either. In fact, in these circumstances, it was the non-accounting style that led to the highest job-related tension with little difference between budget-constrained and profit conscious styles.

Ross concluded that one possible explanation was that '…a more flexible use of variances for performance evaluation had developed' (p. 8) and managers were now less likely to use variance analysis as a means for apportioning blame. This possibility is consistent with our finding that managers tend to disagree with propositions suggesting that budgets cause gaming and a blame culture.

11.2. Frow et al. (2005): Management Control and Shared Accountabilities

A second study is reported by Frow et al. (2005) and by Marginson and Ogden (2005). They investigated whether traditional budgeting based on responsibility centres inhibited innovation in a major multinational enterprise, a leading player in the global technology industry (pseudonym: Astoria).

Marginson and Ogden (2005) conclude that it did not. In fact, they argue that an expanded management control framework (of which budgeting was but part) gives managers '...the tools for reconciling tensions and possible trade-offs involving budgeting and other activities...' (p. 29). Marginson and Ogden were clearly impressed by the way that their case-study company had developed an organic organisation structure where managers used a team-based approach and were not necessarily constrained by adverse variances and budget overruns.

Marginson and Ogden noted that the general notion in the accounting literature that conventional budgeting deters innovation could be 'far from the truth'. And they concluded 'Overall, our research suggests that the dovetailing of formal procedures supports the resolution of tensions between budgeting and innovation. In the light of this case study, calls for the demise of budgeting may be overstated' (p. 31).

The detailed report by Frow et al. (2005) provides corroboration of some of our findings. The company has a 'performance excellence process' that is 'First and foremost...' a planning process. The process gives effect to strategic decisions through: 'Strategy deployment at the individual level...' where individuals become accountable for specific 'actions, initiatives and deliverables'. Subsequently, there are periodic reviews of progress with particular emphasis on the 3 + 9, 6 + 6 and 9 + 3 forecasts (pp. 277–278). Thus, Astoria has a planning, budgeting and accountability process that reflects our finding that companies do use traditional budgeting methods.

The budgeting process is embedded within wider company processes and is linked with the 'Astoria Improvement Process' (AIP), a systematic approach to problem solving that involves setting goals and priorities, identifying solutions and monitoring results.[9] The AIP is a rational approach to management and, at Astoria, it is set within a culture that espouses a team approach to problem solving. Asked whether negotiating responsibilities led to 'blame-shifting' or 'finger-pointing', 'Most managers stated that this was a rare occurrence' (p. 286). Astoria therefore avoids confrontational budgeting by providing tools that envisage team working and developing a cooperative management culture.

11.3. Comment

Budgeting in the twenty-first century may appear to be similar to that designed in the early twentieth century and investigated in the second half of the twentieth century. Budgets are prepared, in detail, in advance of the financial year to which they relate and they are set out by responsibility centre. However, the replies to this survey suggest that budgets are used in flexible ways, and there is very limited evidence of the various misfortunes that might follow in the wake of budgeting. Budgets *can*

---

[9] The Astoria Improvement Process is similar to other tools that date back at least to Kepner and Tregoe's (1965) work: 'The Rational Manager'.

lead to problems and managers have noted that they can be time consuming, bureaucratic and rigid. Also, some managers have complained of failure to create managerial ownership of budgets and the, sometimes unfortunate, interventions of senior managers. However, most managers are satisfied with their budgeting systems, and it seems that a balanced view of the advantages and drawbacks of budgeting systems is needed. We conclude that while the technical features of budgeting remain unchanged and, with technological help, budget preparation and use has been intensified, twenty-first century budgeting can be relatively enlightened and the advantages of budgeting systems often outweigh unfortunate side effects.

Overall, this study suggests that traditional budgets still have a major role in many organisations. Budgets can be important for control in companies operating in stable environments. In these circumstances, top managers should balance their desire for centralised control with the inclusion of junior staff in managerial processes. Budgets may also be important in providing a means of planning and including junior staff in more uncertain situations. This study indicates that managers continue to regard budget processes as important. Where companies do go 'Beyond Budgeting' they do so by adding additional techniques or analytical detail rather than reducing traditional budgeting.

Part 2

Budgets and Organisational Structure

In the survey we asked respondents if they would be prepared to be interviewed and a number agreed to this. The second stage of the research was therefore based on a series of interviews. The initial aim was to confirm the findings of the survey and to provide more insight into the changing uses of budgeting. In the event, we found that understanding the uses of budgeting required an understanding of context and, in particular, of organisational structure. This led us to develop a model of structure that eventually helped us to provide a provisional reconciliation of our findings with those that advocate "Beyond Budgeting".

In part 2 of the book we set out a review of the relevant literature relating to budgets and organisation structure, our field study based on interviews with financial controllers/directors and some operational managers and our conclusions concerning budgets, structure and the "Beyond Budgeting" thesis.

Chapters 4 and 5 complete a review of the relevant literature. Chapter 4 develops the literature review by considering the relationship between budgeting and organisational structure. As our research proceeded we became increasingly aware of the importance of placing budgeting in organisational context and this chapter provides the theoretical background needed to interpret our results. Chapter 5 helps to place budgeting in a wider context by briefly reviewing the transaction cost theory of organisations and the markets, hierarchies, and clans taxonomy of control systems. The final contingency variable, "strategy" is introduced and the unexpected results of studies linking strategy with control systems reviewed. The consequences for control theory as set out by Simons are then summarised.

Chapters 6 to 8 set out the research. In chapter 6 we summarise the views of our interviewees, confirming the results of the questionnaire survey and introducing the key idea that that, to understand budgeting, its interaction with organisational structure and other coordination and control systems must be studied. Chapter 7 develops this theme by describing the structures of the companies visited and reflecting on the extent to which the field study companies actually need their budgeting systems. Finally, in Chapter 8 we introduce another case: a Finnish company that was not part of the original survey. This case provides further insights into decisions about organisational structure and facilitates a summary of the key issues raised by the whole research project.

Chapter 4

Budgets and Structure

▌ 1. Introduction

When businesses are small, there may be little need for budgeting or, indeed, for control systems at all. However, as organisations grow, they usually develop specialised functions in operations, marketing, finance, human resource management and so on. Planning and coordinating the growing organisation eventually becomes too much for a single person and systems are needed. In this chapter, we first trace the growth of organisations as they move from *personal* to *administrative* control systems.

Growth of a company will almost certainly mean specialisation and proliferation of different functions with a consequent need for coordination and control systems. However, the precise form of such systems can vary considerably depending on the particular circumstances the company faces and the technologies it uses. We shall see that companies may opt for *mechanistic* or *organic* structures and systems. Mechanistic systems tend to be needed when the organisation faces a predictable environment and uses standard technologies. Organic systems come into play when the environment is uncertain and operations more unpredictable.

In the nineteenth century, even large organisations could be controlled by a centralised head office. However, the twentieth century saw organisations not only grow large but also diversify their operations. Eventually, diversity and complexity threatened to overwhelm the head office executives, still charged with making all the key operating decisions across their increasingly large and diverse empires. Chandler traced the way that large companies met this challenge by decentralising their operations and, to Chandler's analysis, we add the insights of Goold and Campbell who recognised that large decentralised companies could be managed in different ways depending on the decentralisation strategy adopted.

Finally, we note that the manufacturing techniques of the late twentieth century such as just-in-time production methods tended to increase operational uncertainty and so there was a tendency towards organic organisation structures. In addition, increased competition and the need for constant innovation tend to encourage more organic rather than mechanistic structures.

2.   The Growing Organisation: Departmentalisation

2.1.   Control of Large Departmentalised Companies

As companies grow, they usually expand both the scale of their operations and the diversity of their functions so that, for example, a production company may become involved in marketing and distribution. Chandler (1962) described this process in a number of companies including a wholesale butcher, a cigarette maker and from the expanding electrical engineering industry:

> *General Electric and Westinghouse each had a manufacturing department to administer a number of scattered works or factories, a sales department to supervise a nationwide spread of district offices, an engineering department responsible for design and a finance department (pp. 28–29).*

Growing companies built organisations of specialised, *differentiated* functions with experts in production, marketing, engineering and finance. These specialist departments then needed a system that would *integrate* their differentiated functions in pursuit of company objectives.

Budgetary control provided just such a system. Functional directors could set out objectives and plans that were embodied in the budget. The budgetary control system facilitated the delegation of authority and tended to reinforce hierarchical structures where each individual was responsible to a single manager, himself or herself responsible to a superior. Each manager was responsible for achieving part of the plan, and the budgetary control system allowed comparison of actual performance with the budget plan.

The growth of companies in the first half of the twentieth century almost certainly encouraged the take-up of budgetary control systems and, reciprocally, these systems facilitated the growth of companies by allowing delegation without loss of control.

2.2.   Size, Structure and Budgetary Control

As the Aston School of researchers showed, larger organisations tend to be more formal, specialised and decentralised, and one would expect their budgeting to differ from that of smaller, more centralised organisations. In fact, Hickson et al. (1969, p. 387) noted that, although activities tended to be more formally structured as technology became more integrated, the 'Correlations with technology are overwhelmed by those with size…'

Bruns and Waterhouse (1975) investigated the use of budgets in organisations of different structures and sizes, hypothesising that:

> To the extent that budgets are used as control devices in centralized organizations, we hypothesize that they will be used in a more **interpersonal manner** than in decentralized but structured organizations.

On the other hand:

> The individual in a structured situation may perceive himself and others as having greater control in their areas of responsibility. For these reasons we hypothesize that budget-related behaviour will tend to be **administrative** in character rather than interpersonal.
>
> (p. 182, emphasis added)

These expectations were confirmed in a study of 26 organisations. Managers in structured organisations under administrative control felt greater involvement in budgeting processes while managers in centralised organisations felt they had limited influence.

Bruns and Waterhouse also hypothesised that:

> Since subordinate managers have less authority and may perceive themselves as having less control in centralized organizations, any attempt to hold individuals responsible for directly meeting a budget is less likely to meet with much success and is likely to produce negative attitudes toward budgets (p. 182).

However, despite their lack of influence and requests to explain variances from a budget they had not set, managers in smaller, centralised companies did not express dissatisfaction. Bruns and Waterhouse speculated that this might be because the boss is seen as 'always right' in centralised organisations or because satisfaction is induced by strong interpersonal relationships.

Merchant (1981) duplicated the work of Bruns and Waterhouse. He surveyed production managers in 19 electronics firms ranging in size from 400 to 95,000 employees and found that size, diversity and decentralisation were correlated (though not significantly). He confirmed that managers in larger, more diverse, decentralised firms participated more in formal budgeting and felt that meeting budgets was important for their careers. There was also a strong positive correlation between the participation and the importance of meeting budget with motivation and attitudes. Splitting the sample of firms into 'large' and 'small' revealed:

> ...some support for the general contingency theory notion, because the administrative uses of budgeting, especially high participation and greater importance placed on meeting the budget, appear to be more strongly related to good performance in the larger firms than in the smaller firms (p. 824).

These studies lead to the conclusion that budgetary control tends to be operated in an *administrative* style in, usually larger, well-structured organisations. The budgetary control system can help delegation by setting clear limits for managerial action and, within these limits, managers can feel that they have more control.

3. Mechanistic Versus Organic Structures: Environmental Uncertainty

As firms grew larger, one might have expected an inexorable shift to more specialised, functional, hierarchical organisations. Bureaucratic, structured organisations may seem to be an inevitable outcome of growth and mass production. However, Burns and Stalker (1961) showed that the advantages of administrative control may come at a cost, with loss of flexibility and innovation and, possibly, less job satisfaction. They discovered that a bureaucratic organisation may not be well suited to a company facing rapid change.

Burns and Stalker studied 20 firms as they strove to develop expertise in the electronics industry. They argued that Scottish firms, encouraged by the Scottish Council to enter the industry in order to combat declining traditional markets, failed, at least in part, because they continued to employ bureaucratic, *mechanistic* management organisations. Some English firms developed their electronic expertise in a more integrated fashion and succeeded, partly, because they adopted more *organic* structures. Burns and Stalker summarised what they meant by the terms mechanistic and organic:

> In mechanistic systems the problems and tasks facing the concern as a whole are broken down into specialisms. Each individual pursues his task as something distinct from the real tasks of the concern as a whole, as if it were the subject of a sub-contract. 'Somebody at the top' is responsible for seeing to its

relevance. The technical methods, duties, and powers attached to each functional role are precisely defined. Interaction between management tends to be vertical, i.e., between superior and subordinate...Management, often visualized as the complex hierarchy familiar in organization charts, operates a simple control system, with information flowing up through a succession of filters, and decisions and instructions flowing downwards through a succession of amplifiers.

Organic systems are adapted to unstable conditions, when problems and requirements for action arise which cannot be broken down and distributed within a clearly defined hierarchy. Individuals have to perform their special tasks in the light of their knowledge of the tasks of the firm as a whole. Jobs lose much of their formal definition in terms of methods, duties and powers, which have to be redefined continually by interaction with others participating in the task. Interaction runs laterally as much as vertically. Communication between people of different ranks tends to resemble lateral consultation rather than vertical command. Omniscience can no longer be imputed to the head of the concern (pp. 5–6).

Organic structures are not necessarily 'better' than mechanistic structures. A rayon manufacturer, in a very stable environment, had a clear and effective hierarchical system and this was contrasted with an electrical engineering concern where '...nobody on the staff had a title except the managing director; at least nobody had a definite function to which they could keep...' (p. 85). In this company, anyone could speak to anyone and committees were regularly convened as a means of giving all those with relevant knowledge the chance to contribute.

The organic approach adopted by the electrical engineering concern led to some managerial insecurity, but Burns and Stalker concluded that the insecurity and, sometimes, inefficiencies of organic structures were a price to be paid for ensuring that the organisation could cope with changing circumstances.

In a prescient observation they noted that:

...the emptying out of significance from the hierarchic command system, by which cooperation is ensured and which serves to monitor the working organization under a mechanistic system, is countered by the development of shared beliefs about the values and goals of the concern (p. 122).

Thus they anticipated Ouchi's work on 'Markets, Bureaucracies and Clans' (title) and Simons' 'Levers of Control' (title) as well as the 1990s management drive for employee 'empowerment' and the 'Beyond Budgeting' interest in network rather than hierarchical organisation.

Finally, Burns and Stalker realised that, while the mechanistic and organic structures were not 'better' than each other, neither were they exclusive choices:

> ...*the two forms of system represent a polarity, not a dichotomy; there are... intermediate stages between the extremities empirically known to us. Also the relation of one form to the other is elastic, so that a concern oscillating between relative stability and relative change may also oscillate between the two forms. A concern may (and frequently does) operate with a management system which includes both types (p. 122).*

Lawrence and Lorsch (1967)[1] confirmed the importance of matching structure with the environment in their study of six organisations in the plastics industry. They expected production departments, facing more certain conditions than marketing or research departments, to have the most formal structures and this was true in five of the six organisations.[2] Production departments had more levels in the hierarchy and a higher ratio of supervisors to subordinates. In four of the organisations the research laboratories, facing the most uncertain environments, had the most informal structures.

Lawrence and Lorsch found that, in the two highest performing organisations, functions were highly differentiated from each other and (hence) well matched to their environments. In these organisations, there was effective integration of highly differentiated functions through 'integrators' who were effective 'because managers valued their knowledge and expertise' (p. 65). The four less successful organisations also used integrators, but, in contrast to the more successful firms, the integrator's influence depended more on position and their direct reporting line to the general manager. Lawrence and Lorsch, therefore, provide support for the importance of organic organisation with less hierarchical dependencies when dealing with more differentiated functions in uncertain environments.

Following the pioneering work in the 1960s, assessment of the environment (especially its rate of change) became a key component in organisational and accounting contingency research. Chenhall (2003) summarised a stream of accounting research by noting that uncertainty has been associated with broad scope and timely information, more subjective evaluation style, participative budgeting and more interpersonal interaction. He also noted that different functions need different control styles so that, for example, Research and Development, facing high environmental uncertainty, needs more participation than, say, production departments. Figure 1 is adapted from Chenhall's analysis.

---

[1] The original book was published in 1967 but references are to the 1986 reprint of the original.
[2] Production department structures were most formal in four organisations and tied equal first in a fifth. In the sixth organisation, production department structure was second most formal.

More mechanistic	More organic
Budget control and constrained style	Participative budgets, flexible budgets
Reliance on accounting controls	Low reliance on accounting controls, budget slack
Narrow scope: historical, financial	Broad scope: flexible, integrative
Sophisticated controls	Sophisticated integrative mechanisms
Performance and cost focus	Competitor (external) focus
Operating procedures	Clan (values and beliefs) control
Output and results controls	Social controls
Behaviour and action controls	Prospect controls
Patriarchal control centralised from the top	Personnel (peer) controls
Diagnostic controls	Strategic, interactive controls

Figure 1   Comparison of mechanistic and organic modes of control. (*Source*: Adapted from Chenhall, 2003.)

4.   Pooled, Sequential and Reciprocal Structures: Technology

In the 1960s, it became clear that organisation structure was contingent on both organisational size and the nature of the environment, and Woodward (1965) added a third contingency variable when, following a thorough study of almost all the manufacturing companies in Essex, she showed that organisation structure was related to technology. Firms became more specialised and bureaucratic with increasing tiers of managers as they moved from unit/small batch production to mass/large batch and then to process production.[3] This is not inconsistent with the work of Burns and Stalker. Mass production of standardised products is likely to be conducive to a mechanistic structure with rigid demarcation of duties and design.

Thompson (1967) made an important theoretical contribution by providing a categorisation of technology organisation that has been in use ever since. He noted that operations may be pooled, sequential or reciprocally interdependent. Pooled interdependence refers to relatively self-contained operating units carrying out similar activities. Sequential interdependence arises when the output from one department is passed to the next in serial fashion. And reciprocal interdependence is characterised by work passing back and forth between departments and complex dependencies.

---

[3]Note that, although technology has been recognised as a contingency variable since Woodward's work, Hickson et al. reported that size dominated the technology variable in their study.

Mintzberg (1979, p. 22) notes that teachers in a school provide an example of pooled interdependence, for, while sharing common facilities, they work alone with their pupils. Further examples were supplied by Macintosh (1994, p. 121) who referred to banks and insurance companies as examples of organisations that have many branches that '...get on with the job...without regard to actions in other branches.' Our study provides another example, a company that includes a retail chain with multiple outlets (see Figure 2).

Pooled organisations often exhibit strong decentralisation so that, for example, teachers, bank branch managers and shop managers can have considerable autonomy. However, paradoxically, this might be facilitated by strong *centralisation* of certain functions. For example, the McDonalds fast-food chain practices extensive decentralisation to local franchise managers. At the same time, there is total centralised control over product and the precise manner of its delivery. In some companies, extensive decentralisation might only be possible within a framework that specifies certain aspects of the operation in considerable detail.

Sequential systems are commonplace in manufacturing industry where the production of large volumes of standard product can require a series of clearly defined and possibly tightly coupled processes. The linkages between melting, re-melting, rolling and finishing in a steel mill provide an example of sequential processes (see Figure 3).

Sequential, inter-locked operations, with standardised products and processes, are likely to require relatively sophisticated, specialised, local infrastructure. Operations in a steel mill may be supported by planning, scheduling, purchasing and engineering functions and, as in Burns and Stalker's rayon manufacturer, for

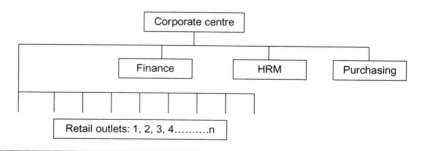

Figure 2   Corporate structure in a retail organisation.

Figure 3   Sequential processes in steel manufacture.

this, a carefully demarcated organisation structure may be very effective. Mintzberg (1979, p. 316) had this in mind when referring to the machine bureaucracy that '...depends primarily on the standardization' of its work processes for coordination' and therefore '...the technostructure – which houses the analysts who do the standardizing – emerges as a key part of the structure.'

Finally, reciprocal interdependence involves work being passed back and forth between organisational units. In a manufacturing environment, this might arise if customers specify their individual requirements. Facilities cannot be laid out in advance for maximum efficiency and product moves to and fro. Reciprocal interdependence is also likely to arise in creative endeavours where, for example, design, marketing and sample manufacture interact in unpredictable ways to meet the perceived demands of customers. A non-business example is provided by Macintosh (1994, p. 122) who refers to a psychiatric unit for children with learning disabilities where diagnosis and testing of both children and their parents required psychiatrists, psychologists, educators, social workers and occupational therapists to undertake work and exchange information in an initially unpredictable sequence.

4.1 Control of Processes in Pooled, Sequential and Reciprocal Structures

Macintosh and Daft (1987) used Thompson's categorisation in order to investigate the management control systems used within organisations. These researchers investigated budgeting in 90 departments drawn from 20 organisations based in the US and Canada. Managers were interviewed and asked questions designed to elicit their views on the use of budgets, for example, by rating the level of difficulty of budget targets on a nine-point scale from 'very easy to achieve' to 'almost impossible to achieve'. In order to measure the degree of interdependence, managers were shown diagrams illustrating the three types of interdependence defined by Thompson (1967) as pooled, sequential and reciprocal.

Macintosh and Daft expected pooled organisations to have independent operating units that shared resources with: 'The low level of interdependence [leading] to standardized coordination through rules and procedures.' The linkages in sequential interdependence were expected to increase demands for control and coordination: 'Here accounting and control systems may be used to facilitate planning and scheduling, and also encourage feedback to coordinate workflow between departments.' Finally, it was expected that 'Reciprocal interdependence places a heavy demand on management for coordination. Standardization and accounting information often are not sufficient for coordination, so face-to-face interaction and mutual adjustment may be required' (p. 50).

In analysing their results, Macintosh and Daft controlled for the size of the budgetary unit; as we have already observed and as the authors point out '...a substantial literature indicates that size is associated with greater use of bureaucratic rules and other impersonal control' (p. 54). They found:

- As expected, pooled structures correlated positively with the use of standard operating procedures but negatively with the use of both budgets and statistical reports.

- There was also support for the authors' expectation that the use of budgets and statistical reports would be correlated with sequential interdependence. Several variables were correlated in a positive direction and there was significance at the 10% level.

- Also as expected, as reciprocal interdependence increased there were negative correlations between the use of standard operating systems and the budget. However, contrary to expectation, the use of statistical reports seemed to play an expanded role in planning, target setting and coordination.

Overall, Macintosh and Daft provide convincing evidence that the extent and type of interdependence plays an important role in determining the emphasis given to different aspects of the management control system. Their work also showed that it might be necessary to understand the role of the budget and other management sub-systems such as standard operating procedures and statistical reports in order to judge the effectiveness of management control in particular contexts.

Summarising, Macintosh (1994, p. 119) noted that pooled organisations will tend to standardisation; serial organisations to sophisticated planning, coordinating and measurement; and reciprocal organisations to control systems that focus on feedback from the product or service.

5. Controlling the Organisation: Matching Structure and Control to Function

This analysis indicates that, as businesses grow, they develop more specialised functions with integrating devices (such as budgets) and generally become more administrative (as opposed to interpersonal) in character. The uncertainty they face and the nature of the technologies they use also have important implications for their control systems.

In practice, businesses can use a variety of control systems and Burns and Stalker saw organic and mechanistic structures not as alternatives, but as extremes on a continuum. Companies could adopt structures that fell between these poles and could switch their position on the continuum depending on circumstances.

Not only this, companies may use different forms of structure and control in different parts of their organisation. As we have already noted, different functional managers are likely to face differing degrees of environmental uncertainty and, facing different problems and using differing technologies, one might expect them to need different structures and controls. Thompson took the issue of functional specialisation and differing levels of uncertainty as central in his analysis of organisational structure:

As a point of departure, we suggest that organizations cope with uncertainty by creating certain parts specifically to deal with it, specializing other parts in operating under conditions of certainty or near certainty (Thompson, 1967, p. 13).

Thompson argued that different parts of the organisation can thus tune their structures to the degree of uncertainty faced. He proposed that organisations will seek to insulate their operating cores by buffering them from environmental disturbances. In manufacturing operations, this is most obvious in the use of inventory to buffer not only the manufacturing process from disruption of supply and unanticipated demand but also different parts of the manufacturing process from each other. In service operations where the operating core may only be able to operate smoothly at a certain level of activity, rationing and other devices may be used to buffer the core from erratic demand.

Thompson argued that the use of buffering techniques allows structures, systems and controls in the organisation's operating core to be designed in accordance with the maxims of technical rationality. Meanwhile, 'boundary spanning' functions that deal with the outside environment face more uncertainty and, logically, need different (more organic) structures and systems.

There is only limited direct research into the inter-relation between function and control systems. However, Lawrence and Lorsch (1967) showed that production departments faced less uncertainty than marketing departments and research and development departments. Mia and Chenhall (1994) investigated the environments of production and marketing managers, hypothesising that marketing managers would need more broad scope management accounting information than production managers. As expected they found that production managers from five mass production environments characterised their operations as standardised and routine with few exceptions while marketing managers thought their tasks were not highly analysable and there were many unexpected and novel decisions. They concluded:

...a higher usage of broad scope MAS information was associated with enhanced performance for marketing activities but not for production at conventional levels of significance (p. 10).

6.   Summary: Structure and Control in the Unitary Organisation

As organisations grow, *personal* control is likely to give way to *administrative* control and budgetary control systems provide a means of coordinating the activities of increasingly diverse technical specialists.

In relatively certain environments with standardised products and services, well-defined roles and operating procedures supported by sophisticated control systems can ensure product or service is delivered to specification, on-time, at acceptable cost and the traditional, hierarchical, mechanistic organisation can be effective. If the environment is relatively uncertain then more organic organisation is likely to be preferred. Roles and relationships are then not well defined and budgeting, operating in a participative, interpersonal manner, may become important for planning rather than for control.

These observations apply to the firm as a whole and also to its disparate parts. Different structures and control systems may be adopted in different parts of the same firm. In fact, Thompson took a key issue in choice of organisation structure to be the isolation of different kinds of function *so that* they may adopt different control systems. If the operating core can be buffered from uncertainty then systems can be developed that aim for operating efficiency.

The specific nature of operations also affects structure and systems so that pooled, sequential or reciprocal organisations may be adopted. Pooled organisations, with their 'carbon copy' structures may have tight procedures and standards but less need for budgeting. Sequential organisations, perhaps producing complex products and services, may use sophisticated budgeting and other coordinating mechanisms. Relatively unpredictable reciprocal organisations rely on spontaneous mutual adaptation in order to achieve coordination and control.

This concludes our overview of structure and control in possibly large, but unitary, organisations. What happens when organisations become *really* large? That is the subject of the next section.

7.   The Very Large Organisation: Decentralisation

7.1.   The Need for Decentralisation

Chandler's (1962) classic *Strategy and Structure* showed that companies of a certain size and complexity needed to adopt something other than functional (whether mechanistic or organic) structures. Growing companies tended to centralise and, by the 1920s '...the organization builders had worked out fairly standard designs for administering the several functional activities from departmental headquarters and

the enterprise as a whole from a central office' (p. 40). But the weakness of this '…
dominant centralized structure …[was] A very few men were still entrusted with a
great number of complex decisions' (p. 41).

Centralised firms with heavy investment in consolidated manufacturing facilities
needed assured markets to keep them busy so firms tended to expand geographically
and to diversify their product ranges. 'By placing an increasing intolerable strain
on existing administrative structures, territorial expansion and to a much greater
extent product diversification brought the multidivisional form' (p. 44). Chandler
concluded that, as companies grew and diversified, it became almost necessary for
them to move towards a decentralised, divisional, product–market-related structure.
Two of Chandler's most celebrated examples relate to the Du Pont Company and
General Motors.

7.2. Du Pont

Du Pont had expanded rapidly and, even before the First World War, had undertaken some diversification to keep its plants busy. Expansion based on demand for
explosives in the 1914–1918 war intensified the pressure to find new business and
the company began to manufacture artificial leather, pyroxylin and then paint and
varnishes. However, even in the post-war boom years, the new ventures were not
particularly successful:

> *'The more paint and varnish we sold,' one report wryly noted, 'the more
> money we lost' (p. 92).*

A committee of Du Pont executives carefully analysed the company's problems and
concluded that separate divisions should be created for Paint & Chemicals and for
Pyroxylin & Articles. All operating decisions would be delegated to responsible
general managers, an executive committee would oversee the divisions and central
departments would both support and control the divisions. However, the President
rejected these radical recommendations, clinging to the old ways that had worked
well in the past.

Despite the official rejection, movement towards divisionalisation nevertheless
took place and matters were brought to a head in 1921 when the company was making considerable losses. Faced with a crisis the company was then reorganised into
five operating divisions (Explosives, Dyestuffs, Pyrolin, Paints & Chemicals and
Fabrikoid & Film) supported by a number of central departments. The executive
committee could now concentrate on the affairs of the whole company and the division managers could adopt operating policies suited to their specific industries. The
company did not look back.

7.3. General Motors

General Motors had grown rapidly under William C. Durant who presided over the growth of an empire consisting of automobile assemblers such as Buick, Cadillac and Olds and component manufacturers such as Weston-Mott (axles and wheels) and Champion (spark plugs). However, a slight recession in 1910 saw Durant lose most of his executive power to bankers who put up $15 million to save the company.

The new managers attempted to introduce central departments for purchasing, accounting and production but met resistance from powerful managers such as Chrysler at Buick and Leland at Cadillac and Durant returned to the helm in 1915. As before, Durant expanded through take-overs and, encouraged by the post-war boom, capacity was drastically expanded in 1919. However, a recession in 1920 revealed massive overstocking and, disastrously, Durant tried to support the company's share price using borrowed money. He left the company in 1920 and Pierre Du Pont was persuaded to take over. He was deemed the only man who could provide reassurance to the investing public.

Pierre Du Pont turned to Alfred P. Sloan who, concerned by the (lack of) organisation within General Motors, had already undertaken an 'Organization Study'. This was based on two principles. First, each operation's chief executive would have full authority over their operation. Second, certain functions had to be organised centrally.

The organisation was introduced with general managers of autonomous operating units supported by a number of central staff departments (Legal, Research, Patents, etc.). The operating units were organised into four groups: Car, Accessory, Parts and Miscellaneous, each operating under a group vice-president. The new structure led to rationalisation and clarity:

Cadillac sold in the highest-priced position, Buick the next, followed by Oakland and then Olds, with Chevrolet in the largest volume, lowest price market (p. 143).

Sloan emphasised the autonomy of operating units and the advisory role of central staff departments. Autonomy was also paramount in transfer pricing policies:

Whether the products of a division went to other General Motors divisions or outside, they were sold at the going market price... 'Where there are no substantial sales outside,' Donaldson Brown pointed out in 1927, 'such as would establish a competitive basis, the buying division determines the competitive picture – at time partial requirements are actually purchased from outside sources so as to perfect the competitive situation' (p. 144).

7.4. Divisionalisation and Decentralisation

In the twentieth century, many companies followed the lead of Du Pont and General Motors and most companies of any size had decentralised product/market-related structures. Part of such an organisation structure might appear as in Figure 4. Decentralised divisions report to a corporate centre that might include a variety of staff functions that support the divisions. There can be many divisions, each with its own functional organisation and contemporary organisations can be very complex. There can be many layers with corporate 'centres' themselves reporting to yet higher corporate levels. At the same time, divisions can be internally decentralised into product/market business units.

7.5. Managing the Decentralised Company

Chandler had shown that, in order to manage diversity, large companies were almost compelled to decentralise their organisations. However, companies operate in very different industries that require varying technologies and permit economies of scale at differing levels of volume. It would not be surprising if major companies, while decentralising their organisations, nevertheless adopted different approaches to managing this decentralisation. This is what Goold and Campbell (1987) found. These researchers investigated the styles of 16 large, diversified, British companies. Following interviews with executives in these companies and study of company documentation, they concluded that the companies could be classified according to three styles:

1. Core businesses (strategic planning style)
2. Diverse businesses (strategic control style)
3. Manageable businesses (financial control style)

Figure 4   Divisional structure.

Companies pursuing the core business philosophy, such as Cadbury Schweppes, concentrated on a limited number of industries and aimed to become a major player in these industries. The centre can be knowledgeable about a limited number of industries and can coordinate and guide the business units through flexible, strategic planning. Diverse businesses, such as ICI and Courtaulds, tended to create divisions of fairly homogenous businesses and to delegate responsibility to these groupings. The corporate centre cannot be knowledgeable about a range of diverse industries and strategic control emerges at divisional level. Finally there were companies such as Hanson Trust that adopted the manageable business style. Hanson concentrates on basic, understandable businesses that can deliver acceptable earnings per share and dividend growth. 'Those in the operating companies have clear responsibility for running their businesses' (p. 45). Companies like Hanson and BTR build a portfolio of low risk, cash generative businesses that can be managed independently using the financial control style.

Goold and Campbell show us that issues of strategy may be driven from a company's corporate centre (strategic planning companies), from the divisional level (strategic control companies) or from the business unit level (financial control companies). Business unit level managers are responsible for operational decisions and dealing with uncertainties and pressures in their chosen industries and markets. However, their responsibility for formulating strategy depends on the sort of corporate entity to which they belong.

8. Contemporary Organisations

The key ideas of centralisation versus decentralisation and mechanistic versus organic structures became well understood and these concepts have stood the test of time. However, their application has changed as organisations have faced an increasingly globalised, deregulated and competitive environment together with developments such as flexible manufacturing, just-in-time production, total quality management, lean methods and workforce empowerment.

Parthasarthy and Sethi (1992) suggested that flexible manufacturing methods should be associated with increased product–market diversity, flexible response and quality leadership, and they proposed that company strategy should reflect this. They expected flexible automation firms to develop more linkages with suppliers, distributors and customers; to adopt more team structures and for shop-floor personnel to possess diversified skills. Their propositions are obviously consistent with the view that flexible methods require more organic structures.

Abernethy and Lillis (1995) explored these ideas and specifically hypothesised that more integrative liaison devices are needed when flexible manufacturing technologies are implemented. They constructed measures for degree of manufacturing flexibility and extent of integrative liaison devices and undertook semi-structured interviews in 42 firms. The results were as expected: positive correlation between increasing flexibility and more use of integrative devices; negative correlation between increasing flexibility and efficiency-based performance measures. Dividing the sample into two groups revealed significant differences between more and less flexible firms:

> ...the relationship between performance and the use of integrative liaison devices was positive and significant for firms committed to flexibility... expanded responses from General Managers indicated that...It was considered more important to get the structural arrangements right than the design of the performance measurement system for firms pursuing flexibility. Informal and organic management structures, development of lateral linkages, and the development of organizational culture which encouraged individuals to identify with corporate goals, appeared to carry strong implications for effective strategy implementation (p. 251).

Kalagnanam and Lindsay (1998) investigated the impact of JIT methods on management control systems. JIT can lead to dramatic reduction in inventory. In organisational terms, there is a reduction in the buffers between the operating core and boundary spanning activities, and this exposes operations to more uncertainty. Kalagnanam and Lindsay argue that, in addition, JIT systems need to be more flexible in response to market changes and customer needs and to embody a philosophy of continuous improvement. All of these aspects of JIT suggest that a more organic organisation structure would be more appropriate.

Three case studies confirmed Kalagnanam and Lindsay's expectations. In the first case hierarchy had become less influential; everybody was consulted; decision making had speeded up and there were ongoing efforts to empower workers and decentralise tasks. In the second case current practice was continuously questioned, management was based on consensus decision making within teams and a network control structure had been adopted. The third case featured a larger organisation so that formal communications were still prevalent. However, there were physical changes such as relocating production engineers closer to manufacturing and there was more direct communication between marketing, engineering, design and quality departments.

The cases were followed by a survey that yielded 155 usable responses and, of these, 68.4% had implemented JIT to some extent. Analysis showed that, relative to traditional mass production firms, the JIT firms had more organic structures and showed higher rates of improvement.

As one might, intuitively, expect, the changes of the late twentieth century that rewarded more flexibility and diversity have encouraged more organic organisational structures. Research confirms the continuing value of the mechanistic–organic bipolar scale in measuring organisation structure and reaffirms the characteristics associated with the organic structure: integrative devices, lateral arrangements, open communications, etc.

9.   Future Organisations

The pace of change in the late twentieth and early twenty-first centuries has led some authors to ask fundamental questions, and Beinhocker (2007) supplies a wide-ranging attack on traditional economic theory together with suggestions for organisational design. He argues that traditional economics, modelled on the equilibrium mathematics of nineteenth century physics, does not reflect what happens in real, dynamic, open economies. In particular, it fails to account for innovation and growth by treating technological shocks as exogenous perturbations to equilibrium systems. Beinhocker argues that evolutionary theory provides a much better basis for understanding the way the economies evolve. Entrepreneurs and managers cannot deduce 'optimal' action in dynamic, complex systems. Instead they search for new physical and social technologies, and only by experimenting do they find out which ones work better than the old methods.

In practice, Beinhocker sees business units fighting in competitive product–markets for market share and profit and this leads him to raise two questions. First, what is a business unit? Second, how should the unit be organised and what strategy should it adopt?

We have noted how contemporary organisations can develop complex structures and the definition of a business unit was an issue that perplexed us in our field study. Bockenheimer argues that:

> ...the key attribute of a business is that it provides the focal point for interactions. Thus, in distinguishing between a business and product and service lines, one should look for coherence across a set of dimensions such as a common set of customers, competitors, geography, technologies or suppliers...

> There is inevitably some ambiguity and subjectivity in drawing these boundaries, and the issue of what constitutes a business unit versus a service line is the subject of regular debate in many companies... [I] assume that management teams are best placed to make these distinctions... business units as defined by the companies themselves (pp. 281–282).

The second issue concerns the organisation of the business units so as to succeed in the evolutionary landscape – the marketplace. Beinhocker sees the selection of business plans as a sequential process that proceeds first within hierarchical organisations so that some plans are rejected and some implemented and then, second, in the marketplace as consumers decide which products and services to purchase. 'Market economies are systems of evolutionary competing hierarchies' (p. 289).

Given the thesis that economies do not settle to some optimal equilibrium but rather proceed dynamically on evolutionary principles, Beinhocker argues that '*We may not be able to predict direct economic evolution, but we can design our institutions and societies to be better or worse evolvers*' (p. 324, emphasis as in original). For Beinhocker this means developing a portfolio of strategic options so that the company has the best possible chance of identifying a strategy that will be successful in the market. Although companies need to be efficient in producing their existing products and services, they also need to be adaptable in creating the next generation of strategies and products.

Beinhocker notes that the structures adopted by large corporations tend to be good at executing, producing existing products for existing markets, but they are not so good at adapting to changing circumstances. As we have seen, as companies grow they need to organise because, otherwise, the number of relationships between organisational members would mushroom exponentially. Beinhocker gives 'Two Cheers for Hierarchy!' and writes:

> *Organizing the network into hierarchies reduces the density of connections and thus reduces the interdependencies in the network. Hierarchies are critical in enabling networks to reach larger sizes before diseconomies of scale set in (p. 154).*

Hierarchies can be broad and flat if problems can be solved in parallel. However, for complex, sequential problems the hierarchy will tend to be narrow and deep. Citing Airbus as an example, Beinhocker argues that the 'Execution organizations, with their big, deep hierarchies, are designed to solve large, complex problems and excel at control, efficiency and accountability. They are not designed for undertaking many small tasks in parallel...' (p. 366). This may mean that large, complex organisations need separate structures for their creative people, working on the strategic possibilities that will facilitate adaptation in the future. The problem is greater for complex, hierarchical organisations than for those that can adopt pooled organisation structures.

If Beinhocker attempts to develop a theory of economic and business organisation, Hamel (2007) adopts a pragmatic approach in pointing to '*The Future of Management*'. He suggests that companies such as Whole Foods Market, W.L. Gore & Associates and Google provide indications of the way management can change so as to become more innovative and adaptive.

At Whole Foods employees operate in teams that have considerable autonomy. The company avoids bureaucracy and fosters trust by both making employee compensation data freely available and limiting the salary of any individual to no more than 19 times the average salary. Empowerment is linked to accountability for: 'Every four weeks, Whole Foods calculates the profit per labour hour for every team in every store. Teams that exceed a certain threshold get a bonus in their next paycheck' (p. 73).

At W.L. Gore & Associates innovation flourishes. There is no hierarchy; operating units are small, self-managing teams; and operating size rarely exceeds 200 employees. Compensation is determined by a committee of an individual's peers based on information collected from at least 20 colleagues. Evolutionary ideas are embedded: 'Gore wins big not by betting big but by betting often...' (p. 95). And, echoing Beinhocker: 'While Gore's leaders understand that it's tough to *plan* for innovation, they have no doubt that it's possible to *organize* for innovation' (p. 96).

At Google '...the founders have sought to recreate...the same fertile innovation climate that is found within Silicon Valley itself' (p. 103). This company generates many new products through its exceptionally bright employees working in small autonomous teams. While as many as 80% of these products fail, the aim is to find the breakthrough product(s) that will take off in the market. Financial rewards include annual bonuses of typically 30–60% but can be much greater for an idea that generates abnormal profits. Once again 'management' is limited and the company functions on 'openness, transparency, and a lot of lateral communication' (p. 117).

Hamel summarises what he sees as the pattern for future management: Darwinian selection through markets; managers accountable to employees and customers not shareholders; iconoclasts encouraged and leadership decentralised; organising to encourage diversity and experimentation and a mission that can energise everyone.

Hamel provides examples of highly successful companies that follow the evolutionary ideas set out by Beinhocker. And the reader will remember the key 'Beyond Budgeting' example, Svenska Handelsbanken, which has some of the same characteristics as the Hamel examples. It might seem, therefore, that the future of organisations is towards ever more organic structures with flat hierarchies and democratically managed and remunerated teams. However, care must be taken in extrapolating from a few examples. All these companies can be organised into relatively small units where teams compete with each other and other companies. Whole Foods and Svenska Handelsbanken are pooled organisations while Gore and Google are self-consciously innovative companies that focus on the generation of new ideas rather than execution. Flat organisational structures are easier to arrange in these companies than in those companies that focus on efficient execution of complex processes.

10. Summary

This analysis of organisation structure and control has shown how companies can adopt different structures, control systems and cultures as they grow and/or face differing environmental challenges. Small companies are likely to adopt *interpersonal* control systems and, if they use budgets, are likely to use them in an interactive manner. Managers in these companies tend not to criticise the interpersonal style, either because 'the boss knows best' or because of strong interpersonal loyalties.

As the company grows it is likely to establish specialist functions such as production, marketing and finance and this places a premium on *integrative* mechanisms and systems such as budgeting. Now the use of the budget is likely to be of a more administrative nature, managers are more involved in the budgeting process, take it more seriously and see meeting budget as an important element of their performance. The traditional approach to budgetary control seems tailor-made for these circumstances with delegation of authority and responsibility and managers able to exercise their initiative within clearly defined limits.

The discovery of *organic* management structures rather upset the clarity of the hierarchical, budget controlled, vision of a *mechanistic* organisation structure. It was realised that, in rapidly changing environments, it might be necessary to cut across the traditional, hierarchical structure by emphasising personal contributions based on knowledge and ability rather than instructions given by a superior and ultimately a direction set by the head of the enterprise. Late-twentieth century research has reaffirmed the importance of organic control systems to cope with more competitive, uncertain markets, and it seems that the growth of organic structures is now as inexorable as once was the growth of mechanistic structures. Organic structures have been found to be effective even in the operating cores of organisations where JIT and increased flexibility demand more organic structures and controls. And management thinkers have argued that, to innovate and adapt, companies need flexible, task-oriented teams motivated by achievement rather than conformity to bureaucratic norms. Having said this, it must be remembered that, in order to deliver complex products and services there is still a place for hierarchical, well-organised and efficient structures.

The growth of organisations in the twentieth century raised a further question: how to manage and control an organisation of several thousand employees engaged in diverse industries and markets with widespread geographical coverage? The answer came in the form of the divisionalised, decentralised organisation. Such organisations are now ubiquitous, often with international, if not global operations. Businesses that operate in diverse product–markets across extensive geographical areas have set up decentralised business units with their own operational managements. These units operate semi-autonomously thus relieving the pressure on senior executives and facilitating informed operating decisions at local level.

The precise degree of autonomy permitted to the business units depends upon the philosophy of the group and the number of diverse industries in which it operates. A focused group, operating in a limited number of industries, will tend to limit the autonomy of its units, because senior managers are likely to have a good understanding of the group's product–markets. At the other extreme, a conglomerate, operating in diverse industries, is likely to adopt extensive decentralisation and delegation.

In Goold and Campbell's terms, the first group is likely to adopt a strategic planning style while the second adopts a financial control style. There is a third possibility that falls between these, the strategic control style where the group's divisions, operating in related industries, can adopt the strategic planning style for their business units. However, the divisions themselves, operating in disparate industries, are treated as autonomous units by the central holding group.

Chandler's analysis shows why companies decentralise and Goold and Campbell provide insight into how decentralised operations might be managed. In particular, they show that business strategy might be developed at corporate, divisional or business unit level depending upon whether a strategic planning, strategic control or financial control style is adopted.

The particular strategy chosen might be to defend existing product–markets, to prospect for new product–markets, to build or harvest, etc. There are some apparently obvious links between choice of strategy and control systems, but empirical research has generated some unexpected results. We conclude our review of the literature in the next chapter by considering budgets in the wider context of organisational structures and control systems.

Chapter 5

Structure, Strategy and Control

1. Introduction

Research has shown that budgeting can have different characteristics depending upon the size, structure, technology and environment of an organisation. These contingent variables affect not only the organisation as a whole but also its individual departments so that a range of structures and control systems can be used in the same organisation.

In this chapter, we first place structures and control systems in a wider context by reviewing contributions from economic and organisational theory. Some economists argue that *transaction costs* drive organisational structure because, if complex products and services are traded, the market framework suffers from increasingly onerous contracting costs. Eventually, it becomes advantageous to dissolve the market through common ownership of supplier and consumer and the hierarchical form of organisation becomes more efficient. This analysis can be applied to the growth of business and, following Ouchi's analysis, extended to include not only market and hierarchical but also clan-based[1] forms of organisation.

The market/hierarchy/clan analysis concludes our analysis of organisational controls and facilitates an analysis of budgeting and other control systems. Using a simple 3×2 matrix of input/process/output versus formal/informal control systems, we suggest that budgeting is most obviously appropriate for formal control over inputs and processes while market-based organisation can be used when formal control over outputs is desired. Clan controls and organic structures provide informal approaches to control over inputs and processes.

Having summarised the role of budgeting in the context of wider control systems, we introduce the last important contingency variable – strategy. There had been references to the links between strategy and structure as in Chandler's (1962) work, *Strategy and Structure*, but not until the late 1970s were working taxonomies of strategic types identified. With the identification of cost leadership/defender and niche/prospector strategies, it became possible to look for links between strategy, structure and control systems, and it was generally supposed that defenders would make heavier use of control systems than prospectors. When empirical research cast doubt on this assumption, a further round of organisational theorising led to the publication of Simons (1995) work, *Levers of Control*, and we conclude our review with a summary of his findings and suggestions.

2.   Control Systems Theory: Hierarchies, Markets and Clans

2.1.   Hierarchies and Markets Within Business Organisations

The previous chapter set out the typical stages in the growth of a business, from personal control to bureaucratic, hierarchical control and to the need for decentralisation in very large organisations. Both personal and hierarchical controls have limitations. Personal control is only effective when the scale of operations can be understood by a single person, and pure hierarchical control can operate only while operations are sufficiently homogenous for a single management team to control them. As the hierarchical organisation grows large and diversifies, it tends to decentralise with business units becoming relatively autonomous. The interaction between business units becomes more market oriented, possibly with transactions at arms length using market-related transfer prices. The relation between the business units and the corporate centre can also move towards a market relation, especially in

---

[1] Some authors prefer reference to culture-based controls but we stick to Ouchi's terminology in this chapter.

financial control groups. The centre can act like a shareholder, rewarding successful units with capital injections while withdrawing capital from unsuccessful units.

2.2. Hierarchies and Markets in Economic Theory

In economic theory, the choice of hierarchical or market-based organisation has been recognised since Coase (1937) asked what determined whether a firm should integrate or rely on the market. Arrow (1969) drew attention to the key role of transaction costs in impeding or blocking the creation of markets, and Williamson (1981a,b) developed transaction cost analysis into a major area of theory. Markets are efficient when transaction costs are low, as for example, when mass produced goods are exchanged for cash. However, for complex exchanges, time-consuming contracts are needed and checking their execution may involve costly governance structures. Then transaction costs become significant and firms might combine rather than employ resources in negotiating and enforcing contracts. A large hierarchical organisation can become more efficient than a group of firms interacting through a series of markets. In hierarchical organisations, employees recognise the legitimate right of superiors to dictate day-to-day activities and (partially unspecified) employment contracts overcome the excessive transaction costs associated with the alternative market solution: an ongoing web of ever-changing contracts.

Ouchi (1980, pp. 132–133) summarised 'The Market Failures Framework'. As transactions become more complex, a 'contingent claims contract' might be used to specify contractual commitments in differing future states. However, all such states cannot be predicted and, therefore, the (partial) contract will work only if the parties trust each other. The alternative of agreeing smaller, sequential 'spot' contracts fails because, if the product/service is unique, the supplier develops specialised expertise and gains an advantage over other suppliers. They withdraw and the 'market' fails.

For Williamson, specialisation and asset specificity drive the market/hierarchy choice because specialised investment leads to seller and buyer becoming locked in a relationship. The seller, having a specialised process, needs the buyer and the buyer cannot easily purchase elsewhere at comparable cost. The tight relationship is likely to lead to common ownership (and hierarchical control). For example, Williamson (1981a, p. 556) notes that, where the output from one process feeds another, closely located, process '...the common ownership of site-specific stations is thought to be so "natural" that alternative governance structures are rarely considered.' However, '... the joining of separable stations – for example, blast furnace and rolling mill, thereby to realize thermal economies – under common ownership is not technologically determined but instead reflects transaction-economizing judgements.'

This theory, developed to explain why firms might choose integrated common ownership over the market, has implications for internal organisational forms.

The initial transition from personal to hierarchical control can be interpreted in terms of a saving in transaction costs as small firms, trading in a complex network of markets, move towards integration and hierarchical control. However, the growth of these hierarchies and, especially, the diversification of large companies into diverse products and markets itself impose heavy transaction costs. The cost of referring decisions up and down the hierarchy and the costs imposed on top executives striving to handle multiple products, markets and industries threaten to overwhelm the organisation. In many organisations, this has been met by the introduction of internal market-based structures so that semi-autonomous business units trade with each other and relate to the corporate centre on an arms-length basis.

2.3.   Hierarchies, Markets and Clans

We saw in the last chapter that organisations do not have to be structured as mechanistic hierarchies with closely defined positions and job descriptions. In changing circumstances, tight definition of roles may be counterproductive and Burns and Stalker described organic structures, where positions, roles and duties are not prescribed in detail, as an alternative to mechanistic structures. In organic structures, the glue that binds the organisation is not the invisible reporting lines that define duties and responsibilities but common beliefs and values to which organisational members subscribe. Ouchi (1980) later referred to this sort of organisational control as *clan* control.

Bureaucracies rely on hierarchical surveillance and standards to evaluate performance. However, performance may be difficult to evaluate because the task is unique (so there is no standard for comparison) or because of ambiguity (e.g. several demands have to be simultaneously met) or because individual contributions are difficult to identify. Then bureaucratic control can become problematic, and Ouchi suggested clan control based on shared values and beliefs as an alternative. Employees are socialised to such an extent that they regard their personal interests as congruent with those of the organisation. Ouchi summarises the conditions under which different forms of control are most appropriate:

> ...*market relations are efficient when there is little ambiguity over performance, so the parties can tolerate relatively high levels of opportunism or goal incongruence. And bureaucratic relations are efficient when both performance ambiguity and goal incongruence are moderately high...*

> *What form of mediation succeeds by minimizing goal incongruence and tolerating high levels of ambiguity in performance evaluation?... The answer is what we have referred to as the clan, which is the obverse of the market relation*

since it achieves efficiency under the opposite conditions: high performance ambiguity and low opportunism (p. 135).

This market, hierarchy and clan analysis of control systems provides insights into the transition of growing organisations from markets to hierarchies and then back to the use of markets as very large companies decentralised. Clan controls, appropriate to organic organisations, provide a counterpoint to mechanistic, hierarchical controls as beliefs and values replace reliance on rules and instructions.

3. Control Systems in Context

3.1. Taxonomy

We have now reviewed a range of key contributions to the literature including:

- interpersonal versus administrative control,
- mechanistic versus organic structures,
- hierarchical versus market versus clan controls.

Additionally, there are numerous categorisations of control systems and Langfield–Smith (1997) summarised the following contributions to the literature:

- formal versus informal (Anthony et al., 1989);
- output versus behaviour (Ouchi, 1977);
- market, bureaucracy and clan (Ouchi, 1979);
- administrative and social (Hopwood, 1976);
- results, action and personnel (Merchant, 1985).

Although this can appear confusing, there are obviously many overlaps between the various categories and we suggest that a simple two-way analysis can help to make sense of them. The two dimensions we have in mind are the focus of control (inputs, processes or outputs) and the method of control (formal or informal) (see Table 1).

This analysis shows us that budgetary control is most likely to be associated with *formal* organisational control and, especially, when that control is over *inputs and processes*. Budgeting is especially useful when outputs are unambiguously specified and the relationship between outputs and inputs is well understood. The following analysis is intended to show how budgetary controls interact with other controls over

Table 1 A Taxonomy of Control Systems

		Focus of control		
		Input control	Process control	Output control
Method of control	Formal systems	*Budgetary control* for authorisation of financial resources. Qualifications, training, induction schemes for control over personnel.	*Mechanistic* structures with administrative systems for control over action. Standards, procedures, *budgets*, bureaucracies, hierarchies and role definitions.	Specification of required outputs: product and service quality and volume; financial metrics for performance evaluation. *Markets* for product; incentive schemes for results.
	Informal systems	Company values and culture leading to peer pressure and *clan* control over personnel.	*Organic* structures with lateral communications and reliance on interpersonal relationships.	If outputs are ambiguous or difficult to evaluate subjective social controls may be needed.

inputs, processes and outputs and how different packages of controls and structures are appropriate in different circumstances.

3.2. Formal Control Over Inputs

Extensive controls over both human and financial resources are common. Control over HR can involve years of training, qualification and extensive recruitment procedures. Control over financial resources can be provided by the budget and can be extensive and detailed, for example, preventing the switching of budget funds between expense categories, or relatively flexible where the total budget is specified but its specific uses are not.

Input controls become particularly important when processes cannot be precisely specified. Professional work falls into this category where pupils, students and patients have different needs; construction projects are unique; businesses face different tax problems and so on. Professional entrance examinations and continuing professional development become important controls for teachers, surgeons, engineers, accountants, etc.

Input controls are also important when there are multiple and/or ambiguous outputs and the relation between these and inputs is unclear. At a macro-economic level, the limitless demand for healthcare can be met by a budget that provides a means of rationing resources. Within business organisations some services may be 'free at the point of delivery'. There is then a danger that users will demand more of these services (legal advice, training support, HR support and advice, etc.) and well-intentioned support staff will try to build up departments to meet demand. The budget can provide a necessary constraint on such activities if charging for them is difficult or inappropriate.

3.3. Formal Control Over Processes

As Macintosh (1994, p. 126) notes, formal systems that aim to get repetitive work done *efficiently* are ubiquitous. 'Routinely they deliver newspapers, carry conversations over long distances, transport people back and forth to work, stock supermarkets, educate children...'. For these tasks, at the operational core of organisations, standardised procedures, budgets and hierarchies are often effective and, as Thompson noted, organisations may actually be structured so as to remove uncertainty from their operating cores.

In pooled organisation structures with relatively simple business units, procedures are likely to be specified very clearly and performance can be readily assessed by comparison with other units or competitors. Paradoxically, clear specification of tasks in a decentralised organisation is likely to be supported by the strong *centralisation* of functions such as product/service design, purchasing and information systems.

In more complex sequential structures, repetitive tasks are amenable to standardisation and bureaucratic process controls with observational hierarchies, manuals, etc. to ensure that routine operations are carried out efficiently. Budgets, schedules and other planning devices become important in coordinating sequential technologies.

3.4. Formal Control Over Outputs

When inputs and processes are less easily related to outputs, detailed budgetary control is less effective. However, if the desired output is well defined, formal systems that centre on the achievement of results, not the method of achieving them, can be used. Output measures based on *effectiveness* replace the focus on process *efficiency*. For example, a football manager is evaluated on the basis of the team's results, not on the effort expended in analysing the opposition. In business 'payment by results' is commonplace. For example, it is difficult to say what makes good salespeople but their results are both clear and measurable and they can therefore be rewarded according to performance.

Output control is closely linked to market control and often has implications for remuneration through incentive schemes. There is an implicit market exchange: the employee delivers the outputs and, in exchange, receives promotion, incentive bonuses, share options, etc. The output may be a product or service – on time, of requisite quality at acceptable price or it might be a financial measure such as target profit, return on investment or residual income. In the latter cases, there would almost certainly be other non-profit targets and constraints. At the very least the profit or return would need to be ethically delivered and without compromising future growth.

In this study, the most important example of output-based performance measurement is in the extensive use of profit and investment centres. When managers are responsible for complex operations it is not easy to specify exactly what they should do. Indeed managers' jobs are often characterised by their unpredictable variety. However, if profit or investment centres can be constructed, managers can be measured, not by what they do, but by what they achieve. In practice, this raises issues of measurement and a number of metrics have been proposed: return on investment, economic value added, cash flow return on investment, etc.

3.5.   Informal Controls Over Inputs

Tradition has always been an important social control, and shared beliefs and values can provide a very important control mechanism – clan control. If values are deeply engrained in every manager and worker, then costly and expensive process and output controls might be avoided. The workforce can be trusted to do what is best for the organisation. In the last 30 years, many businesses have set out mission statements delineating their core values and, if employees share a set of values and beliefs, then clan control is a viable alternative to more formal methods.

More importantly, in complex, ambiguous situations, possibly with multiple outputs, formal systems of control become inappropriate and there is likely to be increasing reliance on both formal and informal input controls. The highly trained professional soldier, both competent and patriotic, is well equipped to face difficult and unusual situations and extreme examples include the Japanese kamikaze pilots of the Second World War and the suicide bombers of more recent times.

3.6.   Clashes Between Input Controls (Professionalism) and Formal Control of Outputs (Managerialism)

Our review tends to lead to the conclusion that, in different circumstances, different forms of structure and control are most appropriate: organic structures and clan controls for uncertain environments, mechanistic structures with procedures and budgets for predictable environments, etc. However, we should also note that, just as organic and mechanistic structures are not mutually exclusive choices, neither are control systems. It is perfectly possible to instigate more than one control system and these can be reinforcing or they can lead to tension.

Extensive training and the inculcation of values and beliefs are common in the professions and this input-oriented form of control can lead to clashes with the, typically managerial, output-based approach. For example, professionals in health, law enforcement and education often claim the importance of professional judgement in their decisions while managers and government attempt to impose instrumental, output-based targets. The multiple dimensions of health care – waiting times, speed of emergency response, appropriateness of treatment, dignity of the patient, probability of acquiring hospital-based infections, etc. – make it difficult to set output targets for them all. Targets can conflict and over-zealous enforcement can (and does) lead to unfortunate consequences as managers and health workers collude in adopting devices such as redefining trolleys as 'beds', corridors as 'wards', etc. Another example concerns police targets based on the number of arrests, and this has led to a number of examples of trivial charges being brought against essentially honest members of the public. Meanwhile, effort can be diverted from addressing serious crime.[2]

3.7.   Informal Control of Processes

As we know, hierarchic structures, formal procedures and budgeting can be very effective in stable situations. However, as product and task diversity increase, it may be necessary to introduce new elements into the structure and/or rely less on formal hierarchy and more on task-centred methods. The structure moves from 'mechanistic' towards 'organic' and informal and lateral communications increase. These may be promoted by matrix organisation structures that reflect the importance of projects, tasks and ability to contribute rather than position, procedures, standards and rules.

Organic structures become important in dealing with increasing environmental uncertainty and this may relate to the whole business or particular departments. They are especially important in boundary spanning departments as these are usually exposed to more uncertainty than operating departments. However, we have seen that modern production management, emphasising flexibility and JIT techniques, faces more uncertainty, and organic systems have become more important in managing the operating core in some businesses. Additionally, if operations involve reciprocal technologies with unpredictable interaction between several departments, a range of coordinating devices may be needed and, again, the structure is likely to tend towards organic and away from mechanistic.

---

[2]Sometimes referred to as 'what you measure is what you get' – WYMIWYG – although some of the examples suggest that what you measure may be only what you appear to get.

3.8.   Informal Control of Outputs

Finally we note that, sometimes, the outputs are difficult to evaluate and the quality of a book, a film, a play or of a piece of research is notoriously subjective. There are many examples: critics may make or break writers and playwrights and the award of a Nobel Prize is the ultimate accolade for academics. In business, the output of some departments, such as HRM or Risk Management, are normally only assessable by their reputation amongst users.[3]

4.   Strategy and Control

Our review has covered the growth of hierarchic organisations, the choice of mechanistic or organic structures and a variety of control systems depending on the focus of control (input, process or output) and the nature of the circumstances faced. The control system can be influenced by the degree of uncertainty faced by the company or department, size, technology used, size, etc. Additionally, it has been shown that organisational strategy can impact on structure and control systems.

Chandler's analysis showed how large, diversified companies opted for decentralised organisation structures, and Goold and Campbell's further analysis identified the different approaches that might be adopted in managing decentralisation. This analysis suggested that 'strategy' might be driven at corporate, divisional or business unit level. It did not address *how* strategy might be determined.

From the late 1970s, a number of models were suggested that could help in analysing strategy and in guiding its formulation. Langfield-Smith pointed to three influential contributions: the defender–prospector–analyser typology of Miles and Snow (1978); Porter's (1980, 1985) identification of cost leadership and differentiation as generic strategies and the build–hold–harvest–divest strategic missions of Gupta and Govindarajan (1984). Langfield-Smith notes that some strategic combinations are feasible while others appear infeasible. Most obviously, a prospector might be expected to adopt a build strategy based on differentiation while a defender might be expected to focus on cost leadership and a hold or harvest product/market position.

Theorists expected some common sense matching between chosen strategy and control systems. Miles and Snow (1978) expected defenders to use hierarchical, mechanistic structures with centralised systems focused on problem solving rather than the location of new product/market opportunities. Porter (1980) expected similar structures and systems for those following a cost leadership strategy. Conversely,

---

[3] In abnormal circumstances, after some disaster, outputs might be easily assessed. For example, the risk management operation at Barings Bank clearly failed to prevent the trader, Nick Leeson, engaging in trades that bankrupted the operation.

theorists expected prospectors following differentiation strategies to use more organic structures with control through interpersonal coordination rather than formal systems. Macintosh (1994) neatly summarised the expected linkages (Table 2).

Perhaps surprisingly, some of the research into practice conflicts with these expectations. Merchant (1985) found little difference between firms pursuing different

Table 2   Typology of Strategy, Structure and Control

		Key characteristics		
		Strategy	Structure	Control system
Type of organisation	Defender	Aggressively maintain a prominent position in a carefully chosen, narrow product-market domain	Traditional centralised functional organisation	Efficiency focus with close detailed and tight controls
	Prospector	Create turbulence by continually bringing new products to the market	Organic management arrangements and product group organisation	Effectiveness focus accenting innovation, entrepreneurial effort and self-evaluation at lower levels
	Analyser	Highly selective in its stable sphere and rapidly copies successful innovations in its dynamic domain	Dual core organisation: centralised functional for its stable domain and organic for its dynamic sphere	Tight controls and an efficiency focus for the stable sphere, looser controls with an effectiveness focus for the dynamic domain
	Reactor	A well-defined but obsolete strategy or a 'running blind' strategy	Politics and careerism dominate over any logical arrangement of authority and responsibility	Treated as merely a bookkeeping system

Source: Macintosh (1994, p. 95). Published by kind permission of Wiley-Blackwell, Oxford, England

growth strategies. And Simons (1987) found that successful prospectors emphasised tight budget and output controls while defenders used control systems less intensively. This unexpected finding caused a re-evaluation of the manner in which control systems might be *used*.

Dent (1990) set out several reasons why and how prospector companies may use an apparently tight budgeting system:

- interactive use of the budget could encourage organisational learning;
- in a decentralised, entrepreneurial company tight budget controls might provide important boundaries that set important limits on the extent of managers' risk taking activities;
- a prospector company might use financial targets as the only practical means of capturing the breadth and uncertainty of activities undertaken by its decentralised, entrepreneurial business units.

Insofar as defender companies might use budgetary control less intensively than expected, Dent noted that these companies, producing standardised product in stable environments, might rely on non-financial systems to control their processes rather than on budgetary control.

5. Simons 'Levers of Control'

5.1. Overview

Following extensive field work, Simons (1995) set out his analysis of and prescriptions for control systems in use. He began by noting that:

> *Data that I had collected from over one hundred companies revealed a puzzling anomaly: the most innovative companies used their profit planning and control systems more intensively than did their less innovative counterparts (p. ix).*

Simons set out to show that managers use '*Levers of Control*' (title) based on belief systems, boundary systems, interactive systems and diagnostic systems. This echoes several of the themes developed in our literature review: belief systems relate to clan control and organic structures; boundary systems link to input controls; interactive systems imply participation; diagnostic systems link to traditional feedback (or feed-forward) standard costing and budgeting systems. Simons produces a convincing synthesis of these ideas together with a range of practical examples.

5.2.   Belief Systems

Like Ouchi (and Burns and Stalker before him), Simons expects belief systems to provide 'values, purpose and direction for the organization' (p. 34). He noted that leaders and managers could develop a system of beliefs that would '…inspire and guide organizational discovery' (p. 36). They could be powerful weapons in generating organisational commitment and their ability to help satisfy individuals' emotional needs could over-ride individuals' self-interest. Simons provides the 'credo' of Johnson and Johnson as an example of a company mission statement and reported that, in a 1991 seminar, 68 of 72 participants had formal mission statements or similar documents – but 15 years previously only 6 would have answered yes. Companies became very interested in mission statements in the 1990s. The Bain biannual survey of most popular tools and techniques ranked mission statements first in 1993 and second in 2000 and 2004. They were still popular in the 2006 survey but had slipped to fifth.

5.3.   Boundary Systems

Simons draws attention to the important role of boundary systems. He points out that 'Although boundary systems are essentially proscriptive or negative systems, they allow managers to delegate decision making and thereby allow the organization to achieve maximum flexibility and creativity' (p. 41). Perhaps counter-intuitively, boundary systems can actually encourage initiative because the absence of rules and guidelines leaves employees open to *ad hoc* sanctions by their superiors if (unwritten) codes of behaviour are transgressed. The implication is that the use of belief systems needs to be counterbalanced by boundary systems that '…communicate the acceptable domain for search activity…' (p. 41). Drawing on previous research, Simons notes that high uncertainty, low trust and lack of shared values tend to increase the need for boundary systems.

Simons also notes that 'Performance pressures create a need for codes of conduct…[and]…Firms that use diagnostic control systems… to pressure employees must create strict guidelines to make sure that certain undesirable behaviors will not be tolerated' (p. 47). With impeccable timing, as Simons' book went to press, Nick Leeson's unauthorised trade in derivatives was bankrupting Barings bank. And issues of ethical behaviour and control erupted anew as the twentieth century closed with the dotcom stock market boom and the Enron scandal of 2001 that took down not only Enron but also its auditors and advisers, Arthur Andersen. As Simons says, boundary systems are often driven by specific events and the Sarbanes-Oxley Act of 2002 was a response to mismanagement and misdemeanour in the late 1990s.[4]

---

[4] It will be interesting to see what new 'boundary systems' will be devised to try to avert a repetition of the banking crises of 2007–2008.

5.4.   Diagnostic Systems

Simons' treatment of diagnostic control systems follows conventional wisdom with feedback of variance information triggering corrective action. The particular output variables to be monitored should be chosen with care, and Simons mentions the balanced scorecard as a systematic method of identifying variables in the four dimensions: financial, customer, process and innovation. As we know, the level of targets has long been a subject for research and Simons provides a neat summary of the issues:

> *The same diagnostic system, a profit planning system for example – can be used to provide motivation; to coordinate plans and resources; to provide benchmarks for corrective action; and as a basis for performance evaluation and reward ...Motivation...may require...“stretch” targets...Coordination may require a level that reflects the most probable outcome. Early warning may require setting goals at lower acceptable limits... Ex post evaluation may require eliminating uncontrollable factors from performance results (Simons, 1995, p. 74, with reference to Barrett and Fraser, 1977).*

Simons goes on to mention some of the dysfunctional consequences of diagnostic systems that can occur if the wrong variables are selected: over-emphasis on inappropriate issues, lack of emphasis on important issues and gaming behaviours. As examples of the latter, Simons mentions employees avoiding difficult customer queries by passing the query to another department and IBM marketing personnel who received credits towards their product quotas even though sales might be through independent retailers – so they spent time trying to identify such 'free' credits. He also notes that managers may indulge in smoothing data, biasing and even illegal acts.

5.5.   Interactive Systems

Finally, Simons deals with interactive systems designed to promote discussion between tiers of management. Competitive pressure often stimulates innovation, and interactive control systems provide a means of channelling creative thought in response to continuing change in markets, products, technology, etc. Interactive control systems can take many forms but, according to Simons, they have four defining characteristics:

1. an important and recurring agenda;
2. frequent and regular attention at all managerial levels;
3. face-to-face interaction;
4. a catalyst for continual change (p. 97).

Later he adds five 'design considerations':

1. reforecasting based on current information;
2. simplicity;
3. involving multiple levels of management;
4. provide a trigger for revised action;
5. based on information relating to strategic uncertainties in the business (p. 109).

His examples include Pepsi's routine, exhaustive and interminable examination of market share data and Turner Construction Company's use of project team meetings. In the latter case, the company's strategy revolves around customer service (not cost) and, among other things, strategic risk relates to loss of reputation and mix and quality of staff. The company has devised an interactive system that '...is really forcing our managers to keep revising their strategy with our clients on each job' (p. 101).

Simons' analysis leads to the conclusion that the manner in which control systems are *used* is important. While output targets and standards are intrinsic to diagnostic control systems, according to Simons they should be anathema in interactive control systems where participants are expected to share problems and opportunities and propose solutions, thus fostering organisational learning. 'For these reasons, control systems *cannot* be used interactively if incentives are linked by formula to fixed, *ex ante* goals' (p. 118).

The divergence between incentives in diagnostic and interactive control systems can lead to confusion, especially because profit planning systems can be appropriate as interactive (as well as diagnostic) control systems. In the face of diversity, complexity and competitive markets, the profit planning system can be easily updated for changes in supplier and customer markets and action plans can be simulated taking account of expected competitor reactions. However, incentives for an interaction-oriented control system should encourage interaction, not output-oriented behaviour:

> Bonus payouts, for example, would not be determined solely by reference to preset formula; instead, bonuses would be determined by a senior manager's subjective judgement about how well participants have performed in the circumstances (p. 120).

And:

> Rather than treating the profit goal as a fixed target, the interactive profit planning process would require bottom-up revision of the profit goal periodically...(p. 121).

Thus, Simons suggests that apparently similar systems might have very different uses and apparently minor differences in system design can have significant consequences. A field study by Dugdale et al. (2006) of 41 UK manufacturing companies revealed that about half (18) had executive incentive schemes and, while financial measures were extensively used, eight companies included 'personal performance' as an element in their scheme. Simons supplies a theoretical explanation for these empirical findings.

6.   Summary

6.1.   Overview

In Chapters 1 and 2, we showed how budgetary control emerged in the early twentieth century, the identification of budgeting problems and research into the contingent variables that might affect the operation of budgeting systems.

In Chapter 4, we concentrated on the interaction between budgets and structure. In centralised organisations budgeting tends to be interpersonal; in decentralised organisations administrative. Organisations face different degrees of environmental uncertainty and organic structures are needed to deal with greater uncertainty. Different parts of the organisation also face differing levels of uncertainty and the operating core may be buffered from the uncertainty that boundary spanning functions face. Thus, not only might different organisations need different structures and control systems so might different parts of the same organisation.

The particular control systems needed in the operating core vary from an emphasis on procedures and output measures in pooled structures to increased use of coordinating mechanisms such as budgets in sequential structures to more interpersonal control in reciprocal structures. Finally, we followed Chandler's analysis of the growth of very large corporations and their need to decentralise while Goold and Campbell showed that the specific nature of this decentralisation depended on the extent of product-market diversity faced by the corporation.

In this chapter, we have briefly reviewed the economic analysis of organisational structure choice and the use of market, hierarchical and clan controls to deal with different circumstances. Market, output controls are effective when *performance* is well defined; hierarchical controls are effective when *processes* are well defined and clan controls become (particularly) important when *neither outputs nor processes are well defined*. The relationships between these categorisations and budgeting are summarised in Table 1. Then we went on to review the interaction between organisational strategy and control systems. Some unexpected results caused a further review of control systems and, in particular, through the focus on the *use* of budgeting and other controls. The following sections summarised the different control systems that might be used.

Chapter 6

The Field Study

1. Introduction

The survey revealed that both financial and non-financial managers saw budgets as important and attitudes to budgeting, if not overwhelmingly positive, were certainly not negative. These findings were at odds with the 'Beyond Budgeting' thesis that budgets are now having unfortunate consequences and need to be replaced with systems more appropriate to the twenty-first century.

A second phase of the research was undertaken with the aim of checking the survey results and gaining additional insights into contemporary budgeting practice. Visits were made to eight of the companies that had participated in the survey and interviews undertaken either with a finance manager or with both finance and non-finance managers. A semi-structured interview style was adopted, which allowed the interviews to be directed yet still allowed the interviewees to introduce topics they considered important and/or enlarge on particular issues. The structured interview guide is shown in Appendix 2 (p. 209).

The division of budget use into planning and implementation/control/evaluation that emerged from factor analysis provided a sensible framework for analysis of the interviews, and there was plenty of evidence of budgets used for both planning and control.

This chapter is divided into sections dealing with organisational context; company products, customers and competitors; budget preparation, use of budgets and attitudes to budgets.

We conclude that our survey results that managers find budgets important and useful are supported by the field study interviews. Although, in some companies, managers might disagree with particular uses of budgets, they did not criticise budgeting itself. Rather they took issue with specific activities, especially senior managers' use of budgets to impose what might considered unrealistic targets and over-detailed analysis of actual results and variances. In general, managers felt that budgets could be used to support responsible managers and managers should be afforded sufficient flexibility so the budget set a target but not the detailed means of its achievement.

2. Organisational Context

Brief details of the companies we visited are summarised in Table 1.

2.1. Size

Six of the eight organisations have turnover of £20–100 million per annum and units of this size may be seen as 'manageable'. In one case, Aircraft, the unit is much larger, the product division we visited is, itself, a pan-European organisation with billions of pounds turnover. The sheer complexity of inter-relationships in this company probably makes it difficult to break into smaller units although the recent introduction of 'centres of excellence' suggests a desire to identify manageable units.

2.2. Ownership

Systems and WRL are private, UK-based companies; the rest are part of larger groups. Foundations is part of a large UK construction group. Jam is part of a large UK group of food manufacturing companies, itself owned by a venture capitalist. Laboratory Instruments is part of a large, diversified, South African group. Frozen Foods is owned by a German private company. Food Ingredients is part of an Irish company quoted on the Irish stock exchange. Aircraft is part of a major pan-European operation.

2.3. Corporate Level (One Company)

At Food Ingredients we entered the organisation at a corporate level. Food Ingredients Europe, while itself part of a wider organisation (being one of five divisions), comprises a number of country-based operations that themselves have profit responsibilities. Our interviewee responded to our questions from a head office perspective and hinted at the need for centralisation and common practices.

Table 1 Organisational Context

Company	Organisational context
Aircraft	Multinational company formed as a result of a joint venture in 2001. We visited one of the product divisions which reports to a European headquarters. Since formation there has been centralisation, some decentralision and then the formation of 'centres of excellence'.
Food Ingredients Europe	Part of an Irish group listed on the Irish stock exchange. There are five divisions in the group: dairy, foods, and three specialising in ingredients (Europe, US and Asia). Food Ingredients Europe with 20 plants throughout Europe is organised and accounts by country. Food Ingredients Europe has central HR, IT and payroll functions.
Foundations	A £56 million turnover company that is part of a group of six companies that, itself, forms part of a larger group. Foundations are divided into four 'areas' – Major Products, South, North and Scotland. These product-oriented areas are supported by finance and other central functions.
Frozen Food	Part of a German-owned private company with other business units in Holland, France and Germany. Frozen Food has turnover of about £60 million and is organised into five divisions – Farm Foods, Local Authority, Food Service, Healthcare, Services (supplies the other divisions).
Jam	Jam Ltd is, itself, part of a large UK food group. Until 2000 the larger group was part of a highly decentralised conglomerate (only 20 or so Head Office staff) when it was sold to a venture capitalist. The new owner planned to float the Jam group on the stock exchange. Jam Ltd has three product streams: speciality, industrial preserves and suet.
Laboratory Instruments	We visited a Welsh manufacturing plant which, together with a sister plant in the Midlands, form Laboratory Instruments, itself owned by a South-African group. The Welsh plant has six manufacturing departments. Marketing and systems are centralised at Head Office, based at the sister plant in the Midlands.

(Continued)

Table 1   *(Continued)*

Company	Organisational context
Systems	A private company with turnover of about £18 million organised into three divisions: marine, transport and battle/space. Marine is the largest division. Systems operates 'as if' it is a public company and there are plans to float on the stock exchange.
WRL	A private, family-owned company organised into three divisions – wholesale, retail and leisure. Total turnover is about £25 million per annum (although, of course, in this company, gross margins are relatively low). A small Head Office (10 people) provides finance, HR, etc.

2.4.   Profit Centres (Five Companies)

Five companies – Foundations, Jam, Systems, Frozen Food and WRL – had to deliver profit targets. Managers were conscious of the consequences of their operating decisions for the profitability of their unit. Sometimes they expressed a desire for greater autonomy. These 'strategic business units' were, themselves, usually divided into profit-oriented units, sectors or areas supported by central functions such as IT and HRM.

2.5.   Cost Centres (Two Companies)

We entered two companies, Aircraft and Laboratory Instruments, at cost-centre level. Although Aircraft's UK operation employed thousands of people in several locations, it is not accountable for profit – profit is earned by the whole trans-European product division. Decentralising profit responsibility at Aircraft would raise numerous transfer pricing problems because of the complexity of manufacture.

The Laboratory Instruments plant focuses almost exclusively on manufacturing and the services needed to support its manufacturing operations. Marketing, finance and other functions are based at Head Office with the other manufacturing plant. The Welsh plant produces plastic products while the Head Office plant produces glass product and both benefit from a common divisional sales force.

2.6.   Level of Demand

All the companies had solid demand for their products with references to 'strong demand' at Foundations, Laboratory Instruments and Jam. There was also a rapid growth at Systems, from £10 to £18 million revenue in the past 5 years, and at Frozen Foods where turnover had doubled in the past 7 years. Food Ingredients has been growing by acquisition while the total market for food ingredients has been relatively stable. Demand for aircraft had fallen significantly after 9/11 and had then remained stable but was now picking up with a projected increase in production of almost 50%.

2.7. Economic Pressures

There were economic pressures on all the companies:

- Aircraft had suffered a sudden fall in demand after 9/11 and, additionally, the previous, pre-joint venture owner had exerted considerable pressure on the company during the 1990s in order to generate 'shareholder value'.

- Laboratory Instruments had suffered a dip in profitability because of cost pressures, especially through the impact of increased oil prices on the cost of plastics. The group was presently blocking capital expenditure because Laboratory Instruments was not meeting CFROI target.

- Jam operates in a very competitive market because much of its product is sold, either directly or indirectly, to the major supermarket chains. Supermarket procurement managers have relatively short periods to prove themselves and, partly because of this, there is always downward pressure on prices.

- Similarly, Food Ingredients is under price pressure in that its customers sell into the competitive retail market.

- Frozen Food differs from the last two companies in its very explicit niche strategy, aiming to expand its Farm Foods and Health market sectors while maintaining its (dominant) share of the less profitable Local Authority market.

- Foundations has operated in a fairly stable market competing for market share with two other major players and several smaller companies.

- The pressure at Systems seems to be generated from within the company as it chases aggressive growth targets. All the consulting engineers at Systems are expected to build potential customer contacts in order to expand the business.

- WRL had been cash rich but expansion into retail and leisure industries led to losses and the introduction of tight control systems.

2.8. Influence of Plans to Float on the Stock Exchange

Budgeting in two companies was influenced by plans to float on the stock exchange. Systems, a small, privately owned company, intends to float and this aspiration influences planning. The Managing Director drives hard for growth, sometimes persuading a division to set an (over) aggressive budget.

Jam, part of a large, £1.6 billion food group, was also driven to set aggressive budgets by its venture capital owner as a prelude to floating on the UK stock exchange. (Depressed shares in food producers delayed the floatation but this has now been achieved.) Before changing ownership Jam had been part of a large, decentralised conglomerate. However, now some centralisation is taking place and, in the year before our visit, the group had insisted on extra 'task' to improve the budget.

3.   Products, Customers and Competitors

Details of the companies' products, customers and competitors are set out in Table 2.

The companies we visited are generally successful (there may be some self-selection as successful companies may be more willing to participate in the study). We were struck by the way companies had developed key competencies and defended their markets against, usually, relatively few important competitors. This is especially obvious at Aircraft where a few global companies compete in oligopolistic markets. Our interviewee felt that the competitors needed each other to stimulate continuing improvement in the industry. He noted that his company had an advantage in the

Table 2   Details of the Companies' Products, Customers and Competitors

Company	Products, customers and competitors
Aircraft	Produces mainly large jets, selling to airlines worldwide. There is a limited number of suppliers of large jets although more competitors come into play for smaller aircraft.
Food Ingredients Europe	Produces food ingredients such as crumb and flavourings selling these to businesses in the food industry. Sales are often within the producing country to customers on long-term contracts. There are three or four UK competitors, but all are significantly smaller than Food Ingredients.
Foundations	Specialist in piling processes (driven and rotary), preparing site foundations for further construction work. Major customers include large builders and some sales are to other members of the wider group. Some of the contracts can be very large including motorway and stadium construction. There are two other major players and some smaller competitors in the UK market.

Table 2   (*Continued*)

Company	Products, customers and competitors
Frozen Food	Produces frozen food but focuses on selling ready meals to several market sectors including meals-on-wheels services for Local Authorities and hospitals and direct sales, mainly to the elderly. The company also supplies some bulk food to wholesalers. There are relatively few competitors in the niche markets with just one major competitor in each of the Local Authority and Farm Food markets.
Jam	Produces industrial preserves, premium preserves and suet. 40% of sales are inter-group but the large supermarket chains have a major influence either as direct customers or indirectly as the ultimate customer for Jam's products. There are four large UK companies in the preserves industry.
Laboratory Instruments	Produces plastic laboratory instruments such as dishes and pipettes together with associated items such as rubber bungs. Sells to the NHS (pathology laboratories), to schools and industry. There is strong demand for the company's products in France and Italy.
Systems	Supplies professional consulting services that have expanded to include hardware in a total package. Customers tend to be large organisations such as the Ministry of Defence and the Space Agency with recent work for a European navy. There are few obvious competitors with the company filling a need that its customers cannot readily fill from their internal resources.
WRL	Wholesale operates from a single warehouse supplying cash and carry delivery services to WRL's own retail chain and to independent retailers and chains. Retailing is based on 15 outlets and is under pressure from Tesco Express, etc. The leisure/hotel business provides a golf course, fitness centre, etc. for leisure clients and conference facilities for business clients.

'home' (European) market but, nevertheless, it was still possible to win business in America – and competitors could win business in Europe.

Food Ingredients, Jam and Frozen Food all operate in the food industry. However, their key competencies are very different. Food Ingredients emphasises bulk production and this can involve heavy investment in automation. The company seems to dominate through cost leadership although our interviewee noted that the ability of the company to deliver complementary products from its Ingredients, Dairy and Foods divisions was also important. Jam also supplies business to business with much of its output being taken by other companies in the group and by the large supermarket chains. Manufacture of preserves requires specialist expertise and a key selling point for the company is its ability to support its customers in their production processes, incorporating preserves into cakes and other products. Jam has systematically promoted special preserves rather than industrial preserves over several years and has succeeded in improving gross margins through this policy. Whereas Jam supplies large retailers, Frozen Food has attempted to develop markets where it is in contact with individual buyers. This company has consciously set out to find diverse markets and to provide services (such as freezers and microwaves) that were uniquely related to the product offered. For example, for customers who want convenience, they simply insert the correct cooking code into the microwave oven.

Foundations' operations are limited mainly to the UK and its expertise in piling technologies assures it close consideration by potential customers. Engineers need close links with customers and a Scottish office is imperative for business to be won north of the border. For Systems also, engineering consultants need good relations with clients and all consultants are expected to be alive to possible new business.

Laboratory Instruments produces standard products, but laboratory equipment has to be produced to close tolerances and its use in sensitive industries such as health mean that quality of sterile equipment can be very important. The company has a well-established brand name and a solid presence in the UK and some European markets.

WRL has wholesale, retail and leisure arms and its key advantage is local presence. In recent years, it has had to build competence in the retail and leisure sectors after purchasing a chain of retail grocery outlets and a hotel. Tight control over wages together with revenue targets in the shops has turned that business round.

4. Budget Preparation

Details of budget preparation processes are summarised in Table 3.

4.1. Budget Preparation – Timescale

All the companies set financial year budgets and preparation usually begins 3 or more months before the budget takes effect. At Aircraft, Systems and Frozen Foods, there are explicit links to longer-term strategic plans. At other companies, strategy is important but the link with budgeting is less specific.

Table 3 Details of Budget Preparation Processes

Company	Budget preparation
Aircraft	Budgeting is longwinded and is approved separately through two management chains thus causing reconciliation problems. There was more devolution through Centres of Excellence and a 'middle-up' approach has evolved. Ownership issues were being addressed, specifically through control of contingencies and 'risk' funds.
Food Ingredients Europe	Preparation begins in August with assumptions for purchase prices and volumes. There is sophisticated profitability analysis by customer using manufacturing overhead rates and distribution costs by customer. After consolidation (October), senior management may require improvements but not so great that ownership is lost within the country divisions.
Foundations	The budgeting timescale had reduced by 1 month (to 3 months). Key information from geographical areas includes budget revenue/margins and utilisation estimates for each production process. More detail is provided for major contracts. The parent group insists that budgets be realistic with improvements supported by timed and costed plans.
Frozen Food	An indicative 5-year plan and forecast for the current year begins the process with the first budget review in August. Managers are 'leant on' and the budget is finalised. Everyone tries to keep some budget 'protection' and, with rapid growth, the company has been more than meeting budget. After finalisation the budget is driven right down the organisation by the Commercial Managers.
Jam	A fairly long (November–April) but well-organised process. Both interviewees referred to a columnar 'early warning' budget that is easy to amend for changing expectations on new business. The Financial Director wants to include only business with a greater than 50% chance of being won. However, there can be group pressure to increase budget revenue. Estimating gross margin is difficult because it depends on next year's harvest.

(Continued)

Table 3   (*Continued*)

Company	Budget preparation
Laboratory Instruments	The budget timescale has been reduced to 3 months (June–August). Sales forecasts are prepared by Head Office Marketing and driven down to piece part level using standard MRP software. Managers make capital and overhead requests and the resulting draft budget used to be reviewed by the Managing Director. Sadly, he recently had a heart attack, but, as a qualified accountant, he was well qualified to review budget drafts which, when approved, became 'Plan 0'.
Systems	5-year plan and profit targets set by the Board in October form the basis for detailed budgeting (January–March). A time-consuming process involves numerous iterations – authorisation took place after the start of the new financial year. The budget is set out by contract – 'above the line' if judged to be more than 50% chance of winning them. The FD tends towards realism while the MD may insist on more aggressive targets. There is a separate, more conservative, 'board budget'.
WRL	Budget preparation is short commencing in January for financial year beginning in March. The FD helps managers and reviews the budgets, insisting on realism. Sales are projected and estimates of expenses take account of the national minimum wage – important in this business. The Board tends to accept the budget presented by the FD. More ownership would be desirable, involving more managers in the process.

Some processes are longwinded. At Aircraft, the process takes 7 months starting with a 3-year plan in May/June. Although it should be complete in November, the budget often does not take effect until February in the financial year. At Systems, the process takes 6 months from long-term planning in October to budget preparation January–March. However, in 2004, it was a further 2 months into the new financial year before the budget was signed off. At Aircraft and Systems, it was hoped that more efficient methods with fewer iterations would be developed.

At Frozen Foods and Food Ingredients, the budgeting process begins in August, more than 4 months before the budget takes effect. However, at these companies and at Jam, there was no particular dissatisfaction with long but well-organised processes.

At Foundations and Laboratory Instruments, the parent groups now expected budgets to be prepared in a *shorter* period than previously (both reduced by approximately 1 month). Current year forecasts would be more accurate and budget data more reliable.

Finally, WRL's relatively unsophisticated budget process, steered personally by the Financial Director, requires less than 2 months.

4.2. Budget Preparation – Ownership

'Ownership' of the budget by responsible managers was an important issue in most of the companies. There was explicit reference to this at Aircraft, Jam, Systems, Frozen Food, Food Ingredients and WRL.

In principle, if profit-accountable managers prepare and accept their budget, one would expect them to be motivated towards its achievement. This did seem to be the case where these conditions were met – particularly at Foundations and Frozen Food. At both these companies, the parent group accepted proposals for realistic, achievable budgets and, at Foundations, the group *insists* on realism. In these companies, targets are driven down to major contracts/areas and to commercial managers responsible for market sectors. A similar situation had existed at Jam and our interviewees seemed highly motivated by the autonomy they had had under a previous owner. They stressed the importance of feeling that this is *my* budget and felt that what was a very positive culture could be affected by the present group's insistence that 'task' be added to the budget, without the agreement of the managers affected.

There was an example of the deleterious consequences of insisting on an over-aggressive budget at Systems. In one division, the divisional General Manager had failed to prevent an unrealistic budget being set and, when this had not been achieved, managers within the division had been demoralised. Ownership issues also arose in the family owned, WRL, where personalities came into play and there were very different degrees of commitment. Our interviewee commented that one divisional manager simply 'tells me what he thinks I want to hear'.

Aircraft provides an example of some of the problems that can arise in a large, complex organisation. Aircraft has undergone a series of organisational changes as some functions were first centralised at European Head Office then partly decentralised and then 'centres of excellence' with some degree of autonomy set-up. There had been problems reconciling central and local analyses even though they were based on the same initial data. Budget iterations involving cost centre managers had proved unwieldy and a 'middle-up' approach to initial budgeting adopted. However, this had excluded some key local personnel and so it would be modified again. The treatment of 'risk funds'[1] and risks/opportunities was an issue and 'ownership' of these symbolically important budget resources was important. Our interviewees

---

[1] 'Risk funds' relate to budgeted expenses that will be needed if a specific risk is incurred.

thought the budget should be managed at a level where a responsible manager had control over risk funds and could offset risks and opportunities in order to achieve the *overall* budget target.

4.3. Budget Preparation – Detailed Analysis

We were impressed by the analyses that supported the budget in all companies. Where possible, at Foundations, Systems and Jam, budgets are developed by contract with probabilities of success estimated at Systems and Jam. At Systems, the 'above the line' budget includes contracts judged more than 50% likely with others 'below the line'. At Jam, a columnar 'early warning budget' is set out by contract; revenues and variable costs are amended for latest intelligence on projects as small as £2,000–3,000. The Financial Director wanted only better than 50% likely projects included but group could insist that other projects be included to create an acceptable budget.

Where the contract approach is not possible aggregate data is used. At Foundations, budgets for geographical market areas are derived from projections of turnover, gross margin, staffing, rig utilisation and anticipated capital expenditure. At Food Ingredients, our interviewee referred to detailed analysis of profitability by customer and to plans to further analyse budgets by function. At Frozen Food, there was reference to a sensible expected value for the mature and stable Local Authority business and attempts to estimate timing and profitability of possible new business in more dynamic sectors.

As one would expect, in the cost centres, Aircraft and Laboratory Instruments, the focus was less on business sector profitability and more on authorisation of spend to support corporate strategies. At Aircraft, the 'recurring spend' element of the budget is based on orders for aircraft that are reliable for up to 3 years into the future. One of our interviewees was a Procurement Manager, and it was clear that there was very detailed knowledge of material and component prices, negotiated with suppliers that were incorporated into budgets. The 'non-recurring spend' element of the budget for development projects and maintenance/servicing of an ageing fleet of aircraft in service required a different approach. There was a system of senior management review for proposed new projects and a major 'bottom-up' exercise was underway to estimate the resources needed to service the fleet. At Laboratory Instruments, standard products are produced in large numbers and a traditional standard costing system supports preparation of the budget. Finished product volumes are estimated by Sales and Marketing staff at Head Office and these volumes are converted into piece part and material and labour requirements.

4.4. Budget Preparation – Targets

There were varying pressures in the budget setting processes. At Aircraft, our interviewee saw the initial centralisation of functions and budgeting as an attempt to strip out the contingencies (padding) that had traditionally been included in some company budgets. He did not think this was an issue for UK operations that had been pressured by the drive for 'shareholder value' in the 1990s. The subsequent devolvement of more responsibility back to local level had been undertaken after a 'more level playing field' (across Europe) had been achieved. At Laboratory Instruments, our interviewees were clear that there was little scope for game playing by attempting to 'pad' the budget. Production costs simply had to be as tight as possible in order to contend with a difficult economic climate.

At Jam and Systems, there were conflicting pressures. Local managers at Jam felt that the budget needed to be realistic but they were under some pressure from corporate managers to include less likely contracts and to accept 'task' cost savings. At Systems, it was clear that divisions might be under pressure from the Managing Director to set aggressive budgets. However, the Finance Director wanted budgets to be carefully justified with an emphasis on realism.

At Foundations, our interviewee showed us the instructions issued by Group requiring that, above all, group companies were expected to set realistic budgets. Any improvement plans had to be supported by specific, timetabled actions and improvements. No specific budget profit target was laid down in advance although managers were aware of normal expectations. Frozen Food also developed realistic, achievable, budgets but this was not so much a consequence of corporate culture as of a successful management team ensuring that targets satisfied Head Office and were achievable. Pressure was generated at Food Ingredients, but our interviewee noted that this did not compromise ownership of the budget by the country divisions, and she also commented on the 'gaming' of divisional managers who wanted achievable budgets so that incentive payments would subsequently be made.

5. Budgets in Use

Issues concerning the use of budgets are summarised in Table 4.

5.1. Budgets for Influencing and Controlling Behaviour

There is evidence of the use of budgets for control in all these companies with the most obvious examples in the cost centre, Laboratory Instruments, and at the profit centre, Systems. The Managing Directors of both the companies were important in setting the culture.

At Laboratory Instruments, unauthorised spending outside of budget 'risked a ton of bricks on your head'. The Managing Director was a qualified accountant who took considerable interest in preparing budgets and monitoring actual performance against budget. Our interviewee said that managers took budgets seriously; 'they

Table 4   Issues Concerning the Use of Budgets

Company	Budgets in use
Aircraft	Budgets are pushed down to operational areas and linked to biannual Personal Development Reviews. There was concern that Group line-by-line control was too detailed: our interviewees thought managers should be able to trade risks and opportunities to achieve their targets.
Food Ingredients Europe	Adverse variances lead managers to cut back to stay within budget. By the same token managers tended to take agreed budgets as theirs to spend (and feared future cutbacks if they did not). Managers seek authorisation for expenditure outside budget.
Foundations	The Finance Director and Managing Director avoid excessive control. Cost-centre managers may need to be reminded to take necessary actions outside budget but area managers with margin targets to meet are less likely to be constrained by budgets.
Frozen Food	Locally, the budget provides control with line-by-line variances checked carefully. However, for the company as a whole, the budget does not provide a 'true' target because of contingency funds (padding). The parent expects the company to outperform the budget.
Jam	Locally, use of budgets is 'definitely not like the local government mentality of spending the budget'. Variances are investigated but managers are expected to be able to explain them. The budget sets expectations but 'not the method of getting there'; managers are expected to balance shortfalls and opportunities. The use of budgets within the business unit contrasted with group introduction of 'task' without agreement.
Laboratory Instruments	Managers take budgets seriously: 'they have no choice' and the Technical Manager noted that, if budgets are exceeded without authority, 'you risk a ton of bricks on your head'. The company culture was partly driven by the Managing Director who is a qualified accountant.

Table 4   (*Continued*)

Company	Budgets in use
Systems	Sales targets are very important and the Managing Director is 'good at ranting and raving' if targets are missed. A lot of costs are fixed and overhead is not charged to projects so that operating managers concentrate on controllable margin.
WRL	The retail business is now tightly managed based on weekly targets for sales and for labour hours. Institution of financial control was vital in stemming losses in this division. Control in the leisure division could be better if reporting against budget were extended to managerial levels below general manager.

have no choice'. There are also corporate controls exerted through bureaucracy (a capital freeze until CFROI targets are met) and initiatives (climate creation workshops that would pave the way to 'employee value creation').

At Systems, failure to meet budget targets might mean 'a good kicking to start with' and the Managing Director was 'good at ranting and raving at people' if targets were missed. Hierarchical issues arose between operational mangers and the company board. There was reference to personalities in this relatively small, privately owned company with the Managing Director pushing hard for aggressive targets while the Finance Director wanted realism. Our interviewees would prefer less detailed 'final' changes to the budget and less detailed monthly reviews.

The second cost centre in the study, Aircraft, posed particular problems because of its size. It seemed that there had been a reduction in central pressure with the removal of a 'local' (UK-based) profit statement when the joint venture took effect but an increase in micro-management of detailed month-to-month and forecast-to-forecast results. This had led to some changes in local behaviour so that, for example, only significant changes led to forecast revisions. Our interviewee at Aircraft referred to a 'young' organisation (because the joint venture had been recently formed) and the relationship between senior management and local management was still emerging. The treatment of 'risk funds' was an example of an issue under negotiation that needed to be addressed at the 'correct' level of management.

Systems seemed to have a heavy, personal, control culture and, at another profit centre, Frozen Food, budgets also seemed important for control because (line) variances from budget received close attention. At Frozen Food, the budget was also used to manage the relationship with the corporate centre. Contingencies in the budget ensured that the real target was stricter than budget and the parent company expected the company to beat its budget. Managers used the budget as a flexible guide and, for example, if results were going to be better than expected there may be more investment to protect key markets.

In the three remaining profit centres – Foundations, Jam and WRL – our interviewees tended to emphasise managerial responsibility rather than control. An indication of this were the references, at Foundations and WRL, to the need to educate managers to take action even if this involved unbudgeted spend.

Foundations is part of a relatively decentralised group and the group adopts what seems to be a mature style insisting on realistic budgets and listening to local management arguments. When Foundations was missing a budget target the Financial Director explained the situation to group: the target could easily be met but the actions necessary were not in the best interests of the group. The group response was to pay the incentives even though, strictly, targets had not been achieved.

Jam had been part of a very decentralised group and managers were expected to be flexible. The budget sets the financial profit but '... not the method of getting there'. Variances direct attention but are not a 'big stick' and '... no one is going to have a heart failure if you overspend in one area and underspend in another.' A team culture means that, if there are problems, managers ask what can *we* do to put things right. The group was now centralising some functions and this had caused some tension. There was resentment of centrally imposed tasks that were judged unreasonable and concern that a group mandated transfer pricing scheme would undermine the company commitment to service and good customer relations. The group style might cause local managers to adopt an overtly negotiated approach to the budget – offering what you think you can get away with.

At WRL, the Finance Director wanted the divisional managers to take a greater role in preparing and managing budgets. At this, family-owned, company personalities loom large and, for example, the Finance Director would like the manager of the Leisure Division to be more proactive in sharing budget information with his team.

At the corporate organisation, Food Ingredients, we had the impression that budgets did have consequences for control although we were not given examples of senior management behaviour. Our interviewee, nevertheless, thought that divisional managers adjusted their behaviour, cutting back on expenditure if they were underperforming against budget. There was a suggestion of gaming in this company with managers trying to pad budgets if possible and treating the budget as 'theirs to spend' once it was approved.

5.2.   Resetting the Budget

All these companies set a budget for the financial year and did not amend it. Interestingly, two companies, Aircraft and Systems, had experience of resetting the budget during the financial year but neither currently making such changes.

- At Aircraft, our interviewee felt that there was too much work involved for relatively small benefits gained. He referred to the need for a sensible 'work-life balance' and felt that finance staff had had too much work to do to make the changes.

- Systems had reset the budget in line with latest quarterly forecasts and operational managers found this desirable because they did not have to reiterate old explanations and excuses. However, the board had taken the view that, if the budget could be changed, managers did not take it sufficiently seriously and discontinued the practice.

6.   Overview and Attitudes to Budgeting

A summary is provided in Table 5.

Table 5   Overview and Attitudes to Budgeting

Company	Overview and attitudes to budgeting
Aircraft	Budgets are 'essential' and gaming was not considered a problem as contingencies had been removed. Budgetary control is needed but it should be at the 'right' level – allowing management of risks and opportunities. The treatment of 'risk funds' was important, possibly because local control symbolised ownership of the budget by local managers.
Food Ingredients Europe	Budgets are important in providing everyone with 'a framework of what they are trying to achieve'. The format needed to facilitate comparison of budget with actual results. Managers are expected to be positive because they 'had a say' in setting the budgets. It is time consuming and there is game playing – as country managers try to set easy budgets so that bonuses can be earned.

(Continued)

Table 5 *(Continued)*

Company	Overview and attitudes to budgeting
Foundations	The Financial Director did not think that budgets caused problems. He had to persuade the IT manager to spend 'non-budgeted' money but this sort of issue did not seem to be a real problem.
Frozen Food	It's 'pretty important' and 'it's what we focus on weekly: sales and cost against budget'. The budget is important for control and also for implementing strategy. Although time consuming this was not a major problem. Accuracy was difficult to achieve because of the 'noise in the system, from the bottom to the top'. This was now a bigger problem because of the link between bonuses and budgets.
Jam	Budgets are important in crystallising targets, managing by exception and planning (inventory, space, transport, etc.) There is no obvious alternative and new ideas may just be budgeting in a different guise. The people issues are important and education is needed in order to create the 'right' culture.
Laboratory Instruments	Both the Financial Controller and the Technical Manager thought the budget is important for planning and monitoring. The Financial Controller thought it is important but also referred to it as just a 'tool in the armoury'.
Systems	The Financial Controller thought budgeting: 'The primary financial control tool'. Budgeting could drag on too long and some detail changes were unnecessary. The impact on people was key and very aggressive targets could de-motivate. There were behavioural issues but gaming was not really a problem. Reporting could be too detailed and managers needed to be trusted to deliver the overall result.
WRL	The company needs financial planning and financial control and the Financial Director could not see an alternative to budgeting. The only real problem mentioned was the possibility that managers might not take a sensible decision 'because it wasn't in the budget'. In this company it would also be desirable to gain more ownership of the budget and to involve lower level managers in budget preparation and in responding to financial issues.

6.1.   Aircraft

At Aircraft, budgets were seen as 'essential' and gaming was not considered to be a problem as the 'contingencies' had been removed and there was now a 'more level playing field'. The process was 'evolving' as the new pan-European organisation attempted to establish a sensible process that involved the 'right' levels of management in the stages of the budget process. Our interviewees saw the provision of sufficient freedom to managers so that they could achieve targets by managing risks and opportunities as important. The treatment of 'risk funds' was important in this and the company needed to avoid 'over-managing' month-to-month results (and forecast-to-forecast reconciliations).

6.2.   Jam

At Jam, the managers also saw the budget as important, in crystallising targets, managing by exception and planning (inventory, space, transport, etc.). For the Finance Director, there was no obvious alternative and apparently new ideas might turn out to be budgeting in a different guise.

The culture within Jam was obviously important and there appeared to be a highly motivated, profit conscious, management team that was proud of its track record, wanted to set realistic budgets and achieve them by using exception reporting to direct attention to key areas. Within the company it was clear that budgets were not to be used as a 'big stick'; an attitude of what can *we* do to solve problems was prevalent. There seemed to be more issues concerning group attitudes and there was some resentment of the pressure to set very aggressive revenue targets and cost saving tasks. Our interviewees also took exception to a recent group initiative that would require transfer prices to be set on a cost-plus basis. This would be '4,000% worse' because other group companies would buy from Jam simply on the basis of price and there would be no incentive to meet industry standards of service when supplying other companies in the group.

6.3.   Foundations

Our interviewee at Foundations also viewed budgeting in a positive light and saw no real problems with the process. In this company, there seemed to be fewer conflicts because corporate managers *insisted* on realism in budget planning[2] and appeared to be very reasonable in evaluating performance. The example given where group was prepared to listen to reasonable argument over incentive payments impressed us. Nevertheless, there was a hint of the negative aspects of budgets in the IT manager's concern to remain

---

[2] Our interviewee showed us a corporate memo spelling out expectations.

with the budget. The Financial Director had to keep educating managers so that the budget was used constructively within the company. Interestingly the IT issue related to a cost centre, it seemed unlikely that area managers would be constrained by budgets (unless the target had already been met!) because they had gross margin targets to achieve. As at Jam, there was an interesting comment in relation to transfer pricing. The company had an advantage when asked to quote by other members of the group *but* they could and sometimes did go elsewhere. If this option were removed (by group decision or, presumably, by 'artificial' pricing) then 'the customer relationship would be killed from the start'.

6.4. Laboratory Instruments

At Laboratory Instruments, the budget is important for planning and for monitoring. Gaming and padding were not seen as problems because there was little scope in a production-oriented operation and because the Managing Director had taken a personal interest in budgeting. In this company, the Financial Controller felt that managers 'had their say' in preparing the budget and they got most of what they wanted. It was obvious that group now had considerable influence, primarily because a South African had been appointed as Managing Director and South African initiatives that might have been ignored now had to be implemented. There was group pressure through the current squeeze on capital spending because the company had failed to hit CFROI targets and through the 'employee value creation' initiative.

6.5. Systems

At Systems, even though there were several examples of budgeting problems, the Financial Controller saw the budget as 'the primary financial tool'. The budget was important in planning at this company and our interviewees independently cited examples of decisions arising from the preparation of the budget. At this company, like Aircraft, the budget process was seen as too long and reporting too detailed. Whereas, at Aircraft, this could be traced to large company systems, at Systems the reference was to the 'personalities' involved. The impact that budgets could have on people was well understood and both our interviewees were well aware of a divisional budget that had been too aggressive and led to de-motivation within the division. Echoing comments in other companies, there was a desire to let managers take responsibility for the overall result and for less day-to-day micro-management. In this relatively small, private, company there were no group issues and references were instead to the Board (which included non-executive directors).

6.6.   Frozen Food

At Frozen Food again, there was no doubting the important role of the budget in providing a benchmark for week-to-week comparison with actual results. There appeared to be few problems with budgets and, as in other companies, our interviewee referred to driving the budget through the organisation (via the sector commercial managers). Almost in an aside, our interviewee had said that he wasn't sure that the company was yet ready to abandon budgeting, and as this sort of comment was so rare it was followed up. It seemed that our interviewee had had experience of rolling budgets in a previous company, and he saw this approach as a possible replacement for traditional budgeting. However, his experience did not suggest that such a change would lead to savings in time.

6.7.   Food Ingredients

At Food Ingredients, budgets were, again, seen as important, providing a framework that was understood, providing a convenient format for the comparison of actual results and exerting a controlling influence on managers. The problems were acknowledged, especially the need for time consuming and detailed analytical work in Finance and the inter-related effects of budgeting and incentive schemes on the general managers of the country-based, production-oriented divisions. This echoed a comment in Frozen Foods concerning the use of incentive schemes, and comments in other companies also suggested that the use of incentives linked to budgets could be a mixed blessing.

6.8.   WRL

Budgeting had been mandated by the bank and other creditors when the company needed financial support. As the cash crisis was overcome, the budget was no longer required for external parties but the Board was now much more financially aware, and the appointment of a qualified Finance Director had ensured that budgeting was now routinely undertaken. Budget plans raised questions, such as whether a shop refit would be justified by sales projections and, if projections were unsatisfactory, then action would be taken. Targets for controllable revenues and labour hours at each retail outlet were set each week. On the drawbacks of budgeting, our interviewee admitted that lack of ownership could be an issue and managers could be inhibited, failing to take action because resource had not been included in the budget.

7. Conclusions from the Field Study and the Survey

7.1. Preparation of the Budget

The field study supports the results of the survey. In these companies, preparation of the budget begins some months in advance of the financial year and preparation can be longwinded with several iterations. Two companies had taken steps to reduce the time taken to prepare the budget and, in some companies, there was recognition that it was a time-consuming and expensive process. This did not lead automatically to dissatisfaction but, in two companies, the interventions of senior managers were criticised.

7.2. Revisions of the Budget

The survey revealed that budgets were usually unchanged throughout the year and none of the eight companies visited currently contemplated revisions to the budget after it had been agreed. However, in two companies, revisions had been made in the past. The comments of managers in these two companies were enlightening. At Aircraft, it was clear that the financial manager saw the preparation of a second budget during the financial year as very time consuming and imposing an excessive burden on finance staff. By implication he judged the work involved to be disproportionate to the benefits gained. Systems had experimented by replacing the budget by the latest forecast. However, the company had gone back to comparisons with the original budget because senior managers felt that 'updating' the budget was allowing managers to escape accountability for their original budget commitments. For their part, operational managers preferred replacement because it avoided having to repeat the reasons for divergence from budget throughout the year.

7.3. Changes in Budget Processes

Changes reported in the survey tended towards more sophisticated budgeting techniques and more importance for traditional budgeting. We could observe how this trend worked in practice in some of the companies visited. At Jam and Systems, the budget was prepared by building it up from projections based on individual contracts including estimated probabilities for the likelihood that specific contracts would be won. At Aircraft, the budget was based on firm plans for the number of aircraft to be produced and detailed information concerning components, price contracts and so on. At Foundations, large projects were identified and detailed assumptions concerning volumes, utilisation, etc. provided the basis for budgeting. In general, we were impressed by the sophistication with which budgets were prepared and it was clear that, in most companies, budgets are a key management tool during the financial year.

7.4.   The Importance of Budgeting

The survey showed that the vast majority of respondents continue to see budgets as important. The field study provides confirmation of these perceptions. Table 5 shows that, across the eight companies we visited, budgeting is important with references to it being 'essential', 'pretty important' and the 'primary financial tool'. It 'provided a framework', 'crystallised targets' and allowed 'management by exception'. Although there were some adverse comments, as in the survey, these were outweighed by the generally positive comments about the utility of budgets.

7.5.   Budgets for Planning

Budgets were used for planning. For example, the development of a detailed budget led to a decision to lease more space at Systems and investment to protect markets at Frozen Food. However, budgets might not be the key planning mechanism. At Aircraft, there is a sophisticated planning system that generates the 'official' projected volumes that operates in parallel with the budgeting system.

7.6.   Budgets for Control

In several companies, the budget was a key control device. At Systems, the Managing Director used the budget to gain commitment to ambitious growth targets and then employed it to pressure managers. At Jam, the venture capital owner employed the budget to communicate aggressive targets to managers. At Frozen Food, the budget was used to check monthly results on a line-by-line basis. At Laboratory Instruments, managers take budgets seriously because they 'had no choice'. At WRL, the budget had been a key instrument in convincing the company's creditors that operations were under control. There was little doubt in the field study that budgets had an important role in controlling operations.

7.7.   Attitudes to Budgeting

In the survey, respondents generally *did not* agree with a list of statements criticising budgeting. Where dissatisfaction was expressed it was usually because the process failed to encourage local ownership of budgets. In some cases, this was blamed on senior management pressure. These views were generally replicated in the field study. Most managers did not express dissatisfaction with budgeting and, as observed earlier, budgets were thought to be key instruments in managing the companies we visited.

Having said this, there were specific examples of problems with budgets. At Aircraft and Systems, budgets were considered longwinded and there was discussion of the importance of ownership by local managers. At both these companies and Jam, the intervention of senior managers was not always seen as helpful with imposed targets at Jam and Systems and some loss of ownership at Aircraft. At Foundations and WRL, despite the financial managers being positive about budgets, there was recognition that managers might not take desirable actions in order to stay in budget. These financial managers were active in persuading managers to break the budget where appropriate (and after gaining authorisation). Generally, budgets were not considered to lead to gaming or de-motivation but, if sufficient pressure was exerted, these consequences were possible. At Jam, managers hinted that they might be less forthcoming than hitherto in anticipation of the tasks that corporate managers might expect. And at Systems, managers felt that the budget combined with the 'disincentive scheme' could be de-motivating.

Overall, attitudes in the eight companies reflected the survey results. It was possible to push too hard but most of our interviewees saw budget targets as challenging but not unrealistic. There was only a limited evidence of gaming and the comments at Aircraft, Laboratory Instruments and Systems suggested that there was little opportunity to 'pad' budgets. At Frozen Foods, 'contingencies' were added to the budget before submission to the Group. However, this was no doubt acceptable to Group managers because the company had consistently beaten its agreed budget.

8. Implications for the 'Beyond Budgeting' and Traditional Literatures

8.1. 'Beyond Budgeting': Budget Processes Are Longwinded and Bureaucratic

There was certainly evidence, both in the survey and the field study, that budgeting processes can be longwinded and, to a lesser extent, that they are bureaucratic. This can lead to dissatisfaction and, in two field study companies, action had been taken to reduce the length of time needed to prepare the budget.

8.2. 'Beyond Budgeting': Budgeting Fails to Meet the Needs of Managers in Competitive Environments

The survey indicated that budgets could lead managers to restrict spending instead of taking desirable action. This issue was mentioned in two companies. However, in these two companies, managers were encouraged to take actions that had not been authorised in the budget where they could be justified. In general, there was limited evidence that managers saw budgeting as failing to assist managers. In fact, the reverse seemed to be the case. Budgeting was perceived to be helpful for planning and control and, like Frow et al. (2005), our impression was that managers found budgets to be useful in setting a realistic financial framework rather than inhibiting necessary action.

8.3. 'Beyond Budgeting': Performance Contracts Are Pernicious

There is hardly evidence in the survey or the field study that performance contracts have 'pernicious' consequences. However, there were comments that suggested that incentive schemes had real and sometimes undesirable effects. At Food Ingredients and Frozen Food, there were references that suggested that budgets might be 'managed' with an eye on potential bonuses. And the combination of budget targets and an incentive scheme was subjected to some criticism at Systems.

8.4. 'Beyond Budgeting' and Traditional Literature: Excessive Budget Gaming

Generally, both the survey and the field study indicated that contemporary managers did not see budgets leading to excessive gaming. Nevertheless, there were examples of gaming linked to performance contracts; of budget contingencies in order to manage the expectations of Group managers and of a danger that, once authorised, operational managers might regard budgets as 'theirs to spend'. Overall, managers were aware of the dangers of budget gaming and did not see this as a major issue. However, when budgets are tightly linked with incentive schemes then there does seem to be a possibility of gaming and de-motivation.

8.5. Traditional Literature: The Budget-Constrained Style

In general we saw little evidence of the budget-constrained style. However, some characteristics of this style could be observed at Systems and Laboratory Instruments. In both of these companies, there was pressure to achieve budget together with emphasis on accounting performance measures such as sales growth and cash flow return on assets. In these organisations pressure was generated by individuals, the CEO at Systems and (previously) the Finance Director at Laboratory Instruments. In most of the companies we would have characterised the style as more 'profit conscious' than 'budget constrained'.

8.6. Traditional Literature: Target Setting

The survey indicated that managers generally did not feel that budgets had to be set realistically so they could not be challenging. Neither did they agree that budget targets were too tough. In the field study companies there was some evidence of budgets being set optimistically, especially at Systems and, recently, at Jam. However, even at these companies, there were voices arguing for realism and, generally, companies seemed to set realistic but nevertheless challenging budgets.

8.7. Comment

This study reinforces the received knowledge concerning budgets and their use. It is possible to make budgets over-bureaucratic and to have an over-detailed approach to budgetary control. Equally it is possible to use budgets as a supportive tool in companies that wish to delegate to responsible managers. Our interviewees saw budgets as important for financial control and for planning. In a general way it seemed that a decentralised approach with local management ownership of budgets and a constructive approach to dealing with variances is desirable and seems to work well in those companies where it exists. Overall, both the survey and the field study support the findings of Ross and Frow et al. (2005). The use of budgeting does seem to have moved on since the 1970s with managers generally positive about the benefits of budgeting, aware of the possible risks and prepared to use the budget constructively so long as the culture set by senior managers permits this.

9.   Lessons from the Field Study

9.1. Culture

The relationship with group and senior management was important in all the companies and influenced the local management culture. The five profit centres displayed a range of cultures. Foundations and Frozen Food are decentralised, local management has autonomy and flexibility. Jam had operated in this manner but some centralisation had taken place, there was more corporate involvement and this had led to some tension. Foundations, Frozen Food and Jam seemed to operate with high degrees of trust in local management. This was less obvious at Systems where senior management was driving aggressively for growth and taking detailed interest in both preparation of budgets and subsequent operations versus budget. At WRL, tight financial control had been introduced following a cash crisis and, following a period of centralised control, the Finance Director would like divisional managers to take more responsibility and to share budget information within their divisions. In this family-owned firm there were differing ways of operating across the three divisions.

In the profit centres, although the budget was an unchangeable target, it was felt that managers needed flexibility to cope with changing circumstances. In some companies, such as Foundations, Frozen Food and Jam this seemed to be the way budgets operated. At Systems this was the way that local management would like to operate but senior management exerted considerable pressure through the budgetary system. At WRL more decentralisation was also desirable but this was dependent on the capability of local divisional managers.

Management attitudes at Laboratory Instruments and Aircraft were influenced by the cost centre status of these operations. At Laboratory Instruments our interviewees saw their aim as delivery of product in the required volumes and quality. The standard costing system and the budget provided the tools to support this. At Aircraft our interviewees were subjected to interrogation by central staffs and felt that the degree of detail involved was counter-productive because it encouraged local managers to manipulate reports. A key issue at Aircraft was the ownership of 'risk funds' and this symbolised the extent of decentralisation and the responsibility entrusted to local managers.

9.2. Context

Local culture was important and this was obviously influenced by context. At Jam and Systems the desire to float companies on the stock exchange almost certainly influenced the attitudes of senior management. At WRL the serious difficulties encountered led to budgeting being necessary to reassure creditors. At Laboratory Instruments recent cost pressures had led to a freeze on capital expenditure. At Aircraft the joint venture, trans-European nature of the operation set the context for budgeting and other systems. At Frozen Food the outperformance of the company we visited compared with other companies in the Group allowed the use of contingencies in budgets submitted to Group and increased local flexibility. At Foundations the Group philosophy of realism in budgets helped to foster a realistic and constructive approach within the company.

9.3. Structure

We have already mentioned the influence exerted by structure through the designation of units as profit centres or cost centres and, as the field study unfolded, we became increasingly aware of the importance of the interaction between structure and budgeting. The location of the unit within the overall Group structure, the degree of autonomy granted to the local unit and the organisation of the local unit itself were important in influencing the way that budgets were constructed and used. The next chapter addresses this important issue and leads to a conjecture concerning the reconciliation of our survey results with the findings of the 'Beyond Budgeting' school.

Chapter 7

Budgets and Structures

1. Introduction

Our visits to companies confirmed the importance of budgets. They also revealed the importance of understanding budgets in specific contexts. Typically, large companies have complex tiered structures. Business units usually report to a corporate level that, in large companies, itself reports to a higher level. And the business units, themselves, typically comprised of profit and cost centres, can be complex.

In this chapter, we summarise the organisation structures of the units we visited beginning with the five organisations that could be categorised as profit centres. The following case studies show how managers organise their businesses in order to promote motivation, coordination and control, and the first two companies in particular, Foundations and Frozen Food, provide excellent examples of the complexity that can emerge *within* profit centres.

2. Structures and Budgets in the Profit Centres

2.1. Foundations

Foundations reports to a 'corporate centre', Foundations Group, which itself reports to a UK quoted, corporate holding company. Within Foundations, there are two production facilities that manufacture the concrete piles needed in construction projects. The projects themselves are won and delivered by three geographical areas and a fourth 'area' dealing specifically with major projects.

Foundations' structure is set out in Figure 1. 'Areas' are expected to deliver target margin. They receive product from the factories at full absorbed cost and are expected to cover this cost and the cost of the heavy equipment needed in construction operations. There is a group of central services that support the factories, the marketing/delivery areas and each other.

Foundations Group expects realistic budgets to be prepared. Any improvement plans have to be supported by specific, timed actions and improvements in capital employed must not be just for year-end 'window-dressing' purposes.

Our interviewee emphasised flexibility, especially in the areas, where spending above budget is encouraged if it helps to achieve sales and margin targets. However, he admitted that flexibility is not so easy to achieve in cost centres; for example, the IT manager had to be persuaded to take action when it meant over-spending his budget. The factories are controlled through standard costs based on the specified processes and transfer prices that permit some over-recovery of overhead costs.

We were struck by the extent of decentralisation, down to market-facing areas, responsible for delivering margin targets. Control was exercised through a number of related systems emphasising control of *outputs* (sales and gross margin) in the sales areas, *processes* in the factories (standards and budgets) and *inputs* (budgeted resources) in the support areas.

Even *within* a single unit of a much larger group there were complex issues of coordination and control. As we noted in Chapter 4, differing functions within a business may need different control systems and, within Foundations, there are four marketing/construction areas, two factories that supply the construction areas and service centres that support the production/construction units and each other. The business unit exhibits pooled relationships (the areas that work in parallel) and sequential relationships (factory – site) as well as some reciprocal relationships (IT – HRM – IT, etc.).

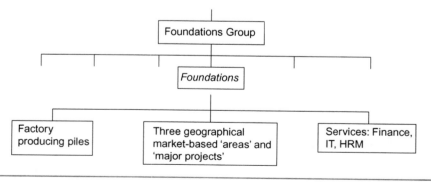

Figure 1 Foundations structure.

Budgets are a taken-for-granted tool for coordinating activities across the factory, marketing areas and service centres. Budgets are also important in setting the fully absorbed cost used in transferring output from factories to areas and in providing a resource envelope for service areas such as IT and Finance. Management bonuses are also linked to the (realistic) budget.

2.2. Frozen Food

Frozen Food is part of a privately owned European holding group with operations in Europe and the UK. Frozen Food is a largely autonomous UK company specialising in frozen meals. It supplies Local Authorities and Health-care organisations and, through 'Your-Food', a premium service direct to individuals. A recent acquisition means the company now has a 'Quick-Food' profit centre producing pasties, pies and similar products, often sold through roadside service outlets. Finally, there is a 'Support Services' profit centre that provides operating services such as transport and refrigeration to the other profit centres (see Figure 2).

Frozen Food has a similar structure to Foundations. Market-based profit centres concentrate on marketing, selling and delivering services. The factories are cost centres delivering product to the commercially oriented marketing and service providing units and, as at Foundations, the operating departments are supported by central service functions such as HRM and IT.

In one respect, Frozen Food is more complex than Foundations: a Support Services profit centre provides services to the other profit centres. This is important in delivering a strategy that focuses on value-adding services for individual customers.[1]

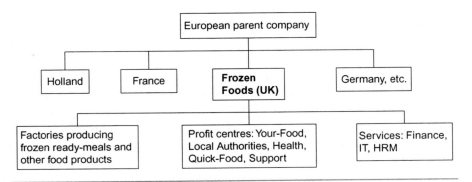

Figure 2   Frozen Foods structure.

---

[1]For example, special cookers can be programmed to prepare frozen ready-meals simply by selecting the correct cooking code.

The Support Services centre provides its services to the other profit centres at a transfer price. Interviewees at Jam and Foundations wanted transfer prices to be at 'arms-length' but at Frozen Foods the response was different. Our interviewee emphasised the importance of a relatively high transfer price so as to prevent the delivery profit centres from 'giving the service away'.

Frozen Food is especially interesting because management chose *not* to concentrate on the profitability of production. Instead, services were identified as the primary value-adding part of the business and commercial profit-centre managers were charged with generating contribution margin over and above the variable cost of production and attributed marketing, selling, distribution and service costs.

Like Foundations, Frozen Food uses a combination of control and coordination systems. There is standard (variable) costing in the factories, target margin in the market-facing commercial areas and budgeting to provide overall coordination and control of resources. A specialised Support Services centre, supplying its services at managed transfer prices, is an integral part of company strategy.

At both Foundations and Frozen Food, the strategy is focused away from the production units towards the output-targeted delivery profit centres. At both companies, transfers from production units are cost related and the production units are expected to operate efficiently to standard. Importantly, in both companies, the major 'value-adding' part of the business is in the marketing/delivery units so, as we later realised, these are the logical areas to which revenue should be attributed and for which contribution/profit targets should be set.

2.3.   WRL

WRL is a private, family-owned company. Historically, the company was a retailer, but eventually concentrated on wholesaling. In the 1990s, aiming to provide a captive market for the wholesale business, the company re-entered the retail trade by purchasing grocery shops. Being cash rich, the company also took an opportunity to expand into the leisure business by purchasing a hotel.

In the event, these ventures proved problematic and the company moved quickly from being cash rich to requiring an overdraft. We interviewed the Finance Director who had been recruited in order to institute financial controls in the business. Budgeting was introduced as part of this initiative and the company's creditors insisted on seeing the budget and management reports until the business had once again returned to profitability.

The structure of the business is very natural with three profit centres concentrating on the wholesale, retail and leisure sectors, respectively (Figure 3). Part of the strategy was that the retail and, to a lesser extent leisure, divisions would provide markets for the wholesale division. Retail and leisure divisions are, therefore, expected to purchase from the wholesale division. However, the transfer prices

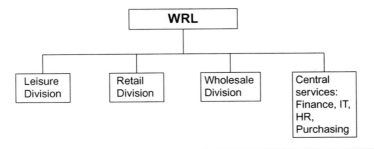

Figure 3   WRL structure.

charged are at 'arms-length'; they are the same as those charged by the wholesale division to other customers. The divisions, therefore, operate largely independently of each other. They do, however, share central services provided by a small head office staff.

In this family-owned and managed company, the operation of budgeting is very dependent on the personalities and capabilities of the managers of the three divisions. Our interviewee felt that he had only to provide support and advice to the retail division. On the other hand, he had to prepare the budget for the wholesale division and had to rework the budget for the leisure division because it was invariably too optimistic. The operation of budgeting also differed within the divisions. In particular, the Finance Director wanted budget information to be more widely shared within the leisure division so that a team approach to tackling problems could be developed.

In this company, operating controls are very important to operational performance. In the wholesaling warehouse, there is an incentive scheme that rewards operatives for speed and accuracy in stock-picking. In the retail outlets, there is rapid feedback of information concerning sales achieved and labour hours worked. As in other companies, control systems have been designed by function. The emphasis is on standards-based efficiency in the wholesale operation but on sales targets and labour costs in the retail operation. Each retail outlet has its targets and, typical of a pooled organisation, can be monitored separately. Transfer prices again come into play; this time following the textbook advice that they should, where possible, be market related, thus allowing meaningful revenue to be attributed to the wholesale division.

2.4.   Systems

Systems provides engineering consultancy services, typically to large companies. The company has identified three markets and designed its structure around these (Figure 4).

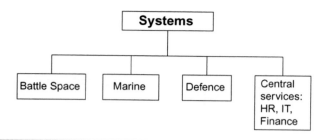

Figure 4   Systems structure.

The similarity to WRL's organisation is striking. However, whereas, at WRL, the distinctions between the three divisions were very obvious, with each serving different markets and requiring differing skills and systems; at Systems these issues are less clear cut. One could imagine a single functional organisation serving all the company's markets. Nevertheless, the company finds it desirable to divide into three divisions, presumably so that engineers can specialise in their particular markets and so that local targets can be set and managers motivated.

At Systems, there is little interaction between the divisions although, sometimes, an engineer who is attached to one division may be needed by another. A transfer pricing issue then arises concerning the payment that should be made for the engineer's time. Time could be transferred at variable rate or fully absorbed cost or the revenue earned could be attributed to the supplying division. In practice, such matters are trivial because there are few transfers between divisions and, if an engineer were working mainly for another division, he or she would transfer between divisions.

2.5. Jam

Jam is our fifth profit centre, and this company is not organised in the same way as the other four. Instead of having identifiable, market-oriented, areas/divisions, the company has adopted a functional organisation with finance, HR, IT and a production operation. Within the production unit three streams are identified: industrial preserves, speciality preserves and suet. However, these are not separate divisions within the company. The reason was not difficult to identify. In this company, the markets for the three products are not easy to disentangle. Much of Jam's output is eventually sold to a limited number of large and powerful customers and, in addition, other parts of the Jam Group also supply these customers. The Jam Group is, therefore, structured so that a marketing division deals with important customers and a large proportion of Jam's product is sold to the marketing division (Figure 5).

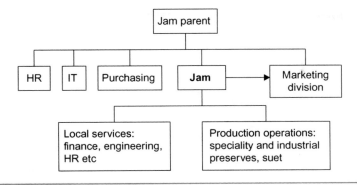

Figure 5 Jam structure.

Jam used to operate as an autonomous unit in a conglomerate operation that operated in a financial control style. However, the group of which Jam was part was sold to a venture capitalist and, under this owner, the Jam group set about centralising its operations. There is logic in this because the company operates both with large customers and suppliers. The group marketing division can negotiate contracts for the whole company with powerful customers such as the supermarket chains. Similarly, a group purchasing department can take advantage of the scale of the group's operations to negotiate good contracts for the whole group.

When we visited Jam, the group was in a state of organisational transition with centralisation of services and more edicts from the centre concerning, for example, more stringent budget targets and instructions that group companies *must* purchase from each other. These changes were probably influenced by the owner's intention to (re)float the group on the London Stock Exchange.

The centralisation was not without its problems. Our interviewees were ambivalent about the centralisation of functions such as IT although they admitted that common group systems would be beneficial and there ought to be some synergies. There was a particular problem with the group marketing division, which tended to concentrate on selling higher margin branded product where possible. This policy operated to the detriment of Jam because the company produced mainly unbranded product. This difficulty was countered by having a marketing person based on the group marketing division but working for (and paid by) Jam.

The Jam structure shows that companies have choices in deciding which structure to adopt. It was possible for a previous owner to choose a financial control style of operation and for Jam to thrive under this regime, building up the speciality preserves, niche business. Equally, the company may prosper in a more centralised operation. When we visited the company a second time, the Finance Director was more relaxed about the changes that had taken place. He was now prepared to argue that transfer prices might be set below full cost so as to encourage more output from divisions within the group. Such a policy would, of course, mean that the contribution of divisions supplying below 'cost' would have to be recognised.

3.   Profit-Centre Analysis

3.1.   Coordination, Planning and Control in Profit Centres

All five profit centres employed budgets and our interviewees thought that they were important, useful and did not pose major problems. However, the particular reasons for employing budgets differed across the five units. Foundations and Frozen Food need systems to *plan* and *coordinate* their production, service and delivery operations. Budgets also help in *setting transfer prices*.[2] Despite obvious structural similarities, the cultures in the two companies differed. In Frozen Food, our interviewee emphasised use of the budget as a *control* mechanism that included checking of individual expense lines against budget. In Foundations, the emphasis was more on encouraging *interaction*, trusting the managers and encouraging them to think outside the budget when needed.

Jam's operation, producing large quantities of preserves and suet, also requires *coordinating* systems in order to translate contract volumes into purchased supplies and production plans. In this company, the internal culture is similar to that in Foundations with an emphasis on *trust* and teamwork. However, there seemed to be a possibility that corporate pressure to achieve very stringent targets might affect the attitudes of managers and the culture within Jam.

At WRL and Systems, there are fewer coordination issues. At WRL, there is transfer of product from the wholesale operation to the retail and leisure divisions but the transfers are at arms-length prices. The divisions, though sharing central services, are relatively autonomous. At WRL, budgets were important for *control*. When the company came close to bankruptcy, a budgeting system was necessary to improve the company's fortunes and to persuade the company's creditors that it should continue to be supported.

At Systems, like WRL, there seems to be little need for coordinating mechanisms but budgets are important for both planning and control. Our interviewees felt that senior managers intervened too much in the detail of budget preparation, but there was no doubt that *planning* decisions flowed from the budget and the comparison of actual results with budget led to rapid and effective action. The emphasis

---

[2]At Foundations, factory product and construction equipment are supplied at full cost plus an element of over-recovery. At Frozen Food, factory product is charged at variable cost while the service centre supplies at a managed transfer price. Transfer prices are based on the budget projections.

on *control* was reinforced by senior management's decision that budget would not be changed during the financial year. The agreed budget could be seen as a contract that managers were expected to fulfil.

3.2.   Drive for Decentralisation

Most obviously, if separate markets can be identified, these examples suggest that companies decentralise. Specialised marketing and delivery operations can then concentrate on the particular characteristics of their markets and customers. At Frozen Food, low margin local authority business differs from high margin private services and the health business differs again with a particularly important customer in the NHS. At Foundations, it is convenient to organise geographically, and this is particularly important if business is to be won in Scotland. WRL falls naturally into three very different divisions providing wholesale, retail and leisure services. And Systems chooses to operate with three divisions specialising in supplying engineering consultancy services to major customers such as the MOD.

It seems that Chandler's finding that large, diverse companies, operating in very different markets, *need* to decentralise their operations is often mirrored in small operations. If they operate in differing markets they tend to decentralise as far as possible. The exceptional case is Jam, a company that is part of a group that chooses to centralise. At Jam, there are countervailing forces because of the need to present a united front to powerful customers. Marketing operations cannot, therefore, be readily decentralised and the Jam group structure leads to interdependencies between group companies. Jam interacts with other group divisions, especially the marketing division and shares more group-based services than the other profit centres discussed.

3.3.   Are Budgets Needed?

A key element in the 'Beyond Budgeting' thesis is that, if companies implement radical decentralisation, they will have much less need for budgeting systems. Although our sample is limited, it seems to us that companies often *do* decentralise. Business units may be part of decentralised groups and, *within* the organisations we visited, decentralisation was further pursued where the companies' markets would allow it. The question then is: why do these heavily decentralised organisations employ budgets?

In order to answer this question, we undertook an analysis of the dimensions that might influence decentralisation within the five profit centres (see Table 1).

Perusal of Table 1 reveals that, *within* business units, there may be a common strategy (Foundations, Jam, Systems); control may be centrally exercised (Frozen Food, WRL, Systems); there may be shared services (all); and there may be transfers

Table 1 Analysis Within Business Units

	Frozen Food	Foundations	Jam	WRL	Systems
Extent of common strategy	Strategy varies across commodity and niche markets	Common strategy but major separate from smaller contracts	Single overall strategy	Retail, wholesale and hotel businesses separately run	Similar across company but for different markets
Control within the business unit	Tight – over individual lines in the budget	Light – managers take action in interests of the business	Light – emphasis on explanation and support	Very important: based on day-to-day systems	Tight – through setting and monitoring the budget
Shared central services	IT, Finance, HRM	IT, Finance, HRM (tried devolving Finance)	Functional organisation structure	IT, Finance, HRM, Purchasing	IT, Finance, HRM, limited Marketing
Intra-business unit transfers	From factories at variable cost, also a designated services unit	From factory at full cost, construction equipment charged out to the areas	No market based units within the SBU but shared production facilities	Retail/hotel must purchase from wholesale at arms-length prices	Limited: if an engineer works for another sector then he/she is transferred.
Shared markets	Very limited	May be a grey area between large and 'major' contracts	Major retailers purchase a range of product: coordination needed	Very limited	Some limited overlap

within the unit (Frozen Food, Foundations, Jam). Although in four of the five profit centres *markets* can be separated, there are still numerous interdependencies within these business units and budgets provide a means of managing these. At Foundations, Frozen Food and Jam coordination of factories, delivery and service centres is necessary and budgeting is part of a package of planning and control systems. At WRL and Systems, coordination is not so important but, like the other profit centres, there are shared services, and, because of the particular issues faced by these business units, budgets have been, and continue to be, important control mechanisms.

It might be argued that, at WRL and Systems, budgets might be abandoned because, so long as their sub-units achieve targets, these companies will be successful. Managers might be more highly motivated and the expense and aggravation of budgeting would be avoided. However, we think that WRL is insufficiently mature for such a course of action and senior managers at Systems use budgets extensively for planning and control. Additionally, at Systems, budgetary control might be seen as an important indication that the company is prepared for stock market flotation.

3.4. Use of Budgets by Corporate Management

Our analysis now moves up an organisational level to the use of budgets by group in managing business units. Two of our five profit centres are private companies that do not have a corporate parent, so our comments here are restricted to the three profit centres, Foundations, Frozen Food and Jam, which are part of larger groups. In these three business units, budgets are mandated and approved by corporate managers.

Although the administration of budgets between group and business units seemed similar, very different cultures prevailed in the three companies. At Foundations, the group insisted on realism and budgets were expected to be achievable. The budget was linked to bonuses but the group adopted a flexible approach when bonuses were at risk. At Frozen Food, the budget was approved by parent managers but this was not problematic because Frozen Food had been so successful. Contingencies in the budget meant that local targets are more stringent than the approved budget. At Jam, corporate managers used the budget to press local managers to accept more ambitious targets.

Our analysis (Table 2) of relations between these business units and their wider groups follows the same pattern as the within-unit analysis of Table 1. This indicates that Frozen Foods and Foundations are relatively independent of the rest of their groups. They have limited sales and purchases to and from other group companies, share very few (group) services with other business units and their corporate centres permit them considerable autonomy. Our conclusion is that, if corporate headquarters in these two companies wished to dispense with budgets, organisational issues would probably not prevent them from doing so. The business units could be set profit and other output targets and/or could be evaluated against the performance of their peers.

In the case of Jam, matters are not so straightforward. This organisation has significant interaction with other group companies, especially through sales to a sister company that trades with the retail sector. This business unit both trades through its sister company and trades directly into retail markets so there are significant coordination issues that include, possibly managed, transfer prices. In addition, Jam shares some corporate services with other business units and suffers a considerable degree of control from the corporate centre. All in all, Jam has a number of inter-relationships that include its markets, interaction with other group business units,

Table 2 Business Unit Level of Analysis

	Frozen Food	Foundations	Jam
Shared strategy	Independent – other units based in Europe with little contact	Independent though part of UK group with some product transfer	Independent, maximises use of local resources
Corporate control	Light – more pressing problems in Europe	Light – mature relations between Group and SBU	Tight – floating on LSE, Group mandates task targets
Shared central services	Minimal services shared between business units	Minimal services shared between business units	Centralising: IT, HRM, procurement
Purchases from other SBUs	None	Minimal	Minimal
Sales to other SBUs	None	Some: at 'arms length' transfer prices	Significant: to the Marketing Division – coordination issues
Shared supply sources	None	Very limited	Shared sources of foodstuffs
Shared markets	None	Very limited	Sales to same major customers – need to maximise corporate negotiating power

shared corporate functions and relations with the corporate centre. We conclude that, in this company, if corporate managers were to dispense with budgets, there would be a number of organisational difficulties to overcome. Alternative coordination mechanisms would be needed and corporate managers would need an alternative control system in order to achieve the tight control that appears to be desired. In this case, budgets provide a means of control and fulfil multiple purposes.

4.   Interdependence, Structure and Budgets

Our analysis of the particular structures within the business unit profit centres that we visited leads us to the generic structures set out in Figures 6 and 7. Figure 6 reflects typical arrangements *between* the corporate centre (parent company) and business units while Figure 7 mirrors these arrangements but *within* business units. Conceptually, interdependence can be analysed into vertical, lateral and external dimensions. In the vertical dimension, the business unit may share corporate services, may be constrained by corporate strategy and may suffer a degree of control both in formulating and in executing plans. In the horizontal dimension, the business unit may buy from or sell to other business units and the transfer prices used in these transactions may be freely negotiated or managed in some way. Externally, the business unit may share finished good markets and/or it may procure goods, services and labour in the same markets as other business units.

Within business units, the analysis in relation to sub-units proceeds in a similar fashion. In the vertical dimension, sub-units may share services, follow common

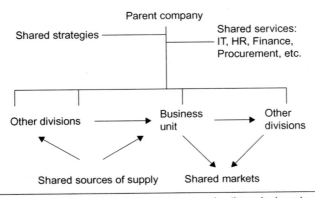

Figure 6   Structural analysis – parent company.

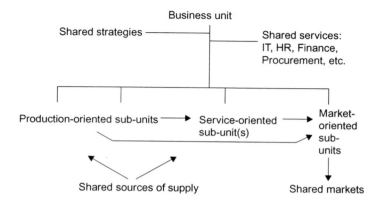

Within the business unit the same issues can arise: interdependence through shared central resources, shared strategies, product/service transfers between units, shared sources of supply and markets, etc.

Figure 7   Structural analysis – business unit.

strategies and be closely controlled. In the horizontal dimension, they may take/supply products and services from/to other sub-units and, externally, they may share factor and/or finished goods markets.

Structures such as those illustrated in Figures 6 and 7 permeate modern organisations and, nested like a set of Russian dolls, different structures can be designed to meet the needs of different organisational levels.

Interestingly, this analysis indicates that interdependence varies depending on organisational level. Foundations and Frozen Food are relatively autonomous business units with few vertical, horizontal or external interactions. However, both exhibit considerable *internal* complexity. This leads us to the conclusion that, structurally, these business units could be managed by setting *output* targets. Arguably, 'budgets' for these units need to be little more than top line sales, profit and investment targets. However, they need budgets or other planning/control systems to manage their *internal* operations.

At Jam, there are vertical interdependencies as the corporate centre provides services and requires a short-term financial orientation, and there are horizontal interdependencies as a group marketing division receives a significant part of Jam's output. Equally, Jam has internal logistical issues with different product lines sharing manufacturing facilities. We conclude that, given the structures chosen, budgeting or other systems are needed at both corporate and business unit levels. It is also worth noting that, under previous ownership, the Jam group was structured so that, despite the potential conflicts between them, group companies operated autonomously.

Under *that* structure, there would be less need for budgeting at the corporate/business unit level.

WRL and Systems are not part of large groups and our analysis is, therefore, limited to *internal* interdependencies. Horizontally, transfers are minimal within Systems and at arms-length in WRL. However, there are shared services and senior managers in both companies to maintain tight control over the sub-units. We conclude that, while in principle the sub-units in these companies might be treated as autonomous units with *output* targets, in practice, vertical interdependencies make budgeting or other control systems necessary.

4.1.   Definition of a 'Business Unit'

As Beinhocker (2007) observed, identifying a 'business unit' may not be easy and, having noted the inevitable ambiguity and subjectivity involved, Beinhocker opted to accept business units as defined by the companies themselves. He argued that management teams are best placed to make the requisite organisational distinctions.

The reader will have noted that we refer to Foundations, Frozen Food, Jam, Systems and WRL as 'business units'. Using Beinhocker's approach, this can be justified by following the lead of local managers: there was no doubt that our interviewees felt that they were responding to our questions on behalf of a 'business unit' in the five profit centres we visited. Nevertheless, why did we not designate the areas at Foundations, the marketing/delivery centres at Frozen Food or the 'divisions' at WRL and Systems as 'business units'? We would argue that that these decentralised units are not 'business units' because of their inter-dependencies. At Foundations and Frozen Food, there are several intra-relationships, including transfers of product/equipment and, at WRL and Systems, the central services are shared by the 'divisions'. At these four profit centres, sub-unit profitability would be subject to a number of assumptions concerning transfer of costs between parts of the larger unit.

Jam was different because of its substantial sales to other parts of the Jam Group. Given that Jam was less independent than other units we visited one could ask why it merited designation as a profit centre? Our answer is that, historically, all Jam's transfers had been at arms-length transfer prices and Jam had had its own central services including finance, HR and IT. These considerations (and the obvious assumption of the managers interviewed) persuaded us that Jam was a 'business unit'.

Our conclusion is that defining a 'business unit' is likely to be based on local managers' perceptions of their role and on analysis of the degree of intra-dependence exhibited by the unit or sub-unit in question. A 'business unit' would normally be responsible for its own revenues and costs and any interaction with other parts of the organisation would be based on 'arms-length' transfers of product or service.

5.   Cost Centres

We classified two of the organisations we visited, Aircraft and Laboratory Instruments, as cost centres. The output from Aircraft is generally transferred to other parts of the group and it would not be easy to attribute revenue to the unit; there are many components in an aircraft and assigning a transfer price to them could be more trouble than it is worth.

Unlike Aircraft, Laboratory Instruments (Figure 8) has an identifiable product that is sold in external markets. The reasons that we classified this unit as a cost centre were: its divorce from markets; absence of meaningful transfer price-based revenue and its concentration on manufacturing. Laboratory Instruments has a sister facility that sells to the same markets and, therefore, it make sense to have a single marketing operation that serves both Laboratory Instruments and its sister plant. The cost of Laboratory Instruments becomes part of the cost of Laboratory Instruments Group and it is at that level that revenues and cash flows are generated. Cash flow return on investment, a key metric for the company, is calculated for the Laboratory Instruments Group.

In the Laboratory Instruments group, product volume estimates are provided by the centralised marketing department and Laboratory Instruments concentrates on delivering product in the required volume, on schedule, to the quality specified. Laboratory Instruments is supported not only by centralised marketing but also by other centralised services such as computing with a common, MAPICS, materials requirements planning system. The emphasis, in Laboratory Instruments, is on efficiency with standard costing and budgeting systems together being used in order to ensure tight cost control.

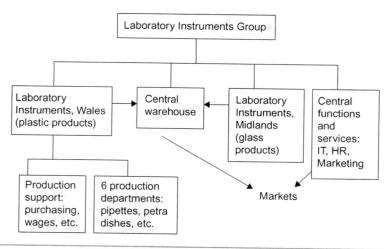

Figure 8   Laboratory Instruments structure.

Laboratory Instruments and Jam have some structural similarities. Like Laboratory Instruments, Jam depends upon a separate marketing operation and shares central services. Crucially, however, Jam transfers product to the group marketing division at arms-length, competitive market prices and, in addition, supplies a significant part of its output directly to market. These features persuaded us that Jam was a profit centre while Laboratory Instruments was a cost centre.

As well as Aircraft and Laboratory Instruments, there are other examples of cost centres in the organisations we visited, most obviously the factories at Frozen Food and Foundations. Like Laboratory Instruments, these companies operated standard costing systems to ensure control of costs and transfer product from the factories at standard cost.

The common feature of the cost centres we identified is the absence of market-related revenue and this alone, we would argue, means that a unit cannot be a profit centre or a business unit. However, the attribution of meaningful revenue is insufficient to designate a business unit. We have argued that the sub-units at Foundations, Frozen Food, Systems and WRL are too interdependent with other parts of their larger units to treat them as business units. Thus, the attribution of meaningful revenue to a unit is a necessary but not a sufficient condition for its designation as a business unit.

6. Implications for the 'Beyond Budgeting' Debate

6.1. Decentralisation

A key element of the 'Beyond Budgeting' thesis is that modern organisations need to go beyond hierarchical, divisionalised structures and adopt flat decentralised structures. This suggestion is partly driven by the Svenska Handelsbanken example, which has demonstrated that such an approach can be very successful. At Svenska Handelsbanken, individual branches drive profitability and budgets are replaced by a motivation system based on performing better than comparable competitors. A sophisticated information system allows 'league table' comparison of branch performance and, as in Macintosh's (1994) observation of systems in the Bank of America, this seems sufficient to motivate good performance from branch managers.

We believe that our analysis is more nuanced than the 'Beyond Budgeting' recommendation, identifying a more complex relationship between organisational structure and budgets in many, non-pooled, organisations. Two of our examples, Frozen Food and Foundations, being relatively autonomous business units, might not need budgets to control them; targets could be set and local managers left to work out how they might be achieved. However, *within* Frozen Food and

Foundations, despite further decentralisation to market-facing sub-units, internal complexity means that, even if budgeting for the business unit itself were abandoned, it is highly likely that local managers would wish to use budgets to manage their internal operations.

Jam is less autonomous than Foundations and Frozen Food; centralisation of a number of functions creates dependence on the corporate centre and a significant proportion of Jam's output is transferred to a group marketing division. There is also internal complexity *within* Jam with volume production across three product ranges and technical expertise to support the production function and to support customers. The interdependency and complexity both between Jam and other group divisions, between Jam and the corporate centre and within Jam itself means that the budgeting is a useful coordinating device at several organisational levels.

Less autonomous are the cost centres, Aircraft and Laboratory Instruments. Activity in these units is dictated by other parts of a wider organisation and, again, the budgeting process provides a convenient coordinating system that helps to identify required production volumes and resources needed.

Our conclusion is that there are organisational limits to decentralisation, which mean that a coordinating system is often needed: budgeting provides such a system. The need for budgets can vary throughout the organisation and budgets (or another coordinating mechanism) may be needed at one organisational level but not at another. Our companies provide a variety of examples. Jam needs coordination both at business unit and within business unit levels. Frozen Food and Foundations need little coordination at business unit level but have complex internal structures with several coordinating/controlling systems. Aircraft and Laboratory Instruments are enormous/large cost centres that need coordination both in their linkages to other parts of their group and internally. The two private companies, WRL and Systems, have divisional structures and, in theory, these could be granted more autonomy, with little need for budgeting. In practice, budgets are useful to senior managers in both these companies for planning and control.

The key point in relation to the 'Beyond Budgeting' thesis is that, in many companies, there are limits to radical decentralisation. At two of our examples, Frozen Food and Foundations, the business units themselves are relatively autonomous, but, even if budgets were abandoned at this level, there is embedded complexity that could see them used within business units. In other examples, such as Jam, Aircraft and Laboratory Instruments, there are interactions between the units we visited and other parts of the organisation as well as internal complexity that suggest a widespread use for budgets.

From the standpoint of organisational theory we note the differentiated and sequential and/or reciprocal organisational structures we observe at Foundations, Frozen Food, Jam, Laboratory Instruments and Aircraft. These can be contrasted with the pooled organisation of Svenska Handelsbanken. With few coordination problems and sophisticated operational controls, Svenska Handelsbanken has abandoned budgeting but this would not be so easy for intrinsically more complex organisations.

6.2.   Budget Uses

Those who advocate moving 'Beyond Budgeting' also draw attention to the multiple and conflicting uses of budgets. They argue that the diverse uses of budgets should be fulfilled by systems designed to meet specific objectives. For example, targets should relate to competitors, not budgets, capital decisions should be based on business need and investment lifetime expectations, etc.

We accept that there are logical problems with the multiple uses of budgets. However, in the cases we have reported, there are few obvious practical problems with the use of budgeting. The managers at Frozen Food and Foundations had little difficulty in dealing with their corporate managers and used budgets internally to guide and control the business. Managers at Jam had more problems with corporate managers but this related to the way the budget was being used to pressure business managers. Again, internally, budgets seemed useful in guiding and controlling the business and in triggering support for managers where it was needed. While budgets could be used to generate pressure (as at Jam and Systems), they need not be used in this way and several companies provided evidence that budgets could be used to plan and control operations. Additionally, the long-established institutional role of budgeting was valuable in reassuring creditors at WRL that financial controls had been instituted and the company should continue to be supported.

6.3.   Conclusion

Our evidence suggests that budgets can be valuable for a number of purposes and can be important for coordinating activities at various levels in an organisation. Having said this, we would advocate that managers consider structures that include autonomous profit and investment centres where this can be arranged. Decentralisation can be helpful in handling diverse markets and our examples suggest that companies do tend to push decentralisation down their organisations. The nature of the product and the markets served set limits to the extent of decentralisation.

If decentralisation to relatively autonomous business units is, broadly, a 'good thing' then the 'Beyond Budgeting' suggestion that such units need not be controlled by complex budgets does make considerable sense. Profit or investment centres are designed to be controlled by their outputs: profit, return on investment, economic value added, cash flow return on assets, etc., and, if the target is agreed then the method of its achievement need not, in theory, trouble senior managers. In fact, if both targets and method of achievement are set out in detail then the control system might be over-specified. One manager could achieve target but not follow process while another followed process but failed to achieve target. Which manager has done what is required?

Given the importance, in this study, of structure, we consider, in the next chapter, a case study which illustrates some of the issues that arise in designing organisational structure.

Chapter 8

Designing
Structure
and Control
Systems

▌ 1. Introduction

This report began with a survey of budgeting practice and the attitudes of financial
and non-financial managers to budgeting. A field study then led us to emphasise the
interaction of budgeting with other organisational control systems. We noted that, in
complex contemporary organisations, analysis is needed at different organisational
levels and there is a range of structural possibilities including different degrees of
centralisation of functions such as HR, finance and IT; choices in the use of cost
centres and profit centres; and differing approaches to the use of transfer prices.

We begin this chapter by introducing another case that was not part of the original survey. By the time we interviewed the Finance Director at Finrock, we better
understood the links between organisational structure and control systems, and the
Finrock case provided further insight. In particular, this case led us to appreciate

the importance of *identifying the key value adding part of the business* when designing organisational structure and control systems.

Having discussed the Finrock case, we summarise the lessons learned from the field study as a whole, and we conclude this chapter by reviewing the whole research study and identifying some possibilities for further research.

2.   The Finrock Case

2.1.   The Company

Finrock is part of a Swedish group, listed on the Swedish stock exchange and operating in 130 countries. The group has a turnover of £7–8 billion and 40,000 employees and is divided into three divisions: Tooling, Materials Technology, and Mining and Construction. Finrock is a Finnish company specialising in heavy drilling and rock-moving equipment. It comprises about 40% of the Finrock group's Mining and Construction division and has a turnover of a little under £1 billion.

The company has grown at a rate of 5–10% per year since 1970 despite growth of output in the mining market of only 2–4% per year. The company is very profitable and there is a 'definite aspiration' by the company's owners to grow the company further during the next 5-year planning period.

The company's major markets are in areas of the world that have extensive mining activities: South Africa, South America, Australia and the US. A key aspect of mining processes is the size of rock removed in drilling. Depending on the size of the seam of ore either too much or too little rock may be removed. A key issue for the company is therefore providing equipment that can help the customer achieve high efficiency in ore removal. Customers want reliable equipment that is well suited to their needs and, of course, at a competitive price.

There is a strong competition in the global market with the Finrock group and a Swedish company each holding about 33% market share. There are also smaller competitors and some important players such as Caterpillar that do not compete across the whole product range. Supplying a wide range of drilling, loading and handling equipment gives the company some competitive edge. Prices are quite transparent and Finrock and its main competitor go head to head for key business.

2.2.   Structure

Finrock has three factories in Finland, France and Canada. The company specialises in drilling and blasting equipment and in loading and handling equipment. Finrock has four product divisions: Underground Drilling, Surface Drilling, Loaders and

Breakers. Selling is organised by region and there are sales regions with 40 sales companies; there may be one or more sales companies per region (see Figure 1).

Like other companies we visited, the group is decentralised with product divisions specialising in the design and manufacture of drilling and related equipment and sales companies providing sales-related services around the world. Transfers of product from the product divisions to the sales companies used to take place at transfer price. However, this made the profits of both sales companies and product divisions particularly sensitive to the negotiated transfer price and our interviewee said that, when he worked for one of the sales companies, he spent 25–30% of his time dealing with transfer pricing issues!

The company has avoided these debates by changing its approach to transfer pricing. Now, emphasis is placed on the profitability of product divisions calculated after an allocation of sales costs. Revenue is attributed directly to product divisions and the sales companies have been 'instructed' to allocate their costs to the product divisions using ABC principles: 'We trust them to do it sensibly'. Factory costs are attributed to divisions directly or using overhead rates (set by machine). Referring to company level administration, finance, HR, etc., our interviewee said that overhead allocation 'will not become a science' and, shrugging, he said they are allocated 'somehow'.

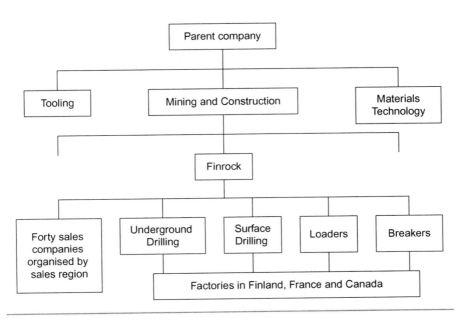

Figure 1   Finrock Structure.

Although transfer prices are now not so important, they still exist because the sales companies are legal entities, operating in several countries and, as Finrock exports 95–97% of its output, transfer pricing for tax purposes is important. However, within Finrock there are now references to 'consolidated profit' and 'local profit'. Consolidated profit refers to the profit of the product divisions and this is now very important for strategic planning and control. Local profit refers to sales company profits. These are not critical for company planning but are important in evaluating the performance of individual sales companies.

The transfer pricing method seems very sensible and, in a sense, allows the company to both have its cake and eat it. Managers of the product divisions have global responsibilities and the structure/control system is devised so that these managers do not concern themselves with transfer pricing issues. Divisional managers can see the profitability of their whole operation. However, the transfer pricing system does allow 'local profit' by sales company to be calculated. Although this is no longer an issue for divisional managers (because they receive a cost allocation from the sales companies), it is still an important performance measure for the sales companies. Sales regions are expected to make 1–3% profit on sales (and transfer prices on this basis have been acceptable to the Finnish and other tax authorities). Generating this margin is important to the sales companies and is influential in pricing policy.

When we reflected on the changes introduced at Finrock, we appreciated the importance of associating revenue with the key 'value-adding' part of the business. At this company, value is added in the complex and engineering-intensive production processes that manufacture, often huge, heavy drilling and rock-moving machines and trucks. Although it is *easy* to attribute revenue to the sales companies, it is much more *useful* to attribute revenue to the product divisions.

The present organisation was introduced some 2–3 years ago, and it had changed the focus of people so that the importance of local profitability had declined and there was greater focus on sales and production issues. Although this organisation seems very sensible, our interviewee nevertheless mentioned that it was under review. Some customers buy product from several regions and the possibility of organising sales by product was under consideration.

2.3.   Budget Preparation

The parent group sets out the budget procedures: timetable for completion, forms to be completed and overall targets for growth, revenues, EBIT, ROCE and capital efficiency. The budget is prepared between October and December, although our interviewee thought this could be shortened. Regional sales managers prepare proposals based on their market intelligence and, initially, there is no discussion with Head Office – although there is much *internal* debate. In fact, considerable analysis is needed to take account of economic fluctuations in this very cyclical business. In an economic downturn, projections may not appear very aggressive, but they are.

Our interviewee conceded that '10 years back' there had been 'sandbagging' of budgets. However, senior managers had developed a better understanding and had learnt to challenge the figures. Any reduction in revenue had to be carefully justified and managers did not want to be embarrassed by, for example, adding 30% to their costs if this would later be uncovered.

2.4.   Budget Uses

The budget has been important for planning and coordinating activity between factories and the regional sales areas. However, procedures were changing and a more dynamic planning process would link activity between production and sales operations.

There are monthly comparisons between actual results and budget (month and year-to-date) and between the budget and full-year forecast. Managers are ambitious and aim for growth 'but not at any price'. Markets can be incorrectly assessed and some markets can be unstable for political and other reasons. However, 'It doesn't mean that someone is killed for that'. Although budgets might be ambitious they are not 'crazy', a degree of realism is important. Sometimes sectors of the business fail to meet budget targets but, 'luckily', there has been compensating performance from other sectors.

Managers need to understand the reasons for divergences from budget. They need to provide a good explanation and, in that sense, they need to 'control' their figures. Some figures should be controlled while others, like variances due to exchange rates, are outside managers' control. (*Ad hoc* adjustments are made to take account of exchange rate changes but these are not carried out on a systematic basis.)

If managers need to spend above budget then they should agree this with their manager. It was recognised that managers needed a certain amount of flexibility – everything could not be set out in advance.

2.5.   Rolling Forecasts

Rolling forecasts are prepared every quarter and 'forecast 0' is prepared at the beginning of the financial year. Occasionally, forecast 0 may lead to changes in the 'final' budget. Rolling forecasts are a relatively new initiative started in the Tooling Division and now extended throughout the group. They are considered especially important in providing production operations with up-to-date information.

2.6. 'Beyond Budgeting'

The 'Beyond Budgeting' debate has probably influenced the introduction and extension of rolling forecasts and more dynamic coordination between production and
sales. However, although dispensing with budgets had been discussed in the Group,
'nobody had the guts to get rid of it'. Our interviewee continued: '[It is] very important for the people that they live with an annual target to achieve. There has to be
something stable in the uncertain world'. He added that 'a hook' was needed to provide some feeling of security and, after all, a year was a short time. Although targets
change every 3 months, people *want* stability.[1] The budget had been expected to dis-
appear, but 'At least in our business and with our people [that] doesn't seem to work'.

2.7. Incentive Schemes

The incentive scheme is related to targets for revenue, gross profit, EBIT, ROCE
and improvement in efficiency. Twenty to thirty per cent of bonus is reserved for
personal targets. The incentive scheme is closely connected to the targets laid down
in the budgeting process. The scheme is regarded as quite generous and everyone is
included from shop-floor workers to senior management. At lower levels, the maximum bonus is 1.5 months salary and this rises to 3–4 months salary at higher levels.
The incentive reward fluctuates. 'Normally they get something but [it is] volatile'.
Managers see the incentive scheme as 'real' and, to earn bonus, there has to be continuous improvement. Divisional managers may receive anything from 0% to 100%
of the possible bonus and the targets tend to be tougher for senior managers than for
the shop-floor workers. Regional managers have a separate scheme based on sales
commissions.

When asked if there might be a problem as managers tried to set relatively
easy targets in their incentive schemes, our interviewee revealed something of the
attitudes in the company. 'Luckily, the divisional managers have a very high ambition to succeed for the company. And after that they want to secure some bonus
for their people'. The process involves a proposal by the manager to his/her
boss and eventual agreement on the target. The agreed targets for the product divisions needed to be consistent with overall targets.

Apparently, the incentive scheme had been criticised in the past and, perhaps 3–
4 years ago, there had been some conservatism in the payment of bonuses. However,
top management had shown their understanding of the business and 'we have been

---

[1]The company suffers considerable instability both because of the cyclical nature of the business and
because metal prices can be volatile. Sales are made in the US dollars and the exchange rate between the
dollar and local currencies is very important to the company.

able to get rid of that kind of thinking'. Now some bonus was paid even if target was not achieved.

2.8. Culture

When discussing the need for managers to agree any overspending with their senior manager, our interviewee emphasised the open communication that was the company's style. He explained that financial results were shared with all the company's employees, including shop-floor workers and this was done on a continuous basis. Measurements were simple and straightforward and employees were proud of being able to deliver the expected results. Two or three times per year there were major company-wide communication exercises and training for union representatives and works councils was also organised.

For our interviewee, it was 'essential' that managers in the divisions felt ownership of their results and had confidence in their ability to contribute to delivering those results.

2.9. Possible Changes

Despite our impression that the company had been influenced by the 'Beyond Budgeting' debate, our interviewee appeared to know little of the 'Beyond Budgeting' movement or its recommendations. He seemed reasonably content with the budgeting procedures in use, referring to the 'intelligent use of the budget' and commenting that group/local relations seemed very sound and sensible. There was 'intelligent pressure' for growth and this was transmitted through the budget and Plan 0. A mature approach to budgeting was adopted and a *lot* of thought had been put into organisation and measurement.

Some changes were planned but our interviewee did not give the impression that budgeting would be eliminated. The changes seemed to be in making the budgeting process slicker, placing more emphasis on rolling forecasts and introducing new methods such as the balanced scorecard.

2.10. Conclusion

This case impressed us because of the changes in control systems that had been introduced. We particularly liked the switch to profitability by product division, unpolluted by transfer price negotiations, while maintaining sales company profitability as important for tax, pricing and motivation purposes. The company had also introduced techniques such as rolling forecasts and, rejecting removal of budgets had, instead integrated new methods with budgeting.

3.   Lessons from the Field Study and the Finrock Case: Structure

The last chapter set out issues concerning the design of organisational structure and we concluded that, although decentralisation might be desirable, there were limits to decentralisation that might impact different tiers of the organisation in different ways. Organisations combine profit centres, cost centres and product/service transfers between these centres in a variety of ways depending on their varying products and markets.

In four profit centres we saw that profitability was driven down to market-facing sub-units. In three of these business units, Foundations, Systems and WRL, value is clearly added as service is delivered to the customer. At Foundations and Systems, engineers work with customers in designing and delivering major projects. At WRL, the retail outlets, the leisure centre and the wholesale operation are the market-facing, value-adding units. In these organisations, the value-adding parts of the business are close to the customer and revenue can be readily attributed to the market-facing, service/delivery operations.

The fourth profit centre, Frozen Food, is similar in that the chosen structure emphasises the service delivered to customers; again revenue can be readily associated with the market-facing delivery units. However, Frozen Food might, instead, have emphasised its factory operations as the key value-adding parts of the business. This would have implied a low-cost strategy with close control over the margins generated at the factory gate. Instead, Frozen Food chooses to concentrate on adding value in the services provided to customers. Factories are treated as cost centres that support the market-facing service/delivery units. Frozen Food has further emphasised its strategic choice by setting up a Services profit centre, ensuring that the services provided generate a healthy margin through managed transfer pricing.

Finrock differs from these profit centres. Its primary value-adding activities are in the design and manufacturing product divisions, not in the sales companies that sell product to customers. It is both easy and necessary to attribute revenue to sales companies, but it has been realised that attributing revenue to the product divisions is more important. This has now been achieved while ensuring that transfer pricing is not a debilitating issue.

We conclude that business units tend to use structures that recognise the key value-adding parts of the business. Revenue is usually attributed to value-adding units either directly or at arms-length transfer prices.[2] Centres that are deemed not to be key value-adding units tend to be designated cost centres and their outputs are transferred on some cost-related basis to the value-adding units. There are many examples in our cases. Corporate centres and business units, typically, have central

---

[2]The exception to this 'rule', in our cases, was the use of managed transfer price in Frozen Food's Service profit centre.

HR, IT and Finance functions and the costs of these functions are allocated to the profit centres. There are factories at Foundations and Frozen Food charging their output at full cost and variable cost, respectively, to profit centres. Foundations also charges equipment hire at full cost to the delivery 'areas'. Laboratory Instruments is a cost centre that transfers output at full standard cost to the larger group and key metrics such as cash flow return on assets are calculated at group. At Finrock, the costs of sales companies are allocated to the key value-adding product divisions.

Obviously, the aim of designing structure and control systems is to encourage desirable managerial behaviour and one can see, in the structures and systems chosen, that certain behaviours are favoured, either explicitly or implicitly. At Frozen Food, the emphasis is on delivering customer service (not frozen meals). At Finrock, the emphasis is on product design, production costs and efficiency. At Foundations, the focus is on service delivered by the geographical delivery areas.

These examples provide insights into the way that structures and systems might be designed and we offer Figure 2 as an overview of the insights this research has generated. It suggests logical links between strategy, structure, control systems, organisational culture and reward systems and these are likely to vary across differentiated organisational functions.

While we believe that organisations might benefit from explicitly working through the connections between strategy, structure, control systems, culture and reward systems, we are not suggesting that this process leads to one 'best' solution. Our cases suggest that there are always alternatives. The Finance Director we interviewed at Foundations explained that the profitability of different processes provided interesting management information and this could have been an alternative basis for organisational structure. Jam had been treated as an autonomous business unit under a 'financial control' style of corporate management, but this was changing with more centralisation of functions, transfers to other group divisions and, possibly, managed rather than arms-length transfer prices. Frozen Food chose to emphasise service delivery rather than low-cost production.

Our analysis suggests that there are a number of linked steps in organisational design:

- Identifying general strategic aims (cost leader, prospector, etc.) and key product/service/markets.
- Identifying key value-adding parts of the business.
- Designing a decentralised structure that emphasises the value-adding operations by attributing revenue to them while recognising limits to decentralisation:
  - interactions between units, sub-units, service centres;
  - extent of local capability;
  - need for central control over strategy and, possibly, operations.

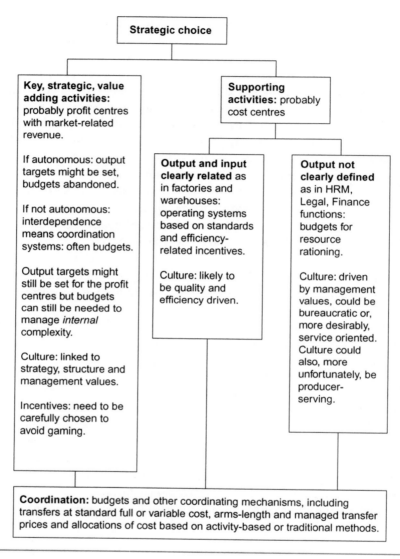

Figure 2   Strategy, structure, control and culture.

- Identifying supporting operations, probably designating them cost centres.
- Designing appropriate coordination and control systems for different parts of the organisation.
- Paying attention to culture and recognising that culture might differ between different elements of the organisation with, for example, efficiency in operations but entrepreneurship in marketing.

4. Lessons from the Survey and the Finrock Case: Coordination and Control

4.1. Systems for Coordination

We have argued that interdependencies within business create a need for coordination systems. Although alternatives could be considered, traditionally, budgeting has been a very important planning and coordination system. Our cases suggest that budgeting (or an alternative) is needed in any business unit that exhibits sufficient diversity and interdependence. Thus, Jam, interacting with other divisions and the corporate centre and managing considerable internal complexity, needs a system to coordinate its operations. Similarly, Frozen Food and Foundations need systems to manage the linkages between profit-oriented delivery units and the factories and service centres that support them. At Finrock, the product divisions have complex interactions with factories and sales companies and, again, coordinating mechanisms are needed.

Textbooks do not see coordination as one of the most important uses of budgets and, likewise, interviewees in our survey saw other functions as more important. However, our analysis suggests that the issue of coordination is important in the 'Beyond Budgeting' debate. The advocates of 'Beyond Budgeting' see radical decentralisation as a vital part of the cultural change that abandoning budgeting entails. However, the key 'Beyond Budgeting' example, Svenska Handelsbanken, is a pooled organisation where budgets are not necessary either to coordinate decentralised branches or to coordinate complexity within the branches.

Our field study companies need coordinating mechanisms either between business units or within the business unit we visited. Our conclusion is that complexity sets limits to sensible decentralisation and many organisations face issues of functional differentiation that require integrative mechanisms. Such issues can arise at various levels of the organisation and structures can be created that reduce the need for coordination at one level but generate a need for such mechanisms at the next level down. Indeed, the traditional approach to decentralisation is likely to create just this scenario. The creation of divisions that have their own IT, HR, Finance, Quality, Engineering and Production functions means that they may operate more-or-less independently of each other and the corporate centre. They may not, therefore, need systems to coordinate operations across the group. However, the divisions themselves, with significant *internal* complexity, need coordinating systems.[3]

---

[3]We note that strategic planning organisations are likely to need coordinating systems across the whole company; strategic control organisations are likely to need such systems within their relatively autonomous divisions, and financial control organisations may only need such systems within their relatively autonomous business units.

None of this is to say that budgets are *necessary* to coordinate diverse functions and activities. However, if budgets were not used, other mechanisms would be needed. Many companies will find the well-institutionalised budgeting system convenient for this purpose. Our interviewee at Finrock explicitly recognised this when he defended budgeting on the basis that a year was a reasonable planning timescale. It was not a very long time, but it was sufficiently long to provide a point of reference for managers and some stability in a changing world.

4.2. Budgets for Control

Undoubtedly, it is in the area of control that budgeting can become contentious. If budgets are used in order to pressure managers then a number of unfortunate consequences are possible. In our study there were some examples of this, notably at Jam where corporate managers insisted on more aggressive targets with apparently little understanding of local conditions and at Systems where the budget could be used as a pressure device both during its preparation and later when comparing actual results with budget. Having said this, it seemed to us that there were more examples of budgets being used constructively. We had little evidence of problems within Jam, Foundations, Frozen Food or WRL with interviewees at these companies talking about the constructive use of budgets to identify problems and support managers. Two of our interviewees were concerned to persuade managers that it could be best to *overspend* their budgets. Finrock provided another example with our interviewee noting that if targets are missed because of changing conditions, 'It doesn't mean that someone is killed for that'. Laboratory Instruments probably had a 'traditional' approach to budgeting and the budget was an instrument of tight control in this company. Nevertheless, as a cost centre producing standard product, it was difficult to say that the use of standard costing and tight budgets was inappropriate.

Budgets can be very important control mechanisms. The survey provided no evidence that budgets could not be both realistic and sufficiently tight, especially in uncertain and competitive conditions. Although there were suggestions of over-aggressive budgets at Jam and Systems, there were more indications of a desire for realism with this being mentioned at WRL and Finrock and being *corporate policy* at Foundations. The survey indicated that budgets are most appropriate as control devices when conditions are relatively stable and this is consistent with the literature.

Our conclusion is that budgets can be an important management tool for maintaining control and, generally, managers understand their advantages and disadvantages well enough to ensure that the former outweigh the latter. In the cases where, arguably, budgets had been used to generate pressure, senior and corporate managers wished to demonstrate improving results as a prelude to stock market flotation.

5. Conclusions

5.1. Satisfaction with Budgeting

Both our survey of financial and non-financial managers and our field study indicated that, broadly, managers were satisfied with their budgeting systems, regarded budgeting as important for a number of reasons, and had a limited number of specific problems.

These findings are very different from the assertions of those who favour 'Beyond Budgeting': they claim that managers are very dissatisfied with budgeting systems. However, our results are consistent with a recent study (Frow et al., 2005; Marginson and Ogden, 2005) that found, in a case company, that managers could reconcile the tensions between budgetary constraints and innovation.

Analysis of our survey data supported the longstanding view that managers are likely to be more satisfied with budgets in relatively stable environments, especially where there is a degree of task certainty. Our survey also indicated, however, that, in relatively certain environments, budgets tend to become more important for *control*, not for planning. Conversely, budgets become less important for control but more important for *planning* as uncertainty increases. These findings are consistent with those of Chapman (1998).

Although managers generally were not concerned by over- or under-ambitious targets, budget padding and budget 'games' some managers did point to possible budgeting problems:

- Budgeting can be longwinded and bureaucratic as observed by those advocating 'Beyond Budgeting'.
- Budgets can constrain managers and discourage them from taking necessary actions.
- The link between budgets and incentive schemes can encourage budget gaming although performance contracts did not seem to have the very pernicious consequences described by Hope and Fraser.
- There were references both in survey and field study responses to the need for local ownership of budgets and the dangers of top managers imposing unrealistic tasks and/or over-involvement in detailed planning.

5.2. Changing Nature of Budgeting

Our survey and field study indicate that contemporary managers usually use budgets productively and do not generally encounter the problems highlighted in the traditional budgeting literature: (over) reliance on accounting measures; the budget-constrained style of management; targets set too stringently; padding in budgets; and budget games. This may, as Ross (1995) speculates, be because managers have learnt to use budgeting systems flexibly and to avoid apportioning blame. We also note that there appears to be less emphasis on the use of budgets to enforce rigid hierarchical control. Argyris (1952) had described the dangers of overly department-centred budgets, but, 35 years later, Umapathy's (1987) survey indicated that fewer firms were fully matching performance reports to organisational authority and responsibility. Complex contemporary organisations, possibly using organic structures in parts of their operations and recognising the importance of teamwork and empowerment, may adopt less department-centred approaches than in the past.

It is likely that cultural change during the last 30 years has affected the use of and attitudes to budgeting. We report only limited aggressive, interpersonal use of budgets with more examples of a constructive, profit conscious style. The managers we interviewed, typically, did have a flexible attitude, would be prepared to listen to reasoned explanations and adopted a team-based approach to problem solving. Budgeting could be longwinded and bureaucratic but this was not necessarily a problem, and linking budgets and incentives could increase the risk of gaming but managers were very aware of these possibilities.

Revolutionary technology and increased management education have encouraged relatively sophisticated techniques in the preparation of budgets and integration of budgeting with non-financial performance measures in general and the balanced scorecard in particular. Instead of the abandonment of budgets, as recommended by the 'Beyond Budgeting' movement, there seems, instead, to have been intensification in the (enlightened) use of budgeting.

We were interested in references to having shortened the timescale needed to prepare the budget. No doubt modern information technology makes this possible and there are obvious advantages in limiting the budget preparation period. First, there is saving staff/management time; second, the information on which the budget is based is more current, third: the projection for the end of the current budget period (the start of the next budget period) will be more accurate.

5.3. Structure and Coordination: The 'Beyond Budgeting' Debate

Our questionnaire survey revealed limited dissatisfaction with traditional budgeting practices, and we were puzzled that, contrary to expectations stoked by 'Beyond Budgeting', financial and non-financial managers were united in regarding budgeting as important and not particularly problematic.

A partial reconciliation of our findings with those of the 'Beyond Budgeting' movement resides, we believe, in the interaction between organisational structures and coordination systems. We have suggested that:

■ The performance of *independent, autonomous* units can be assessed using market-based, output-related measures.

■ Interaction between business units and sub-units makes coordination devices such as budgets necessary.

In our study, the focus was on control *within* operating organisations and we saw sufficient complexity to suggest that a coordinating system, such as budgeting, was needed. The operational managers responding to our survey and participating in the field study were concerned with the coordination of differentiated functions and devising systems for planning and control. The 'Beyond Budgeting' movement, on the other hand, has emerged from study of the relations *between* corporate managers and operating units. Big company executives aiming to control relatively autonomous divisions may see target setting and performance measurement rather than budgeting as the key issues.

It is possible for tiered organisations to adopt output-related measures in managing relationships between corporate and divisional levels and to adopt budgetary systems *within* divisions or other business units. We note that, when a particular organisational tier falls into the 'pooled' category, it may be managed by output rather than process measures. The key 'Beyond Budgeting' example, Svenska Handelsbanken, is a bank with many similar but independent branches. In these circumstances, as Macintosh and Daft (1987) discovered, standard operating procedures (together with, in the case of Svenska Handelsbanken, a centralised information system and rapid feedback to branch managers of their standing in the branch performance league tables) may be sufficient for control.

6. Suggestions for Further Research

There have been enormous changes in the past 30 years. The environment has become more competitive and, in some sectors, less regulated. Managerial culture may be more flexible, supportive and less personally aggressive. Information technology has made more efficient and more intensive budgeting possible. Techniques such as the balanced scorecard and measures such as economic value added and cash flow return on assets have opened up possibilities for organisational control.

All these changes have, no doubt, impacted on the uses of and attitudes to budgeting. Our study and those of Frow et al. (2005) and Ross (1995) suggest that budgeting has been adapted to contemporary conditions. Meanwhile, the 'Beyond Budgeting' Round Table argues that budgeting is past its sell-by date and should be abandoned. We suggest that a technique that is so widely used is well worth further research study, especially as there are diverse views as to its efficacy. Our study has highlighted the importance of setting budgeting in a context that includes strategy, structure, operating systems and culture and reward systems.

We suggest that the complexity of the linkages between these variables is easy to overlook and provides a potentially rich field for research and managerial prescription:

■ *Interaction of strategic choice and structure.* In particular, we suggest that companies can identify the key, strategic, 'value-adding' parts of the business and these will normally designated as profit centres.

■ *Profit-centre management.* 'Beyond Budgeting' recommends assessment of performance by relative market measures rather than by budget comparison. We suggest this is most appropriate for relatively autonomous profit centres.

■ *Complexity within profit centres.* Structures combine contribution/profit centres and cost centres to reflect strategic choice and functional diversity. Transfer pricing and cost transfers should reflect strategic choice.

■ *Coordination and integration of diverse functions.* This research suggests that budgeting is valuable in managing business complexity, especially for planning in uncertain environments, control in stable conditions and rationing inputs where there is neither profit responsibility nor a clear input/output relationship.

■ *Cost centres with clearly defined input/output relationships.* Factories, warehouses and, possibly, call centres might use standard costing systems and traditional incentive schemes so as to encourage and reward efficiency, accuracy and quality.

■ *Cultural controls* complement more instrumental output, process and input controls. We suggest that culture should be related to strategy, structure and function. For example, a prospector strategy might be linked with an entrepreneurial culture in, organically structured profit centres but this might give way to a more bureaucratic, efficiency-centred culture in the organisation's cost centres.

■ *Incentive schemes* provide a link between plans, outcomes and rewards and influence planning, budgeting, decision making and reporting. Incentives include not only cash bonuses but also promotion and recognition, possibly through such devices as 'league tables'. Incentive schemes need to be carefully devised with an eye on possible unintended consequences.

Budgeting operates within a context that includes organisational strategy, structure, culture and reward and omitting some of these variables means that research models can be under-specified. While many studies now control for organisational size and nature, we argue that researchers need to be aware of multiple interacting variables in complex business environments. Among other things, the behaviour of managers in profit and cost centres will be different; organic and mechanistic structures require different behaviours/cultures and budgets may have a range of purposes that may be appropriate (or inappropriate) for particular combinations of strategies, structures and functions.

This concludes our exploration of budgeting in the twenty-first century. While we have only limited support for some aspects of the 'Beyond Budgeting' thesis, the movement has reinvigorated interest in a topic that has widespread and pervasive influence throughout both profit and non-profit sectors. We hope that this monograph encourages further research into this important topic.

Appendix 1

The Survey: Descriptive Statistics

1. IT systems

Does your company use an Enterprise Resource Planning System or Integrated IT System?

	Frequency	Percentage
Yes	29	74.4
No	10	25.6
Missing	1	–
Total	40	100.0

How sophisticated is the IT system in your company?

	Frequency	Percentage
Simple stand-alone system	–	–
	9	22.5
	15	37.5
	11	27.5
Highly sophisticated system	5	12.5
Total	40	100.0

Most responding companies have integrated IT systems and, generally, respondents regard their systems as sophisticated.

2. Competitive environment
How would you describe the competitive situation faced by your company?

	Frequency	Percentage
Very little competition	–	–
Some competition	1	2.5
Moderate competition	10	25.0
Strong competition	17	42.5
Very strong competition	12	30.0
Total	40	100.0

Almost 75% of respondents judge competition to be strong or very strong.

3. Task certainty/uncertainty
The following questions give some indication of the degree of task and environmental uncertainty experienced by respondents. Most respondents feel that they know which methods to adopt and understand whether actions are effective. Responding companies divide between those where environmental changes frequently impact on decisions and those where they have only occasional impact.

In relation to your job, are you certain about which method is best?

	Frequency	Percentage
Never	–	–
Occasionally	3	7.5
Half the time	14	35.0
Frequently	21	52.5
Always	2	5.0
Total	40	100.0

In relation to your job, is it difficult to determine whether the right decision was taken?

	Frequency	Percentage
Never	–	–
Occasionally	24	60.0
Half the time	6	15.0
Frequently	10	25.0
Always	–	–
Total	40	100.0

In relation to your job, do environmental changes frequently affect decisions?

	Frequency	Percentage
Never	3	7.5
Occasionally	22	55.0
Half the time	2	5.0
Frequently	13	32.5
Always	–	–
Total	40	100.0

In relation to your job, are you uncertain how to act?

	Frequency	Percentage
Never	6	15.0
Occasionally	26	65.0
Half the time	6	15.0
Frequently	2	5.0
Always	–	–
Total	40	100.0

In relation to your job, can you tell if actions were effective?

	Frequency	Percentage
Never	–	–
Occasionally	9	22.5
Half the time	9	22.5
Frequently	21	52.5
Always	1	2.5
Total	40	100.0

In relation to your job, are you certain how to deal with environmental changes?

	Frequency	Percentage
Never	–	–
Occasionally	8	20.0
Half the time	17	42.5
Frequently	14	35.0
Always	1	2.5
Total	40	100.0

In relation to your job, do you frequently encounter new problems?

	Frequency	Percentage
Never	–	–
Occasionally	9	22.5
Half the time	9	22.5
Frequently	19	47.5
Always	3	7.5
Total	40	100.0

In relation to your job, do environmental changes frequently affect decisions?

	Frequency	Percentage
Never	3	7.5
Occasionally	22	55.0
Half the time	2	5.0
Frequently	13	32.5
Always	–	–
Total	40	100.0

In relation to your job, are you certain about how the job should be done?

	Frequency	Percentage
Never	1	2.6
Occasionally	7	17.9
Half the time	8	20.5
Frequently	19	48.7
Always	4	10.3
Missing	1	–
Total	40	100.0

In relation to your job, are you in doubt as to how to obtain information?

	Frequency	Percentage
Never	2	5.0
Occasionally	29	72.5
Half the time	7	17.5
Frequently	1	2.5
Always	1	2.5
Total	40	100.0

4. The budgeting process
Does your company set a budget?

	Frequency	Percentage
Yes	40	100.0
No	–	–
Total	40	100.0

As expected, all responding companies set a budget.

How many months before the financial year does the budgeting process begin?

	Frequency	Percentage
One month	2	5.0
Two months	–	–
Three months	8	20.0
Four months	12	30.0
Five months	5	12.5
Six months	12	30.0
More than 6 months	1	2.5
Total	40	100.0

Most companies begin the budget preparation process well in advance of the financial year with 75% taking 4 months or more to prepare the budget.

Top managers drive the budgeting process to ensure that the final outcome will be acceptable to them.

	Frequency	Percentage
Strongly disagree	3	7.5
Disagree	–	–
Neither agree nor disagree	3	7.5
Agree	22	55.0
Strongly agree	12	30.0
Total	40	100.0

The vast majority (85%) of respondents agree or strongly agree that top managers drive the process.

Junior managers have a major input to the budgeting process and can affect the final budget outcome.

	Frequency	Percentage
Strongly disagree	4	10.0
Disagree	10	25.0
Neither agree nor disagree	3	7.5
Agree	22	55.0
Strongly agree	1	2.5
Total	40	100.0

But more than 50% of respondents also believe that junior managers have a major input to the process and can affect the final outcome.

There are usually many revisions before the budget is finalised.

	Frequency	Percentage
Strongly disagree	–	–
Disagree	6	15.0
Neither agree nor disagree	2	5.0
Agree	18	45.0
Strongly agree	14	35.0
Total	40	100.0

Consistent with the length of the budget process, typically, there are many budget revisions with 80% of companies agreeing or strongly agreeing with the statement. Budget setting is time consuming and complex.

Is a budget set for each separate month in the financial year?

	Frequency	Percentage
Yes	38	95.0
No	2	5.0
Total	40	100.0

The vast majority (95%) of responding companies set budgets for each month of the financial year.

5. Budget reporting

*In reporting actual results versus budget for the **period** do you report:*

	Frequency	Percentage
Budget	1	2.6
Actual and budget	1	2.6
Actual, budget and variance	36	92.3
Actual and variance versus budget	1	2.6
Missing	1	–
Total	40	100.0

The vast majority (90%) of companies report actual, budget and variance every month.

*In reporting actual results versus budget for the **financial year to date** do you report:*

	Frequency	Percentage
Budget	1	2.5
Actual and budget	1	2.5
Actual, budget and variance	37	92.5
Actual and variance versus budget	1	2.5
Total	40	100.0

They also report corresponding figures for the year to date.

In reporting actual results versus the previous year do you report:

	Frequency	Percentage
Budget	–	–
Actual	14	35.0
Actual and budget	1	2.5
Actual, budget and variance	6	15.0
Actual and variance	8	20.0
Variance	1	2.5
Not reported	10	25.0
Total	40	100.0

Most companies (75%) provide a comparison with previous year results.

*In reporting **estimated out-turn for the financial year** do you report:*

	Frequency	Percentage
Budget	1	2.5
Actual	5	12.5
Actual and budget	1	2.5
Actual, budget and variance	17	42.5
Actual and variance	4	10.0
Budget and variance	1	2.5
Not reported	11	27.5
Total	40	100.0

Most companies (70%) estimate full-year result and most of these report both the estimated out-turn and comparison with budget.

Is the budget flexed before calculation of variances?

	Frequency	Percentage
Yes	7	17.9
No	32	82.1
Missing	1	–
Total	40	100.0

Despite textbook advice, most (80%) of the companies confirm that they do not flex the budget before calculating variances.

Does your company revise the budget during the year?

	Frequency	Percentage
Not at all	31	79.5
Half-yearly	5	12.8
Quarterly	3	7.7
Missing	1	–
Total	40	100.0

Although most (79.5%) of the companies do not revise the budget during the year, a significant minority (20.5%) claim to do so.

If a revised budget is prepared, is it:

	Frequency	Percentage
For the remainder of the financial year	8	80.0
For the next 12 months	1	10.0
For some other period	1	10.0
Not applicable	30	–
Total	40	100.0

Those companies that do revise the budget almost invariably do so for the rest of the financial year.

If the budget is overspent in a given month, which of the following options best describes the practice in your company:

	Frequency	Percentage
Normally no enquiry is made as the cost-centre manager is trusted to have good reasons for overspends	2	5.0
No action would normally be taken if the overspend was small	2	5.0
Large overspends would be investigated and managers called to account	22	55.0
Any overspend would be investigated and managers called to account	4	10.0
Overspends on particular lines are OK so long as managers are within budget overall	7	17.5
Multiple practices (entered by some respondents even though not available as an option)	3	7.5
Total	40	100.0

Most (65%) of the companies investigate overspends and expect managers to account for them. A significant minority (17.5%) are satisfied if total spending remains within budget.

6. Forecasting
Are forecasts prepared separately from the budget?

	Frequency	Percentage
Yes	36	90.0
No	4	10.0
Total	40	100.0

The vast majority of companies (90%) prepare forecasts.

How often does your company prepare forecasts?

	Frequency	Percentage
Half-yearly	5	14.3
Quarterly	12	34.3
Monthly	18	51.4
Missing	5	–
Total	40	100.0

About half of responding companies prepare forecasts every month while the rest prepare forecasts less frequently, usually quarterly but some just half-yearly.

If forecasts are prepared, are they for:

	Frequency	Percentage
The remainder of the financial year	29	80.6
The next 12 months	2	5.6
Some other period	5	13.9
Not applicable	4	–
Total	40	100.0

Most of the companies that produce forecasts (80%) do so for the remainder of the financial year.

7. The importance of budgeting

In your opinion, how important is the budget in the management of your company?

	Frequency	Percentage
Extremely important	7	17.9
Very important	21	53.8
Fairly important	9	23.1
Not very important	2	5.1
Almost irrelevant	–	–
Missing	1	
Total	40	100.0

Almost all respondents (95%) see the budget as important in managing their companies.

*Please indicate how important the budget is for **planning**.*

	Frequency	Percentage
Extremely important	7	17.5
Very important	22	55.0
Fairly important	10	25.0
Not very important	–	–
Almost irrelevant	1	2.5
Total	40	100.0

Virtually every respondent sees the budget as an important tool for planning.

*Please indicate how important the budget is for **control**.*

	Frequency	Percentage
Extremely important	9	22.5
Very important	21	52.5
Fairly important	8	20.0
Not very important	2	5.0
Almost irrelevant	–	–
Total	40	100.0

Similarly, virtually every respondent sees the budget as important for control.

*Please indicate how important the budget is for **coordination**.*

	Frequency	Percentage
Extremely important	4	10.0
Very important	14	35.0
Fairly important	15	37.5
Not very important	5	12.5
Almost irrelevant	2	5.0
Total	40	100.0

Most (82.5%) respondents also regard budgets as important for coordination but there is a dissenting minority (17.5%).

*Please indicate how important the budget is for **communication**.*

	Frequency	Percentage
Extremely important	3	7.5
Very important	16	40.0
Fairly important	14	35.0
Not very important	5	12.5
Almost irrelevant	2	5.0
Total	40	100.0

There is a very similar response for communication. Again 82.5% see budgets as important while 17.5% did not agree.

Please indicate how important the budget is for **authorisation**.

	Frequency	Percentage
Extremely important	3	7.5
Very important	17	42.5
Fairly important	16	40.0
Not very important	3	7.5
Almost irrelevant	1	2.5
Total	40	100.0

Most respondents (92.3%) agree that budgets are important devices for authorising expenditure.

Please indicate how important the budget is for **motivation**.

	Frequency	Percentage
Extremely important	3	7.5
Very important	10	25.0
Fairly important	12	30.0
Not very important	11	27.5
Almost irrelevant	4	10.0
Total	40	100.0

A very significant minority of respondents (37.5%) do not agree that the budget is important for motivation. Although most respondents agree that the budget is an important motivator, a larger minority disagreed with this statement.

*Please indicate how important the budget is for **performance evaluation.***

	Frequency	Percentage
Extremely important	12	30.0
Very important	14	35.0
Fairly important	9	22.5
Not very important	2	5.0
Almost irrelevant	3	7.5
Total	40	100.0

As with planning, control and authorisation, the vast majority (87.5%) agree that budgets are important for performance evaluation.

8. Satisfaction with budgets

*Do you think that **managers in your company** are satisfied with the budgeting system?*

	Frequency	Percentage
Very satisfied	–	–
Satisfied	12	30.0
Neither satisfied nor dissatisfied	16	40.0
Not satisfied	9	22.5
Very dissatisfied	3	7.5
Total	40	100.0

This question suggests considerable equivocation in assessing budgeting systems. The distribution of replies is almost evenly spread around the most usual response: neither satisfied nor dissatisfied.

Are you satisfied with the budgeting system?

	Frequency	Percentage
Very satisfied	–	–
Satisfied	16	40.0
Neither satisfied nor dissatisfied	8	20.0
Not satisfied	14	35.0
Very dissatisfied	2	5.0
Total	40	100.0

Consistently, for financial managers themselves, there are 40% satisfied but 40% not satisfied or very dissatisfied with their budgeting system.

9. Attitudes to budgeting
To what extent do you agree or disagree with the following statements?
The process is too bureaucratic.

	Frequency	Percentage
Strongly agree	3	8.8
Agree	9	26.5
Neither agree nor disagree	11	32.4
Disagree	8	23.5
Strongly disagree	3	8.8
Missing	6	–
Total	40	100.0

There is some evidence that financial managers see the budgeting process as bureaucratic although 32.4% neither agreed nor disagreed.

Budgets are too time consuming for the results achieved.

	Frequency	Percentage
Strongly agree	5	12.8
Agree	17	43.6
Neither agree nor disagree	7	17.9
Disagree	7	17.9
Strongly disagree	3	7.7
Missing	1	–
Total	40	100.0

Financial managers tended to see the budget as overly time consuming with 56.4% agreeing or strongly agreeing.

The process of setting the budget is de-motivating for managers.

	Frequency	Percentage
Strongly agree	4	10.3
Agree	5	12.8
Neither agree nor disagree	7	17.9
Disagree	18	46.2
Strongly disagree	5	12.8
Missing	1	–
Total	40	100.0

Budget setting is not regarded as de-motivating for managers.

The budgets set are unrealistic.

	Frequency	Percentage
Strongly agree	3	7.7
Agree	7	17.9
Neither agree nor disagree	7	17.9
Disagree	11	28.2
Strongly disagree	11	28.2
Missing	1	–
Total	40	100.0

A minority of 25.6% agreed or strongly agreed that budgets are unrealistic. Most felt that budgets *are* realistic.

Too many managers know how to play budget games – padding costs so as to look good later.

	Frequency	Percentage
Strongly agree	3	7.5
Agree	13	32.5
Neither agree nor disagree	10	25.0
Disagree	13	32.5
Strongly disagree	1	2.5
Total	40	100.0

There is a fairly even split between those agreeing that too many managers know how to play budget games (40%) and those disagreeing with the statement (32.5%).

Budgets lead to a culture of blame, recrimination and buck passing.

	Frequency	Percentage
Strongly agree	2	5.0
Agree	3	7.5
Neither agree nor disagree	9	22.5
Disagree	17	42.5
Strongly disagree	9	22.5
Total	40	100.0

The majority of financial managers (65%) do not agree that budgets lead to unfortunate cultures. Only 12.5% agreed with the statement.

Budgets have to be 'challenging' but that means they are unrealistic.

	Frequency	Percentage
Strongly agree	1	2.5
Agree	8	20.0
Neither agree nor disagree	5	12.5
Disagree	26	65.0
Strongly disagree	–	–
Total	40	100.0

Most respondents (65%) disagreed with the statement that challenging budgets are unrealistic. A minority of 22.5% agreed with the statement.

Budgets are too rigid, it's not easy to revise them when things change.

	Frequency	Percentage
Strongly agree	3	7.5
Agree	13	32.5
Neither agree nor disagree	9	22.5
Disagree	14	35.0
Strongly disagree	1	2.5
Total	40	100.0

Respondents split about evenly between those agreeing that budgets are too rigid (40%) while 35% disagreed.

Planning in financial years is not logical as the business evolves continuously.

	Frequency	Percentage
Strongly agree	6	15.4
Agree	8	20.5
Neither agree nor disagree	8	20.5
Disagree	12	30.8
Strongly disagree	5	12.8
Missing	1	–
Total	40	100.0

Similarly, respondents split between those that thought planning in financial years is illogical (35.9%) and those that disagreed (43.6%). Fewer financial managers were concerned by the financial year issue than by rigidity.

Budgets allow 'streetwise' managers to build empires while others suffer.

	Frequency	Percentage
Strongly agree	1	2.5
Agree	10	25.0
Neither agree nor disagree	13	32.5
Disagree	9	22.5
Strongly disagree	7	17.5
Total	40	100.0

While 40% of managers disagreed that streetwise managers built empires, 30% did agree with this proposition.

Managers simply aim to stay inside their cost budgets instead of taking actions that would benefit the business.

	Frequency	Percentage
Strongly agree	3	7.5
Agree	18	45.0
Neither agree nor disagree	8	20.0
Disagree	8	20.0
Strongly disagree	3	7.5
Total	40	100.0

There is evidence that budgets can constrain managers with over half of respondents (52.5%) agreeing with this proposition.

Linking the bonus system to the budget means that this is the over-riding concern when budgets are set.

	Frequency	Percentage
Strongly agree	4	10.0
Agree	8	20.0
Neither agree nor disagree	13	32.5
Disagree	8	20.0
Strongly disagree	5	12.5
Not applicable	2	5.0
Total	40	100.0

Respondents split evenly between those agreeing that the bonus system can be an over-riding concern (30%) and those disagreeing with the statement (32.5%).

Budgets must be realistic so they cannot be challenging targets.

	Frequency	Percentage
Strongly agree	2	5.0
Agree	5	12.5
Neither agree nor disagree	9	22.5
Disagree	14	35.0
Strongly disagree	10	25.0
Total	40	100.0

As with the question suggesting that challenging budgets cannot be realistic so most respondents (60%) disagreed that realistic budgets cannot be challenging and only 17.5% agreed with this statement.

There is too much emphasis on meeting budget targets rather than on taking actions that are best for the business.

	Frequency	Percentage
Strongly agree	1	2.5
Agree	7	17.5
Neither agree nor disagree	14	35.0
Disagree	15	37.5
Strongly disagree	3	7.5
Total	40	100.0

A minority of respondents (20%) agreed that there could be too much emphasis on budget targets. This would not appear to be an issue in most companies. There was more agreement that managers might stay within their cost budgets instead of taking actions that might benefit the business.

The annual battle with Headquarters to agree a budget is time consuming and unproductive.

	Frequency	Percentage
Strongly agree	5	12.8
Agree	11	28.2
Neither agree nor disagree	12	30.8
Disagree	9	23.1
Strongly disagree	2	5.1
Missing	1	–
Total	40	100

More respondents agreed than disagreed with this statement (41% versus 28.2%). It seems that budget setting can be bureaucratic and time consuming.

Budgets focus too much on the past.

	Frequency	Percentage
Strongly agree	–	–
Agree	10	25.0
Neither agree nor disagree	8	20.0
Disagree	15	37.5
Strongly disagree	7	17.5
Total	40	100.0

Most respondents disagree with the statement that budgets focus too much on the past. A minority of 25% respondents agreed with the statement.

The budgeting process inhibits innovation and change.

	Frequency	Percentage
Strongly agree	1	2.5
Agree	6	15.0
Neither agree nor disagree	12	30.0
Disagree	18	45.0
Strongly disagree	3	7.5
Total	40	100.0

Most respondents (52.5%) disagree that budgeting inhibits innovation and change. Only 17.5% agree with this statement. While there is some agreement that budgets can inhibit managers, it seems that this possibility should be kept in perspective.

Budgets focus too much on financial performance.

	Frequency	Percentage
Strongly agree	3	7.7
Agree	11	28.2
Neither agree nor disagree	10	25.6
Disagree	14	35.9
Strongly disagree	1	2.6
Missing	1	–
Total	40	100.0

There is a more-or-less even split between those agreeing that budgets focus too much on financial performance (35.9%) and those that do not (38.5%).

Budgets inhibit cross-functional process thinking.

	Frequency	Percentage
Strongly agree	3	7.5
Agree	9	22.5
Neither agree nor disagree	14	35.0
Disagree	12	30.0
Strongly disagree	2	5.0
Total	40	100.0

There is also a split between those agreeing that budgets inhibit cross-functional thinking (30%) and those that do not (35%).

As presently constructed budgets are too inaccurate, more resources and technology need to be devoted to them.

	Frequency	Percentage
Strongly agree	3	7.7
Agree	8	20.5
Neither agree nor disagree	11	28.2
Disagree	10	25.6
Strongly disagree	7	17.9
Missing	1	–
Total	40	100.0

Although a minority (28.2%) agreed that budgets are too inaccurate and need more resources, 43.5% disagreed with this statement.

10. The influence of headquarters on budgeting procedures

Does your company have a headquarters/parent company?

	Frequency	Percentage
Yes	37	92.5
No	3	7.5
Total	40	100.0

Most responding companies are part of larger groups.

To what extent are budgeting procedures laid down by headquarters?

	Frequency	Percentage
Whole process laid down in detail by HQ	3	8.1
Process is largely set out by HQ	13	35.1
HQ interested only in the result – but must be presented in their own format	15	40.5
Budget presented in subsidiaries own format	6	16.2
HQ is not interested in budgets	–	–
Not applicable	3	–
Total	40	100.0

Group HQ takes considerable interest in the budget process in most companies, laying down the process (43.2%) and having an interest in the result in all responding companies.

11. Performance and bonuses

Is there a bonus scheme for managers in your company?

	Frequency	Percentage
Yes	34	85.0
No	6	15.0
Total	40	100.0

Most companies operate management incentive schemes.

Which of the following options best describes the bonus scheme in your company?

	Frequency	Percentage
The scheme is based on a single performance measure	8	25.0
The scheme is financially based on a number of financial targets, for example profit, gross margin, cash flow, return-on-investment, residual income, economic value added, working capital reduction and EBIDA.	9	28.1
The scheme is based on non-financial criteria. For example, subjective assessment of a manager's performance.	1	3.1
The scheme is based on a combination of financial and non-financial targets – and the *budget is important* in establishing targets for financial measures.	14	43.8
The scheme is based on a combination of financial and non-financial targets – but the *budget is not very important* in establishing targets for financial measures.	–	–
Missing/Not applicable	8	–
Total	40	100.0

Most schemes are based on financial performance measures (53.1%) although 43.8% are based on combinations of financial and non-financial measures. Almost all incentive schemes have a financial component.

How does the budget relate to assessing managers' performance?

	Frequency	Percentage
The budget is almost irrelevant in assessing managers' performance. Discharge of functional and professional responsibilities is much more important.	6	15.4
Meeting financial targets is important, but they are only part, and not the most important part of a manager's responsibilities	14	35.9
Meeting financial targets and remaining within cost constraints is *very* important. Managers are expected to meet all their non-financial objectives *and* meet financial targets.	19	48.7
Missing.	1	–
Total	40	100.0

Responding companies divide almost evenly between those that see cost constraints as *very* important and those that emphasise other aspects of managers' performance.

12. The importance of non-financial indicators
*Please indicate the importance of non-financial indicators for **quality**.*

	Frequency	Percentage
Extremely important	23	59.0
Very important	13	33.3
Fairly important	2	5.1
Not very important	1	2.6
Irrelevant	–	–
Missing	1	–
Total	40	100.0

There is little doubt that non-financial indicators of quality are very important in almost all companies.

*Please indicate the importance of non-financial indicators for **product/service not to specification**.*

	Frequency	Percentage
Extremely important	15	37.5
Very important	16	40.0
Fairly important	5	12.5
Not very important	3	7.5
Irrelevant	1	2.5
Total	40	100.0

Meeting product/service specification is also very important in almost all responding companies.

*Please indicate the importance of non-financial indicators for **on-time delivery performance**.*

	Frequency	Percentage
Extremely important	18	45.0
Very important	16	40.0
Fairly important	4	10.0
Not very important	2	5.0
Irrelevant	–	–
Total	40	100.0

Measures of delivery performance are also regarded as very important in almost all responding companies.

*Please indicate the importance of non-financial indicators for **schedule adherence**.*

	Frequency	Percentage
Extremely important	7	17.9
Very important	20	51.3
Fairly important	8	20.5
Not very important	3	7.7
Irrelevant	1	2.6
Missing	1	–
Total	40	100.0

Measures of adherence to schedule are also important in the vast majority of responding companies.

*Please indicate the importance of non-financial indicators for **returns**.*

	Frequency	Percentage
Extremely important	5	12.8
Very important	13	33.3
Fairly important	12	30.8
Not very important	6	15.4
Irrelevant	3	7.7
Not applicable	1	–
Total	40	100.0

Measures for returns are not quite so important but, nevertheless, 76.9% of respondents judged them at least fairly important.

*Please indicate the importance of non-financial indicators for **length of order book**.*

	Frequency	Percentage
Extremely important	9	25.0
Very important	9	25.0
Fairly important	4	11.1
Not very important	10	27.8
Irrelevant	4	11.1
Not applicable	3	–
Missing	1	–
Total	40	100.0

The order book is very important or extremely important for half the responding companies. It is not very important or irrelevant for a significant minority (38.9%).

*Please indicate the importance of non-financial indicators for **rework**.*

	Frequency	Percentage
Extremely important	5	13.5
Very important	10	27.0
Fairly important	13	35.1
Not very important	5	13.5
Irrelevant	4	10.8
Not applicable	3	–
Total	40	100.0

Indicators of the extent of rework are also important: 75.6% rate them at least fairly important.

*Please indicate the importance of non-financial indicators for **labour turnover**.*

	Frequency	Percentage
Extremely important	3	7.7
Very important	10	25.6
Fairly important	12	30.8
Not very important	13	33.3
Irrelevant	1	2.6
Not applicable	1	–
Total	40	100.0

The majority of respondents (64.1%) rate the importance of indicators of labour turnover at least fairly important. A significant minority (35.9%) do not consider them important.

*Please indicate the importance of non-financial indicators for **absenteeism**.*

	Frequency	Percentage
Extremely important	2	5.0
Very important	10	25.0
Fairly important	19	47.5
Not very important	8	20.0
Irrelevant	1	2.5
Total	40	100.0

Measures of absenteeism are also important in most companies (77.5%).

*Please indicate the importance of non-financial indicators for **customer satisfaction**.*

	Frequency	Percentage
Extremely important	22	55.0
Very important	15	37.5
Fairly important	2	5.0
Not very important	–	–
Irrelevant	1	2.5
Total	40	100.0

Like measures of quality, specification and on-time delivery, virtually all companies rate measures of customer satisfaction as very or extremely important.

*Please indicate the importance of non-financial indicators for **product/service innovation**.*

	Frequency	Percentage
Extremely important	12	30.0
Very important	12	30.0
Fairly important	11	27.5
Not very important	4	10.0
Irrelevant	1	2.5
Total	40	100.0

Measures of innovation are also important with only 12.5% rating them not very important or irrelevant.

*Please indicate the importance of non-financial indicators for **purchasing** performance.*

	Frequency	Percentage
Extremely important	6	15.8
Very important	9	23.7
Fairly important	12	31.6
Not very important	9	23.7
Irrelevant	2	5.3
Not applicable	1	–
Missing	1	–
Total	40	100.0

Not so important as other non-financial performance measures are measures of purchasing performance with 29% of respondents rating these not very important or irrelevant. Still 71% rated these measures at least fairly important.

*Please indicate the importance of non-financial indicators for **productivity** performance.*

	Frequency	Percentage
Extremely important	11	28.9
Very important	14	36.8
Fairly important	8	21.1
Not very important	5	13.2
Irrelevant	–	–
Not applicable	2	–
Total	40	100.0

Like virtually all the non-financial performance measures listed, productivity measures are also considered important by the vast majority (86.8%) of respondents. There is little doubt that most companies make extensive use of non-financial performance measures and, usually, consider them to be very important.

13. Changing relative importance of budgeting and other techniques
*Please indicate how the **relative importance** of use of non-financial performance indicators has changed over the past 5 years.*

	Frequency	Percentage
Much more important	11	28.9
Slightly more important	19	50.0
No change	8	21.1
Slightly less important	–	–
Much less important	–	–
Not applicable	1	–
Missing	1	–
Total	40	100.0

As one would expect from the results summarised above, most (78.9%) respondents feel that the importance of non-financial indicators has increased during the past 5 years.

*Please indicate how the **relative importance** of traditional budgeting has changed over the past 5 years.*

	Frequency	Percentage
Much more important	5	13.2
Slightly more important	11	28.9
No change	19	50.0
Slightly less important	2	5.3
Much less important	1	2.6
Missing	2	–
Total	40	100.0

Half think that the importance of traditional budgeting has not changed while 42.1% thought it more important with only 7.9% seeing it as less important over the past 5 years.

*Please indicate how the **relative importance** of budgets as a basis for bonus payments has changed over the past 5 years.*

	Frequency	Percentage
Much more important	9	25.0
Slightly more important	7	19.4
No change	18	50.0
Slightly less important	2	5.6
Much less important	–	–
Not applicable	1	–
Missing	3	–
Total	40	100.0

Similarly, 44.4% think budgets more important as a basis for bonus payments while only 5.6% think them less important.

*Please indicate how the **relative importance** of standard costing and variance analysis has changed over the past 5 years.*

	Frequency	Percentage
Much more important	5	13.2
Slightly more important	14	36.8
No change	15	39.5
Slightly less important	4	10.5
Much less important	–	–
Not applicable	1	–
Missing	1	–
Total	40	100.0

Half of respondents feel that standard costing and variance analysis is now more important than it was 5 years ago.

*Please indicate how the **relative importance** of activity-based budgeting/costing has changed over the past 5 years.*

	Frequency	Percentage
Much more important	1	2.8
Slightly more important	11	30.6
No change	20	55.6
Slightly less important	3	8.3
Much less important	1	2.8
Not applicable	2	–
Missing	2	–
Total	40	100.0

Some 33.4% of respondents rate activity-based budgeting/costing more important than 5 years ago. Only 11.1% rate it less important.

*Please indicate how the **relative importance** of economic value added has changed over the past 5 years.*

	Frequency	Percentage
Much more important	5	14.3
Slightly more important	8	22.9
No change	21	60.0
Slightly less important	–	–
Much less important	1	2.9
Not applicable	1	–
Missing	4	–
Total	40	100.0

Similarly, 37.2% of respondents consider economic value added to be more important than 5 years ago.

*Please indicate how the **relative importance** of the balanced scorecard has changed over the past 5 years.*

	Frequency	Percentage
Much more important	7	20.6
Slightly more important	11	32.4
No change	16	47.1
Slightly less important	–	–
Much less important	–	–
Not applicable	2	–
Missing	4	–
Total	40	100.0

Consistent with the increasing importance of non-financial indicators, 53% of respondents consider the balanced scorecard to have become more important during the past 5 years.

All techniques are judged to have become more important and the general impression is of an intensification in the use of traditional budgeting, non-financial performance measures and of other techniques.

The Structured Interview Guide

1. Company background
   a. Ownership
   b. Size – employees, turnover
   c. Products
   d. Markets
   e. Processes
   f. Organisation

2. Budget processes
   a. Who is involved in preparation – top management versus junior managers?
   b. Timescale and number of revisions in preparation
   c. Changes during financial year (if any)
   d. Forecasting – frequency and nature (e.g. for current year)
   e. Intensity of use – managers allowed to exceed the budget?
   f. Remuneration – are bonuses and incentive schemes linked to the budget?

3. Budget importance
   a. Important for what?
   b. Why?
4. Budget consequences
   a. Good results
   b. Unfortunate results
5. Budget changes
   a. Any important changes in past 5 years?
   b. Why?
   c. Are there any changes that you would like to see?
   d. Could you dispense with the budget?
   e. If you could would it be beneficial to use alternative methods?
   f. Do you use ABC, economic value added, balanced scorecard, etc.?
   g. Are non-financial measures important?
   h. Benchmarking?

References

Abdel-Maksoud A, Dugdale D, Luther R. 2005. Non-financial performance measurement in manufacturing companies. *British Accounting Review* 37(3):261–97.

Abernethy MA, Brownell P. 1997. Management control systems in research and development organizations: the role of accounting, behavior and personnel controls. *Accounting, Organizations and Society* 22(3–4):233–48.

Abernethy MA, Lillis AM. 1995. The impact of manufacturing flexibility on management control system design. *Accounting, Organizations and Society* 20(4):241–58.

Anthony R, Dearden J, Bedford NM. 1989. *Management Control Systems*, 6th ed. Homewood, IL: Irwin.

Anthony RN, Govindarajan V. 2004. *Management Control Systems*, 11th ed. New York: McGraw-Hill/Irwin.

Argyris C. 1952. *The Impact of Budgets on People*: Controllership Foundation. New York.

Argyris C. 1953. Human problems with budgets. *Harvard Business Review*, Jan–Feb, 97–110.

Arrow KJ. 1969. The organization of economic activity: issues pertinent to the choice of market versus non-market allocation. *In: The Analysis and Evaluation of Public Expenditures: The PBB-System*. Joint Economic Committee, 91st Congress, 1st Session, Vol. 1. Washington, DC.

Bain Consultancy. 2007. Bi-annual survey of management tools and techniques http://www.bain.com/management_tools/Management_Tools_and_Trends_2007.pdf

Barrett ME, Fraser LB. 1977. Conflicting roles in budgeting for operations. *Harvard Business Review* 55(4):137–46.

Beinhocker E. 2007. *The Origin of Wealth: Evolution, Complexity, and the Radical Remaking of Economics*. London: Random House Business Books.

Boyns T. 1998. Budgets and budgetary control in British businesses to c. 1945. *Accounting, Business and Financial History* 8(3): 261–301.

Brownell P, Dunk AS. 1991. Task uncertainty and its interaction with budgetary participation and budget emphasis: some methodological issues and empirical investigation. *Accounting, Organizations and Society* 16(8):693–703.

Bruns WJ, Waterhouse JH. 1975. Budgetary control and organisation structure. *Journal of Accounting Research* 13(2):177–203.

Bunce P, Fraser R, Woodcock L. 1995. Advanced budgeting: a journey to advanced management systems. *Management Accounting Research* 6:253–65.

Burns T, Stalker GM. 1961. *The Management of Innovation*. London: Tavistock Publications.

Chandler AD. 1962. *Strategy and Structure: Chapters in the History of the Industrial Enterprise*. Cambridge: M.I.T. Press.

Chandler A. 1977. *The Visible Hand*. Cambridge, MA: Belknap Press of Harvard University Press.

Chapman CS. 1998. Accountants in organisational networks. *Accounting, Organizations and Society* 23(8):737–66.

Chartered Institute of Management Accountants. 2005. *CIMA Official Terminology*: Elsevier/CIMA Publishing. Oxford.

Chenhall RH. 2003. Management control systems design within its organizational context: findings from contingency-based research and directions for the future. *Accounting Organizations and Society* 28:127–68.

Chenhall RH, Morris D. 1986. The impact of structure, environment and interdependencies on the perceived usefulness of management accounting systems. *Accounting Review* 61:16–35.

Coase R. 1937. The nature of the firm. *Economica* 4(16):386–405.

Daft RL, Macintosh NB. 1981. A tentative exploration into the amount and equivocality of information processing in organizational work units. *Administrative Science Quarterly* 26(2):207–24.

Davila T, Wouters M. 2005. Managing budget emphasis through the explicit design of conditional budgetary slack. *Accounting, Organizations and Society* 30(7-8):587–608.

Dent JF. 1990. Strategy, organization and control: some possibilities for accounting research. *Accounting, Organizations and Society* 15(1/2):3–25.

Drury C. 2004. *Management & Cost Accounting*, 6th ed. Business Press, Thomson Learning. London.

Drury C, Braund S, Osborne P, Tayles M. 1993. *A Survey of Management Accounting Practices in UK Manufacturing Companies*. London: ACCA.

Dugdale D, Jones TC, Green S. 2006. *Contemporary Accounting Practices in UK Manufacturing*. Oxford: Elsevier/CIMA Publishing.

Elbourne ET. 1926. *The Marketing Problem*, London: Longmans.

Evans-Hemming DF. 1952. *Flexible budgetary control and standard costs; cost control for management*. London: Macdonald & Evans.

Ezzamel M. 1990. The impact of environmental uncertainty, managerial autonomy and size on budget characteristics. *Management Accounting Research* 1:181–97.

Frow N, Marginson D, Ogden S. 2005. Encouraging strategic behaviour while maintaining management control: multi-functional project teams, budgets, and the negotiation of shared accountabilities in contemporary enterprises. *Management Accounting Research* 16:269–92.

Giglioni GB, Bedelan AG. 1974. A conspectus of management control theory. *Academy of Management Journal* 17:292–305.

Goold M, Campbell A. 1987. Managing diversity: strategy and control in diversified British companies. *Long Range Planning* 20(5):42–52.

Gupta AK, Govindarajan V. 1984. Business unit strategy, managerial characteristics, and business unit effectiveness at strategy implementation. *Academy of Management Journal* 25–41.

Hamel G. 2007. *The Future of Management*. Boston, MA: Harvard Business School Press.

Harrison GC. 1930. *Standard Costs: Installation, Operation and Use*. New York: The Ronald Press Company.

Hayes MV. 1929. *Accounting for Executive Control*. New York: Harper and Brothers.

Hickson DT, Pugh DS, Pheysey DC. 1969. Operations technology and organization structure: an empirical reappraisal. *Administrative Science Quarterly* 14(3):378–86.

Hirst MK. 1981. Accounting information and the evaluation of subordinate performance. *The Accounting Review* 56:771–84.

Hirst MK. 1983. Reliance on accounting performance measures, task uncertainty, and dysfunctional behavior: some extensions. *Journal of Accounting Research* (Autumn) 596–605.

Hofstede GH. 1968. *The Game of Budgetary Control*. London: Tavistock.

Hope J, Fraser R. 1997. Beyond budgeting... breaking through the barrier to the 'third wave'. *Management Accounting* 75(December):20–23.

Hope J, Fraser R. 1998. Measuring performance in the new organisational model. *Management Accounting* 76(June):22–23.

Hope J, Fraser R. 1999. Beyond budgeting: building a new management model for the information age. *Management Accounting* 77(January):16–21.

Hope J, Fraser R. 2003a. Who needs budgets? *Harvard Business Review* February:108–15.

Hope J, Fraser R. 2003b. *Beyond Budgeting: How Managers Can Break Free from the Annual Performance Trap*. Boston, MA: Harvard Business School Press.

Hopwood AG. 1972. An empirical study of the role of accounting data in performance evaluation. *Journal of Accounting Research* 10:156–82.

Hopwood AG. 1976. *Accounting and Human Behaviour*. Englewood Cliffs, NJ: Prentice-Hall.

Horngren CT. 1962. *Cost Accounting: A Managerial Emphasis*. Englewood Cliffs, NJ: Prentice-Hall.

Horngren CT, Foster G, Srikant MD. 2000. *Cost Accounting: A Managerial Emphasis*, 10th ed. Englewood Cliffs, NJ: Prentice-Hall.

ICWA. 1950. *An Introduction to Budgetary Control, Standard Costing, Material Costing and Production Control*. London: Institute of Cost and Works and Works Accountants.

Kalagnanam SS, Lindsay RM. 1998. The use of organic models of control in JIT firms: generalising Woodward's findings to modern manufacturing practices. *Accounting Organizations and Society* 24(1):1–30.

Kepner CH, Tregoe BB. 1965. *The Rational Manager*. New York: McGraw-Hill.

Langfield-Smith K. 1997. Management control systems and strategy: a critical review. *Accounting, Organizations and Society* 22(2):207–32.

Lawrence PR, Lorsch JW. 1986, reprint of 1967. *Organization and Environment*. Boston, MA: Harvard Business School Press.

Lowe EA, Shaw RW. 1968. An analysis of managerial biasing: evidence from a company's budgeting process. *The Journal of Management Studies*, October, 304–15.

Lukes SM. 1974. *Power: A Radical View*: Macmillan: New York.

Lyne SR. 1992. Perceptions and attitudes of different user-groups to the role of the budget, budget pressure and budget participation. *Accounting and Business Research* 22(88):357–69.

Macintosh NB. 1994. *Management Accounting and Control Systems: An Organizational and Behavioral Approach*. Chichester: Wiley and Sons.

Macintosh NB, Daft RL. 1987. Management control systems and departmental interdependencies: an empirical study. *Accounting Organizations and Society* 12:49–61.

Marginson D, Ogden S. 2005. Budgeting and innovation: managing the tensions. *Financial Management (CIMA)*, April, 29–31.

McKinsey JO. 1922. *Budgetary Control*. New York: Ronald Press.

McKinsey JO. 1927. The accountant's relation to the budgetary program, N.A.C.A., 1927 Yearbook *reproduced in* Vangermeersch (1990) Relevance Rediscovered, National Association of Accountants, Montvale, NJ.

Merchant KA. 1981. The design of the corporate budgeting system: influences on managerial behaviour and performance. *The Accounting Review* 56(4):813–29.

Merchant KA. 1985. Budgeting and the propensity to create slack. *Accounting Organizations and Society* 10(2):201–10.

Merchant KA. 1989. *Rewarding results: Motivating Profit Center Managers.* Boston, MA: Harvard Business School Press.

Merchant KA. 1990a. How challenging should profit budget targets be? *Management Accounting*, November, 46–48.

Merchant KA. 1990b. The effects of financial controls on data manipulation and management myopia. *Accounting Organizations and Society* 15(4):297–313.

Merchant KA, Manzoni JF. 1989. The achievability of budget targets in profit centers: a field study. *The Accounting Review* 64(3):539–58.

Merchant KA, Van der Stede WA. 2003. *Management Control Systems: Performance Measurement, Evaluation and Incentives*, 1st ed, Harlow, England: Financial Times/ Prentice Hall.

Mia L, Chenhall RH. 1994. The usefulness of management accounting systems, functional differentiation and managerial effectiveness. *Accounting Organizations and Society* 19(1):1–13.

Miles RW, Snow CC. 1978. *Organizational Strategy, Structure, and Process.* New York: McGraw-Hill.

Miller EL. 1982. *Responsibility Accounting and Performance Evaluations.* New York: Van Nostrand Reinhold.

Mintzberg H. 1979. *The Structure of Organizations.* Englewood Cliffs, NJ: Prentice-Hall International, Inc.

Mintzberg H. 1994. *The Rise and Fall of strategic Planning.* Harlow, England: FT Prentice-Hall.

National Industrial Conference Board. 1931. *Budgetary Control in Manufacturing Industry.* New York: National Industrial Conference Board.

Nohria N, Gulati R. 1996. Is slack good or bad for innovation? *The Academy of Management Journal* 39(5):1245–64.

Onsi M. 1973. Factor analysis of behavioural variables affecting budgetary slack. *The Accounting Review* 48(3):535–48.

Otley DT. 1978. Budget use and managerial performance. *Journal of Accounting Research* 16(1):122–49.

Otley DT. 2001. Extending the boundaries of management accounting research: developing systems for performance management. *The British Accounting Review* 33(3):243–61.

Otley DT, Berry AJ. 1980. Control, organization and accounting. *Accounting, Organizations and Society* 5(2):231–44.

Ouchi WG. 1977. The relationship between organizational structures and organizational control. *Administrative Science Quarterly* 22(1):95–112.

Ouchi WG. 1979. A conceptual framework for the design of organizational control mechanisms. *Management Science,* September, 833–48.

Ouchi WG. 1980. Markets, bureaucracies and clans. *Administrative Science Quarterly* 25:129–41.

Parthasarthy R, Sethi SP. 1992. The impact of flexible automation on business strategy and organizational structure. *Academy of Management Review,* 17(1):86–111.

Peirce JL. 1954. The budget comes of age. *Harvard Business Review*, May–June, 58–64.

Porter ME. 1980. *Competitive Strategy*. New York: Free Press.

Porter ME. 1985. *Competitive Advantage*. New York: Free Press.

Quail JM. 1997. More peculiarities of the British: budgetary control in the U.S. and UK business to 1939. *Business and Economic History* 26(2):617–31.

Roseveare H. 1973. *The Treasury 1660–1870: The Foundations of Control*. London: George Allen & Unwin Ltd.

Ross A. 1995. Job related tension, budget emphasis and uncertainty. *Management Accounting Research* 6:1–11.

Schiff M, Lewin AY. 1968. Where traditional budgeting fails. *Financial Executive* May:50–62.

Schiff M, Lewin A. 1970. The impact of people on budgets. *The Accounting Review*, 45:259–68.

Seal W, Garrison R, Noreen E. 2006. *Advanced Management Accounting*. Maidenhead, England: McGraw Hill.

Simons R. 1987. The role of management control systems in creating competitive advantage: new perspectives. *Accounting Organizations and Society* 15(1/2):127–43.

Simons R. 1995. *Levers of Control*. Boston, MA: Harvard Business School Press.

Sizer J. 1968. The development of marginal costing. *Management Accounting*, January, 23–30.

Sloan AP. 1986. *My Years at General Motors*, London: Penguin Books.

Solomons D. 1952. The historical development of costing. *In: Studies in Costing*, Solomons D. (ed): Sweet & Maxwell, pp. 1–52, London.

Sord BH, Welsch GA. 1958. *Business Budgeting*. New York: Controllership Foundation.

Stedry AC. 1960. *Budget Control and Cost Behaviour*. Englewood Cliffs, NJ: Prentice-Hall.

Stedry AC, Kay E. 1964. The effects of goal difficulty on performance. *Behavioural Science* 1966:459–70.

Thompson JD. Organizations. *Action: Social Science Bases of Administrative Theory*: McGraw-Hill, New York, 1967.

Umapathy S. 1987. *Current budgeting practices in U.S. Industry: The State of the Art*. New York: Quorum.

Van der Stede WA. 2000. The relationship between two consequences of budgetary controls: budgetary slack creation and managerial short-term orientation. *Accounting, Organizations and Society* 25(6):609–22.

Williamson OE. The Economics of Discretionary Behavior: Managerial Objectives. *Theory of the Firm*, 1964, pp. 28–37. Englewood Cliffs, NJ: Prentice Hall.

Williamson OE. 1981a. The economics of organization: the transaction cost approach. *The American Journal of Sociology* 87(3):548–77.

Williamson OE. 1981b. The modern corporation: origins, evolution, attributes. *Journal of Economic Literature* XIX:1537–68.

Willsmore AW. 1949. Business Budgets and Budgetary Control, 3rd ed. London: Pitman.

Woodward J. 1965. Industrial organization: Theory and Practice. Oxford: Oxford University Press.

Index

Lightning Source UK Ltd.
Milton Keynes UK
19 February 2010

150369UK00001B/94/P